NO ONE LISTENS TO YOUR DAD'S SHOW

In 2018 Christian O'Connell was one of the UK's biggest radio stars, the youngest DJ ever to be inducted into the UK Radio Hall of Fame and the winner of an unprecedented 25 radio awards. As a stand-up comedian he sold out national tours.

Then he decided to move to Australia. Struggling at first and written off by industry experts, against great odds on-air and off-air his breakfast show on GOLD FM in Melbourne went to the highly coveted Number 1 spot within eighteen months, giving the station its highest ratings in over twenty years, making Christian the first DJ to have Number 1 breakfast shows on both sides of the world.

CHRISTIAN O'CONNELL

NO ONE LISTENS TO YOUR DAD'S SHOW

From number one
to no one

ALLEN&UNWIN

First published in Great Britain and Australia in 2021
by Allen & Unwin

Published in hardback in Great Britain in 2021 by
Allen & Unwin, an imprint of Atlantic Books Ltd.

10 9 8 7 6 5 4 3 2 1

A CIP catalogue record for this book is available from
the British Library.

Hardback ISBN: 978 1 83895 288 4
E-book ISBN: 978 1 83895 289 1

Printed in Great Britain

Allen & Unwin
An imprint of Atlantic Books Ltd
Ormond House
26–27 Boswell Street
London
WC1N 3JZ

www.allenandunwin.com/uk

To Sarah
For calling out my BS since 1996
and
For free-falling through life with me

PS
I hate craft fairs, so do the kids

Contents

My last show on air, London, May 2018

Absolute Radio Studios, Soho

The song ending is by Echo and the Bunnymen, 'Nothing Lasts Forever . . .'

[Song fades]

I pause trying to find the words among the tidal wave of big emotions, I rub my chest soothing my aching heart. It's time.

Time to say goodbye to two million people listening right now, all over the UK.

'I'm not going to say goodbye . . . I'm going to say thank you, for twelve years I got to do this! This was and will always be my dream, I still remember listening to this show, ironing my shirt to go and do a job I didn't want to be doing in sales. I was sleepwalking through my life . . . what a ride that I got to do this for twelve years . . .

'Radio is disposable, I've always understood that, and this show's memory will fade . . .

'You shouldn't feel bad about that . . .

'But it will never fade from my heart . . . this song is all I have left to say . . .'

I start the last song, 'Thank You For Being a Friend'.

I walk round the radio desk to hug my sidekick and great friend Richie. 'Thank You For Being a Friend' acts as a live soundtrack. I take one last look around a room that has so many memories and changed my life, a safe place when life outside was hard. I stroke the light switch I'd hit every morning when I strolled into the studio at 5.30 a.m.

As I head out of the station the entire staff line the stairways to send me off. Clapping, patting, some have tears in their eyes.

Out on the streets of London I hail a taxi and head to meet my family at Heathrow airport, we have a flight to catch.

One way to Australia.

In two weeks' time I will start a new radio show on the other side of the world.

The first message I will get from my new listeners will say . . .

'Fuck off home'

INTRODUCTION

The story I don't want to tell you

If you can't do it anymore, then you could train to become a hairdresser or something . . .

SARAH O'CONNELL

I was 44 when my life fell apart.

I'm bent over a bin. At a radio station. One of the most famous ones in England. The radio station, that is, not the bin.

I tell stories for a living but this one I've tried to hide from, to bury deep. There is always some part of us we are trying to look away from. But if I'm going to honestly tell you the story of why I moved to the other side of the world, it starts at this bin. Like all great stories.

I'm in the post room of the radio station. I'm due to start my show in seventeen minutes. The show has two million listeners and goes all over the UK. It's the Number 1 show.

The clock on the wall above me seems to be going faster and faster. When you excitedly look forward to something, time goes so slowly. I remember on my wedding day, I couldn't wait, it was as if every slow dripping second was a chance for fate to deny me this magical event at midday. When you fear something, time takes on an undeniable magnetic urgency, pulling you rapidly towards events and situations. This clock right now is moving me when I'm trying not to move, I can't. I've somehow added another option to the flight or fight response: bin.

Radio stations have clocks everywhere. Everything is built around time. The news, travel updates, the start and finish of every single show, the length of the songs and advertising breaks, all dictated by time. When I first started working in radio, I suddenly found time and its omnipotent presence utterly terrifying. I even used to jog to the toilet with a stopwatch, like a madman, so I would know exactly how long I had before the song was ending and I was due to start talking again. Then the utter dread if a routine number one suddenly turned into a number two. If you ever hear me play 'Stairway to Heaven', you'll know what's happened. Plant and Page gave all DJs a great eight minutes and two seconds with that epic song.

One radio boss advised me that my success as a morning-show DJ relied on me becoming a 'human alarm clock' to my listeners. I pointed out this was the 21st century and clocks were everywhere: car dashboards, microwave ovens, televisions, phones and those lesser-known devices called watches. This was also the same boss who advised me to donate one of my kidneys to a listener, 'to show I cared'. None of them was asking for a kidney, oh no, he just thought I could run it as some kind of competition. To win my left kidney.

Oprah gave her audience cars, I would give away major organs.

This cold metallic grey clock is a big old-school analogue one that makes a noise when the minute hand moves. It's a clock that exists only in the world of entertainment. You've seen it in every movie needing to show us the impending deadline for the bomb going off/train departing to freedom/high noon showdown/ time-travelling back to the future/time left in the game.

Right now, it feels like an executioner's axe moving ever closer to 6 a.m. and my show and showdown. It's looming over me as I hang on to this bin, fearing I'm about to die.

Clunk goes the minute hand . . . 5.44 a.m.

Normally this time before the show is my special time. The counting down clock excites me. After 22 years on the radio, time is my friend. I try to quiet my excitable racing mind and allow room for what the day's show will be. It's a magical hour before we go live to the UK and I get to do what I love doing. I have the best job in the world. I've dreamt of doing this since I was a kid.

Today is different. The dream has become a nightmare.

I'm looking up at the clock in the post room and I'm frozen, leaning over a bin and vomiting. I'm having what I later find out is called a panic attack. At the time I seriously thought I was going to die.

Clunk.

The executioner's clock hand moves again. It's fifteen minutes until showtime. My feet go icy cold as if I'm losing contact with the very ground beneath me, as if there's nothing holding me to the planet.

My phone goes, it's my producer, I click ignore. I'm terrified, I feel trapped and that fucking clock is going faster and faster towards showtime. I can't move let alone do a four-hour radio show and be funny.

Eventually my now-concerned producer locates me, hugging the bin, eyes bloodshot from being sick and wide with fear. It's not a good look.

'Shit!' he says upon finding me like this.

I see him glance up at the clock. Yeah, I know, it's now 5.48 a.m., twelve minutes until showtime.

But to me, I'm seconds away from dying.

I've never felt more scared in my life. Scared of what's happening to me, scared that I can't do the show and truly scared that I'll never be the same again. Radio is my joy. Why is this now happening to me that I can't even make it into the one place in the world that's my happy place?

My sickening rising thought and fear is that some part of me is broken beyond repair. That I'm about to be found out.

'You look terrible, head home, I'll call the boss now,' my producer says and rushes off, not before taking me in one more time, as if just to make sure that what he sees is actually happening.

Head home and say what?

'Oh, I didn't really fancy it today.'

What exactly would I tell my wife as I come home without doing the show? What would we say to the kids? Dodgy curry? The worry of letting my family down, losing my mind and job, makes it all even worse. As these thoughts and images play out on my mind's projection screen, plus the shame of not being able to provide, not being a strong man, I'm really starting to spin out. It's like my brain's a hamster wheel travelling so fast it's burning up.

I manage to pry my whitened knuckles away from my comfort bin: maybe I'll start taking one on a plane to have alongside people's comfort dogs.

I stumble out of the radio station and suddenly the streets of London feel overwhelming. I almost want to hug the walls to keep me connected to the ground. I feel so weak and small I could fly off into orbit.

I make my walk of shame through London's West End onto Regent Street and the giant burning LED advertising screens of

Piccadilly Circus. Then feel the noise of the roaring rush-hour commuter traffic that I normally broadcast to as their friend in the morning.

Today is not my friend. Morning has broken.

Me.

I collapse into the back of a London black cab; the driver does a double-take when he recognises me.

'Can't be arsed today?' he chuckles. London taxi drivers have been some of my biggest supporters in more than seventeen years of being on air to the city. Today I sink down into the back seat, unable to quite fit the persona he thinks is in his taxi. 'Heavy night was it, OC? Legend mate!'

I nod along politely. 'Yeah, something like that.'

At the time I thought this was undeniably the worst day of my life.

It was one of the best.

PART ONE

1

The man in the shed

Never trust a stranger with your secrets, son.

MY DAD

I was sitting somewhere I did not want to be. A therapist's office.

I always thought if I ended up in therapy, it would be a bit like a lifeguard having to pull you out of life's swimming pool. Therapy wasn't for me.

I was successful, I had awards and a nice house to show me that. The house had a big garden, a crunchy gravel driveway and, get this, I had a big kitchen with a KITCHEN ISLAND!

Look at me, Mum and Dad! Look what I've done!

Therapy was for fuck-ups. And I'm not one of *those*.

But now, I'm going to see a therapist.

As I walked to my first therapy session, I thought of the board game Snakes and Ladders. It felt like I had landed on a snake and I had slid down somewhere I didn't want to be. This was not part of the plan I had for my life now at my age.

The pre–radio show anxiety attacks had gotten so severe I wasn't able to do several shows, blaming a 'viral infection'.

I thought my life as I knew it was over. What a cruel way to come undone, so that I couldn't do the very thing I'd been rewarded for working so hard at and that I loved so much. What was I meant to do now?

My wife was, as ever, a rock. Saying we could sell the house, I could do something else.

This shows what a big-hearted caring wife I have, trying to take all the pressure off me.

But what else did she think I could do? Doing what I do, my skillset is tiny, negligible. At one point she'd said I could maybe open up a hairdressing salon.

What, like when Daniel Day Lewis left Hollywood for a few years to work as a shoe cobbler in Ireland? I'd said a few times how I would have loved to have been a hairdresser. I'd bought a top-of-the-range hairdryer so I could do my daughters' hair after their baths when they were younger, but now I'm opening a salon?

Something else?

There's only ever been this.

I checked the address again on Google Maps. He had said on the phone, 'Walk down the alleyway at the side of my house and let yourself in through the gate five minutes before our session. You'll find my office on the left.'

I did. It was a . . . shed?

What the . . .?

No, this can't be right. I walked back out the gate fearing I'd just broken into someone's garden and would have to give the lamest excuse ever when questioned by a startled homeowner: 'I thought this was my therapist's office,' as I pointed to a shed.

Nope, this was the right place.

And it was a shed.

A very nice shed, but by all objective measures, a shed. To my knowledge, I don't believe Dr Freud worked out of his shed, paint pots in one corner, Sigmund's rusty old lawnmower in the other and the smell of turps in the air.

Not only is a shed a worrying indicator of the quality of a therapist, this one was also late.

As I waited, all I could think about was how I wasn't a 'therapy guy'.

I really didn't want to be here, but I was totally exhausted from worrying about what was wrong with me. I couldn't work. I needed to get my shit together.

Now this therapist was already pissing me off by being late for our first session. He works in his garden, how can he be late?

So, I sat in his shed annoyed at his time keeping. Was this some technique? Was he just watching on a remote camera, sipping his coffee and laughing? It was starting to feel more like waiting for a serial killer than therapy.

He finally wandered in, seemingly distant and cold, which made me feel even more on edge.

He sat down calmly, no apology about the time. Took a big sigh out, showed a welcoming half-smile and said, 'Your name is familiar, but I don't really listen to breakfast radio, tell me about yourself.'

With my job, people can't wait to tell you, 'Oh, I listen to someone else,' when they ask what I do for a living. You wouldn't say that to a plumber when he told you his job, 'Oh, you're not my plumber, I use Ray.'

'Oh sure, yeah Ray's great.'

What is it about my line of work that makes people want to tell me that I'm not their type? If they met Mick Jagger, do they immediately say, 'Oh, I don't listen to you, I'm more a Beatles guy.'

I bet they do.

I'd only come to get help from a therapist because my wife, Sarah, kindly suggested I go. She said, '*You need help.*'

Those caring, kind and tender three words my fragile male ego translated into, '*You're a hot mess and the kids are wondering why Dad is rocking back and forth staring out the window.*'

I started to explain to him why I was there, about the panic attacks.

'I know why you are here, you said on the phone, but it might help to tell me about yourself.'

A quick look on Wikipedia could've fixed that, but I guess that wouldn't give him the chance to charge me by the hour. Plus, in fairness, Wikipedia says I was a thirteen-year-old National Nunchuck Champion in 1986. I guess there are worse lies to have told about yourself.

So, I reluctantly started to tell the man in the shed about myself.

•

I go back to 1998, when I got married at age 25. It was for society's good as much as my own. I still have no idea what my wife saw in me.

When we first met, I had a job in telesales, selling advertising space in a photography magazine. That statement right there, it's enough to drive any woman wild.

I'm talking headset with a mic, crammed into a cubicle in an office with hundreds of others, like battery hens.

My playboy assets were, well, nothing, except a huge crippling debt from university where I'd spent more time at the bar than raising it.

When Sarah and I started dating, my diet was mainly beer and toast, and I was mumbling into my pint glass about wanting to be a radio DJ or a stand-up comedian. I was doing the odd open-mic stand-up spot in London in very rough pubs. This was around 1996. Comedy was huge in London with many comedy clubs and some really great stand-ups.

Meanwhile, I was performing to six drunks on a Monday night in the East End on a milk crate 'stage' (six milk crates taped together). One night a fight broke out between two of the eight audience members. I carried on with 'my set' as everyone turned to watch the drunks fight, and I had the awful realisation that the fight was more entertaining than my stand-up. Which is why now, when I tour, I have two drunks fight on stage as my warm-up.

I had no real game plan. I was drifting and starting to sleepwalk through my life. Part of me was dying, and not just my liver. It was the part that had a dream and a belief that I could do something with my life. Sadly, that part had met the tidal force of real life and how it demands so much from you and cares very little for your fragile aspirations and hopes. It wants to keep you in a lane, to confine you.

Every morning felt like Groundhog Day, my soon-to-be wife would have to kick me out of bed to reluctantly start another day, ironing a shirt while listening to the morning radio and just *wanting to be doing that.*

They—the people on the radio—were, to me, in the Emerald City. I wanted to make my way there. But I had no idea how I could get from my tiny south London flat into a radio studio. I was struggling every morning to get the 7.22 a.m. from Crystal Palace to London Victoria station.

Sarah was a lawyer and hated it, because she has this thing called a soul. We'd drag our heels out the door every morning to begin days neither of us really wanted.

We got burgled a few weeks before our wedding and my financial situation was so dire the thieves left my credit card.

They had rifled through my credit card statements, which was easy to do as they were all in red, and pitied me. They probably thought, 'Should we leave him some money or something?'

I was so broke I even had to borrow the money from Sarah to pay for my own wedding suit. Who marries this loser? If one of my daughters met a guy like me at that point, I'd tell them to walk away.

Our wedding rings cost $150 (£85) for the pair. For the record, two things: I have paid back the money for the suit, and I have offered my wife an upgrade on her wedding ring, something maybe around the $200 (£115) mark, because she's worth it.

I actually love the fact our wedding rings were dirt cheap, it grounds me. It grounds us. It reminds me of where we came from. Burglars pitying me. To my wife, it's a constant reminder of the poor choices she made in life—a good woman thinking I could change.

Just a few months after getting married I was in another sales job I'd been headhunted for. Accidentally, my reluctant sales career was going great. I was now working for a group of radio stations around Britain, selling sponsorships and promotions.

This was my wife's idea. Get a job, any job, as near to radio as possible, and find a way in that way. I said this was a terrible idea as Howard Stern wasn't discovered because one day the morning DJ didn't turn up and they yelled out into the sales office, 'Any of you guys funny?'

However, annoyingly, it turned out to be the first in a very long series of very good ideas my wife had. My wife lives to be right and say, 'Told you so.' If she had been married to JFK, she'd have suggested they not take the convertible and later, as those sniper's bullets hit, my wife would've simply said, 'Told you so.'

Down at the pub after work one night, I heard that a DJ from one of the radio stations had quit the breakfast show. I happened to meet the Australian who ran all the radio stations the company owned and who was in charge of all the DJs. I drunkenly told him that most of their breakfast shows were painfully unfunny, and he offered me an audition at the same time as asking me if I wanted another beer. I said yes to both.

'Either you are as funny as you are here in the pub or you'll be shithouse, either way I'm cool,' he said in what I was to learn is the wonderfully laid-back but brutally honest Australian way.

Opportunity had presented itself. My wife was right, dammit. I woke up the next morning hungover and wondering what I'd agreed to, as I have many times in my life.

Top 5 Things I've Thought Were a Good Idea While Drunk in the Pub

1. Buy a boat with a guy I'd only met that night.
2. Put up a bounty of $1 million to anyone who could bring proof of aliens to my radio studio.
3. Host a TV game show in a bowling alley.
4. Buy a fire engine for my radio show, paid for by my boss as a promotional vehicle.
5. Carry out my producer's vasectomy live on air.

So, in August 1998, just three months after getting married, I got the train out of London early one Saturday morning. The enormity of the opportunity weighed heavily on me and I remember nervously looking out of the train window as the countryside passed by, rushing me towards the moment I'd been waiting for.

In my mind was a constant question: *Could I grasp the brass ring that life was offering me?* How many times does life ask of us, 'Are we equal to the moment?'

As soon as I walked into that dingy windowless studio in the seaside town of Bournemouth, I felt a deep sense of calm. Like I belonged. This was where I was meant to be. The desk, the microphones, the faders. The potential of what you can do with that microphone. To this day, 23 years later, I still get excited when I see a radio studio.

It's always been like that, since I entered my very first radio studio. Something in me comes alive.

•

Like the time when Sarah was in hospital being induced for our first daughter, Ruby. I was told to help calm the situation by going away for a while.

This was a real shame as I'd taken a two-hour course in pressure-point massage to help ease labour pains. I was pressing a special point on my wife's ankle while she was in some distress and I calmly assured her that sweet relief was on its way thanks to ancient Chinese medicine thousands of years old and . . . sadly I had barely begun my magical healing powers when my wife kicked me away like a feral donkey, and at the same time—she can really multi-task, my wife—yelled, *'Fuck off, Chris.'*

'Perhaps your husband would want to go for a walk, get some fresh air . . .'

In other words, get old Dr Quinn, Medicine Man out of here.

So I went to get my wife a cup of tea, because we are English. Forget gas and drugs, a cup of milky tepid hospital tea will be just what my in-labour wife will need. For us Brits, it's one of our five a day.

Off I went around the hospital and I came across their little hospital radio studio and I immediately calmed down.

My first-ever radio gig was on hospital radio. I was seventeen and it was in my hometown's biggest hospital, Winchester Hospital, which had its own in-house hospital radio station.

Hospital radio is a big thing in Britain, and many big-name radio DJs started there. The stations broadcast to the patients, and were run by very well meaning and enthusiastic volunteers. My dad voiced his natural distrust of them, quietly saying, 'There's something weird about volunteers.'

My dad spoke very quietly when making a point, like Clint Eastwood in *The Outlaw Josey Wales*. He'd squint into the distance, like Clint, as he shared some 'life wisdom' with me. Here I've recorded some so that future generations can benefit from this wise man's teachings.

Top 5 Wise Words from My Dad

1. *'Never trust a man with a beard, they're hiding something.'*
2. *'I can tell a lot about a man from the state of his shoes.'*
3. *'Never swim within an hour of eating a heavy meal. You'll live to regret it.'*
4. *'This is how they get you'* when some hidden fee is revealed.
5. *'Don't sell me a dog'*—meaning don't lie to him, nope, I've got no idea either.

Back to hospitals having their own radio stations. At each bedside, on every ward, was a little radio where patients could choose between several proper professional radio stations, or the in-house hospital one, run by these enthusiastic volunteers. I never understood why anyone, in hospital, ill, scared and fighting for their life, would choose an amateur radio station like

WHR FM (Winchester Hospital Radio) and a show hosted by a clueless seventeen-year-old.

I started there after I wrote them a letter and was invited to come in and meet the 'boss', a postman off on medical leave.

When I got there, I was blown away by the quality of the equipment in the studio. State-of-the-art CD players and turn-tables, all paid for by public donations, better than some of the professional radio stations I would begin my career in. It made me question the underfunded hospital barely able to get essential lifesaving equipment, while a pretend radio station was fully kitted out.

The pretend radio station boss, Andrew, and I chatted and after he heard me speak, he was no doubt blown away by the pipes God gave me and offered me a show right there and then on the spot. Prime time. Sunday 10 p.m.

Wait, Sunday 10 p.m.?

Who is listening then?

Especially to a two-hour request show.

One major problem—we had no listeners, so no requests. Therefore, being a young gun, before my show I would walk around the entire hospital with my notepad, asking at the foot of every bed if they'd like a song request.

Looking back now, I shudder in horror at my inability to read the situations I was walking into, in my desperation to get a song request. A mixture of ambition and teenage selfishness blinded me as I would approach a family at the bedside of someone clearly very ill on a respirator and asked if the patient would like a song played. Still not put off by irritated family members glaring at me, I'd shuffle around the bed asking if any of the gathered family would like a song.

Turns out they didn't. The only request people were making at this point was for more morphine. And for me to take my pathetic empty notepad and go away.

Maybe I should've called the show 'Last Requests'.

Six Sundays this carried on until mid-show late one evening heading into my second hour on a very real graveyard shift, I got bored.

There was a Frank Sinatra song playing on a turntable. I stopped it midway, opened my fader and turned on my mic.

'That was for Elsa, but we have just heard she has just passed away so there's no point playing out the rest of that, which means we can *now* play a song for someone who is *alive*.'

I thought this was funny. Look, I was bored, seventeen and looking for mischief. Can I just say there was no Elsa, no one had died, it was a joke. Only we got complaints, which stunned me, complaints meant there were listeners. Awesome!

The hospital fired me.

It remains to this day the only radio station I've been fired from. Can you even 'fire' someone from something they aren't being paid for?

I got sacked that night and cycled home in the dark, fearing that I'd just blown my entire radio career. My days as a bedside DJ were certainly over.

Years later as I looked at this little hospital studio as my wife literally laboured away a few floors above, this all came flooding back, only interrupted by a wild-eyed, bearded, radio volunteer handing me a flyer.

'We're having an audition for new presenters if you're interested,' he said.

By this stage, I was an actual DJ on a London breakfast show, but I didn't tell him that as he'd probably tell me he listened to someone else. I just smiled at the echo of my first start.

My phone snapped me out of the reverie, it was my wife: *'Chris! Where the hell have you been? The baby is coming!'*

'I've been reminiscing about my own life,' didn't feel like the correct response.

Instead, Radioboy leapt into action, as I handed back the flyer to the radio enthusiast grinning a bit too intensely at me. My dad was right, there *is* something weird about volunteers. Don't even get me started on the state of his shoes.

•

Luckily, with my brief but eventful hospital radio career under my belt, I nailed the breakfast show audition in Bournemouth.

I got the gig and my life changed. It really did from that moment.

Steve, my new and first radio boss, actually gave me a lift home afterwards and as we chatted, he played back the audition tape.

He laughed a few times, then said what was to become his catchphrase, 'Shithouse,' after an admittedly very unfunny bit on my audition about missing dog posters, and why don't they put them lower down on a telegraph pole so that dogs can see them. 'Oh that's Kenny' a dog might say. 'Just seen him down the park, now where's my reward?'

'Shithouse' was a word Steve used a lot. Sometimes varying its use from a term for something being very bad, and sometimes merely as a form of punctuation. So in his Australian accent, roadworks would be 'shithouse roadworks', our climate 'shithouse weather' and sometimes my show would get a 'the six o'clock hour today was shithouse'.

Steve took a huge gamble on me and I can never thank him enough. No one else in the country would've put me straight on air with no experience. I know his bosses above him said it was on him to make this work, and he was risking his job for me.

So Sarah and I moved out of London to the Vegas of South England.

Bournemouth.

I was finally starting my radio career.

I took a 60 per cent pay cut, just as I had finally started earning good money in a job I didn't really want to be doing. I had just earned a bonus that month almost the size of my new job's yearly salary. Steve said when he told me the money side of his offer, 'You don't get into radio to make money, that's like a monk getting into a monastery to get laid.'

To be honest, I would've done it for free. I almost was.

When I handed in my notice, my sales job bosses looked at each other like I was mad.

'Two years from now you could be the sales director, with a company car of your choice, BMW or Porsche. Radio is brutal, and you've never done it. Have you thought this over, chasing some fairytale?'

Yeah, every waking day since I was a teenager.

This was the easiest decision of my life.

My awesome wife even quit her lawyer's job! And not for another job as a lawyer—she walked away from something she had been studying years for. Her colleagues thought she was mad. Her mum must've been so impressed that her former lawyer daughter had made a real safe bet in me.

'One day you're going to marry a handsome prince working in telesales with a headset, he will sweep you off your feet with a 60 per cent pay cut to go do a job he's never done before.'

To be fair, her mum never said a bad word and wished us all the best as we chose risk and adventure over law and a company Porsche.

Things were really tight financially, so my ever-resourceful wife started up her own cleaning business. Every weekend I would go help her clean homes and do leaflet drops. It's a good look for the new breakfast DJ, shoving leaflets through your letterbox on the weekend. I didn't care, I was finally at the Emerald City. It wasn't long though before I peered behind the curtain of radio and saw the scared little man running it.

I wish I could say that I was a natural DJ from day one, but I sucked.

Really sucked.

I'd made a deal with Sarah that I'd do it for two years and if it wasn't happening and I wasn't getting better, I'd go back to sales to become that future sales director I was destined to be.

In my first show I got the station's frequency wrong and gave out the big rival's one. They were Power FM, which was 103.2 FM, we were 2CR FM, on 102.3 FM. To me now this seems so incon-sequential in the bigger picture of what radio is really about, but in my raw rookie days, this was HUGE.

Radio bosses talk all the time about 'they', meaning the other stations, and about 'winning' in the ratings. My boss had a copy of Sun Tzu's *The Art of War* on his desk, as I discovered many radio bosses did. In the bosses' minds, we were at war. Getting the frequency wrong was 'a gift to them'. I was told after my first show, 'Shithouse.'

I was also told by the big boss a few weeks later to 'smile when you say the station name'.

'2CR FM,' he said, 'should be said *"Two SEE RRRRRRRRRR"* and smile.' This seemed utter bollocks to me.

I was reprimanded every day for not saying the station strapline as well: 'Today's Better Music Mix from the 80s, 90s and Today.'

This all just seemed so small and petty. None of it was about being funny, entertaining or interesting. But I went out and bought *The Art of War*. If I wanted a successful career in radio broadcasting, it made perfect sense to read an ancient Chinese military text from 5 BC from the mind of a military strategist.

Then maybe on to Winston Churchill's *Dummies Guide to World Wars*. I couldn't understand the connection between war—you know, actual humans shooting at each other and fighting for life and territory—and doing a radio show sponsored by the local carpet showroom.

Having read *The Art of War*, I can confirm that at no point does Sun Tzu say: 'You will need a secret sound competition, and prank calls, oh and some station merch to give away at local fairs, I'm talking car stickers and mugs, shit like that.'

I'm sure the reverse isn't true. I can't imagine that great military minds of today are advising the new generation of leaders and battalion commanders to read Howard Stern's *Private Parts* or Kyle Sandilands' *Scandalands*.

Instead of following this military path, I banked on myself instead, like you can at 25 years of age. I treated the next two years like an apprenticeship. Because Steve was so direct, I learnt very quickly with his feedback. After most shows we would play back a link (a 'link' is what you hear when the DJ speaks, the bit we do in between the songs) that didn't work, which was brutal, but he would find, or try to find, a link that had gone well. I even found I started to mutter 'Shithouse' to myself after yet another fumbled link. He encouraged me to talk about my life more, as when I did it set me out from the rival shows. I bought a notebook and would make notes in it throughout the day as things happened or ideas came up. I still do this every single day. Once, after a row with my wife had calmed, she even said, 'Notebook.' Those notebooks pay for the house!

I put my ego aside and just wanted to get better. To feel my progress. I learnt how to edit and helped out on the evening show, I worked for free on the weekends just to build up my microphone air miles and get more time working out how the studio desk operated so I could use it without even thinking about it.

It was, however, a strange radio station.

When I got there, a 21-year-old man–boy was the traffic guy on the breakfast show and was called 'Richie the Travel Chicken'. Every morning at 5.30 a.m. he'd be at his desk next to me and be angrily putting on his adult-sized chicken outfit, complete with bright red rubber chicken feet. He dressed up as a chicken every day, for the radio. I kept trying to get a rapport with him on air as I found him fascinating and he was funny. Every time he shut me down. He *hated* me. I'd walked in off the streets with no radio experience and took the job he was meant to have, in the studio, and out of an adult-sized chicken outfit.

One day I asked Steve why the traffic guy needed to be in the chicken outfit when no one could see him. Because it's, well, radio. One thing you should be very careful using with radio management is logic.

'He's the most famous thing in this town!' Steve yelled and threw some market research documents at me.

Richie, no, *Richie the Travel Chicken* was really a big deal it turned out. More loved than the local football team, the team captain and just about anything else in town.

A 21-year-old pretending to be a chicken, while reading the traffic news, was the most loved thing in Bournemouth.

I learnt my first lesson about commercial radio: it's nuts.

Sun Tzu didn't have anything on poultry traffic reporters. I was clearly at the leading edge of radio military strategy.

One day in the station carpark, I found Richie crying after a bust-up with the boss about the chicken suit, so I dragged him out for beers. Once he'd taken the chicken head off, a friendship was born, on and off air, that continues to this day.

I even eventually got Richie out of the chicken suit, despite Steve telling us we were crazy, and—no word of a lie—saying it was like 'Nike dropping the swoosh from their logo'.

The next year was one of my favourites of my life. I felt like I'd won life. I was doing the job I'd wanted to do since I was a teenager.

2

Son of Fonzie

That's the last you'll hear of Christian O'Connell.

UNNAMED UK RADIO BOSS,
SPEAKING AT A CONFERENCE IN 2000

'What happened to the chicken man?' asked the therapist.

My mind switched back to the present, and I took a moment to again question why I was in a shed.

'The chicken man, what happened to him?'

For the first time, the therapist seemed animated and interested in what I was saying. Even after all these years, the chicken man's magnetic pull was strong.

I left the 2CR FM breakfast show after almost two years, due to increasing tensions with management.

They wanted me to do dumb competitions like 'Secret Sound' which *every* other show in the world does, which to me felt like filler. You take a sound, say a kettle being filled with water, and play it, taking guesses every day as to what that 'secret sound' may be. And do this for weeks and weeks.

Are you still awake?

We had to do this despite my protests: it had, I was told, come 'from above'.

I had little or no enthusiasm for this on air, which must've been nice for the listeners. We were meant to take guesses every show for four to five weeks to drag it out for ratings. After four shows I'd had enough. A caller was close, so off air I told them the answer and I let them go on air and gave away the whole $10,000 (£5650).

Richie had begged me not to and said we'd be in major trouble. Richie was right.

Immediately after the show, we were marched into the board-room. *Ohhhhhh! Not the boardroom!* Steve the boss was there, and the head of news for some reason, which to this day I still don't know why—was he going to break the story later in the day about the scandal of the secret sound prize going too soon? Worst of all, the managing director was there too. I'd never been in a meeting with him before, so I took this as a bad sign.

The MD was furious that we'd ruined the ratings by giving the answer away so soon. 'What were you thinking?' he asked banging the table, like we were in the courtroom scenes of *A Few Good Men*.

I lied and said I had no idea the listener had the right answer and they changed their guess once they went live on air. He knew I was lying.

Luckily for me, when the ratings came a few weeks later, we got our highest ever results, I couldn't believe it.

The ratings are up?

The ratings seemed like this strange arbitrary judgement you'd be given every three months over your shows. To feel success for the first time making bold choices on what I instinctively felt was right or wrong was a big little moment for me. The lasting takeaway that would forever inform how I did radio was that it was all with no dumb cash giveaway. I didn't want to buy listeners.

But a rift had formed between me and the big bosses.

I then refused to do 'Battle of the Sexes'. This was some ripped-off American radio idea. Every morning it's a man versus a woman. The man gets asked the female-based questions and the woman the male-based questions. You'd get crap like:

To the woman: Where would I find a spark plug?

To the man: What's the name of the male love interest in *Notting Hill*?

After a few weeks peddling this, I refused to do it anymore. This was hot on the heels of #secretsoundgate. I was now regarded as a rebel by senior management. In other words, they saw me as a pain in the arse. I wasn't doing what all their other shows were doing. I thought that this was the right approach, or more correctly, the right way for me. They didn't. Other presenters in the group were getting bigger shows in bigger markets ahead of me. Most breakfast show hosts are pretty lazy and are happy to be spoon-fed ideas. Not all, but most. I wanted to do radio that was funny, real and more inventive, so I did.

I did phone-ins like:

- Have you ever worn a disguise?
- Using Fake ID
- Cruel Games Your Older Brothers and Sisters Played with You
- Psycho School Sports Teachers
- What Was the Christmas Present You Wanted but Never Got?

By today's shock-jock standards this isn't getting the rage of online outrage blogs, but I was making something I believed in.

I made a big effort to not do what all the other radio shows were doing. I once got a clairvoyant on the show and rather than get people calling in about dead relatives, I would only let them ask questions about their dead pets.

Anything weird, amusing or irritating that happened during the day would get talked about on air. I wanted to talk to the listeners and turn it into a conversation. Like you do after those first few drinks with your mates.

I then came up with my first big idea. I had read about a TV show in Europe called *Big Brother,* based on a load of strangers in a house together. I started to wonder if we could do a radio version of it.

The 'Caravan of Hell' was born. I pitched it to Shithouse Steve and to his credit he went for it. We drove out to a caravan showroom and bought the smallest, shittiest, cheapest one we could find. It was covered in rust and mould and I had to paint it.

My idea was to get a few listeners to stay in the caravan and every morning face a challenge live on air. Reality radio, I guess. Back in 1999. The caravan was small so they'd be crammed together. But I needed some money to make it sound big on air or no one in their right mind would enter.

I asked Steve for the annual marketing money for the entire station, he had to see the managing director about this, and then I had to go in and pitch my 'Caravan of Hell' idea. I remember wearing a shirt and tie to help my pitch. The MD just laughed as I bowled into his office. Then stopped laughing when I pitched him my idea.

'And you want me to give you every bit of the entire station's marketing budget for this?'

Somehow, they did and it was a huge success. It even made the local newspapers and TV: the police were called one day as two of the guys almost had a fight, and another guy proposed to his girlfriend live on air.

The show went to Number 1. Over twenty years later, I can still remember what that felt like. Do you know what surprised me about it? It wasn't an ego buzz like I thought it would be.

It was the incredible deeper gratitude that people were enjoying what I was making. That, friends, is the real and simple but great joy about what I am lucky enough to do.

Despite this, I was restless. Or maybe because of it. Even with the show's success, I realised the bosses would never stop trying to turn me into a 'proper radio DJ' like their others. I had little interest in sounding anything like the other DJs. Radio all over the world has been ruined by pin-headed management adopting a cookie-cutter approach.

I was scared of leaving my first radio home, it felt safe and familiar, but Steve gently nudged me towards realising that I needed to leave and make my own path, or I'd lose my edge and any real potential I had.

Now that's a good boss, not thinking about himself.

Although maybe he just wanted to get rid of the guy who killed the chicken man.

•

The man in the shed had warmed up now, chuckling a few times as I told him my stories.

By now I had a few stations offering me jobs. Normally the career path is you go to work for a *bigger* radio station. That's not how it happened for me.

I was about to sign up for one of the biggest stations in the UK, but my agent insisted I check out an opportunity with one of the smallest. They had virtually no listeners but were about to relaunch and their programmer was regarded as one of the best, Giles Squire. The meeting started badly.

Giles opened with, 'I didn't think much of your demo tape,' and I thought of all the swear words I would call my agent for putting me in a room with this jerk. *Who did he think he was? I had three bigger offers!* I'd driven five hours for this interview.

'But I carried on listening,' Giles continued, 'and finally, right at the end, I heard you.'

My demo tape had some of what I thought, at the time, were very funny, topical one-liners. I remember one of them:

I see Michael Jackson is getting divorced, watch out kids, he's dating again.

'Drop the tedious and obvious one-liners,' Giles said.

Ouch.

'Talk about your life, storytelling is what you should do and make your show around, and being in the moment with callers. Be playful and subversive.'

I dropped the ego and started listening to Giles, and at the end of the meeting I shook his hand and accepted the job on the spot from a man who told me I wasn't as good as I thought I was. Which was just what I needed to hear. He told me he would help me get better and I knew he would.

Sarah and I packed up once again as the job was hours away from where we were living in Bournemouth, and got out our road atlas (I know it's easier now using our phones, but the thrill of navigating using a road map and arriving safely is still the best) and mapped our route to a city called Liverpool, maybe you've heard of it, the home of The Beatles and one of Europe's biggest football clubs. We were taking a leap into the unknown once more and heading to a city where we knew no one.

I said an emotional goodbye and thanks to Richie who, despite his younger years, had taught me so much.

Later, I learnt that a week after I left 2CR FM, there was a conference for all the station programmers of the fifteen-odd stations the company owned. The big boss was asked about losing me and the recent good ratings and apparently told them, 'That is the very last we will hear of Christian O'Connell, that is what's called the dead bounce.'

I wrote 'dead bounce' on a post-it note and put it in my new studio when I got there, on one of the studio monitors. Anger can be such a great motivator. I was written off and dismissed so often in my early career, it fuelled me. I wanted to prove them wrong. (All of this was getting me ready for being *really* written off when I came to Australia. But we're a while away from that.)

In my chat with Giles he asked where I wanted to be eventually, and I said a station in London called XFM. Most radio DJs want to be on the Number 1 station—the big name, the big salary, the big ego kick. I was aiming for the Number 13 radio station in London. XFM was a small indie music station that played great music and, most of all, gave their presenters freedom. It was cool and had an attitude. That was where I wanted to be.

Giles said he'd get me there. Neither of us knew I'd only be working with him for nine months before I was offered the breakfast show on XFM.

We loved Liverpool. It's a great city with a big heart. The station was run on a very small budget. I had no sidekick and no producer. There wasn't even an engineer in the station so when the studio broke down, which was once or twice a week, the show would just go off air and I would have to call a help desk in India—I am not making this up. They would guide me over the phone through all the racks of monitors to fix a radio station. This was such a regular occurrence I became on first-name terms with some of the guys in India and I'm godfather to one of their sons.

I became such an expert in how the station worked that one day I turned up with a nasty hangover and tripped a switch that shut the station down, in the middle of the show. I called the boss and told him the Indians were on it but it would take time, quoting 'server issues in Canada apparently', and went to sleep *for an hour* at the back of the tiny studio. I then put the station back on air for the last ten minutes of the show, feeling a little more refreshed, pretending to be furious at my predicament. What a pro.

I had no sidekick to bounce off, so I hired a woman named Lucy who called in frequently and was super smart and funny. I paid her myself—$50 per show was all I could afford—and she had to leave at 8.30 a.m. to go to her actual job as a charity fundraiser.

The show became a talking point in the industry despite being so small when it made national media after I took out a fake advert in a national newspaper, saying:

Britain's First Bullfighting Arena is Coming to the UK, Liverpool

I paid for the fake ad myself, it was recruiting for trainee matadors, no experience needed as full training would be given. A phone number that went to my studio offered more details. No one at the newspaper checked out what I was saying despite the fact that bullfighting is illegal in Britain.

At the time I thought it would be a funny idea and be interesting to record what happened, to see if anyone believed that a bullfighting arena was really coming to the UK and Liverpool.

I had not cleared any of this with my boss and it quickly spun out of control. But not before I'd been invited on BBC radio, defending my fake bullfighting arena, saying, 'Any bulls used will be volunteer ones.'

I was trying to make a point about how even in the year 2000, everyone rushes to outrage without thinking about whether something is for real. Luckily, that doesn't happen anymore . . .

People actually called in, interested in becoming trainee matadors, and I recorded all the calls. I quizzed these people about how fit they were, how were they with the colour red, had they ever used a cape before. In the background I played sound effects of people screaming in pain and I'd casually say to the wannabe bullfighter on the line, 'Oh no! Another failed audition, more mess to clean up, are you still interested?'

The ratings tripled and XFM took the bull by the horns and came to Liverpool to meet me. I remember buying a new jacket to impress them. A jacket that would say *Yeah, I'm ready for a London breakfast show.*

I bought a leather jacket. This is a thing for me, my love of black leather jackets. I had saved my pocket money for my first one when I was fifteen. I remember wearing it as I rode my BMX bike to my girlfriend's house and thinking I was the shit.

This 'I'm ready for the big-time' leather jacket had to make an impression as another brass ring might be offered to me with a London breakfast show. It was skin-tight, tight like Eddie Murphy wore on stage in *Raw* and *Delirious.*

Looking back, I shudder, as after the lunch and interview—not that you can really interview someone for a job on the radio—the man who would be my next boss, another very blunt Australian (there's a pattern forming here) touched my red-hot-off-the-peg leather jacket and said, 'If we offer you the show, you might wanna lose this, Fonzie, unless you're auditioning for *Grease.*'

•

The next morning the boss and chief executive of XFM sat in their hotel rooms and listened to my whole show together. I was only aware of this live audition as the boss texted me telling me minutes before my show started:

'You are about to do the most important show of your life, don't fuck it up'

I texted back, it was 2001 so this took a little time then on an old Nokia:

'No pressure then!'

He sent me one of the greatest messages I have ever received, sort of thing a legendary old sports coach might say to a raw rookie on the verge of being drafted into the majors:

'If you think this is pressure, then you're not ready for London'

I got the job.

After less than three years on the radio, I would have a London breakfast show. Maybe the jacket did help.

They had little confidence in me though. I was unknown and, in London, you are up against big names, radio legends, TV presenters on the radio. I had to take a pay cut to get the show.

A pay cut?

My wife wasn't convinced this time.

I had other offers, with actual pay rises. Which is how it should work with your career. At this rate I'd be a volunteer back on hospital radio again. I asked her once more to trust me and she did. She was really worried about the money, what if we wanted to have children, and why I was so fixated on this tiny station when I should be on a bigger one in London. I told her that the thought of not doing this show and taking this offer made me want to be sick. That's when you know, despite logic and reason, you really are following your heart.

Or an idiot.

Money was so tight when we packed up for the third time that I had to sell my car to afford moving to such an overpriced and expensive city as London. It was the first car I'd ever owned, a second-hand Peugeot 205 (still no BMW or Porsche). I was actually sad saying goodbye to that car. There are so many firsts you don't forget in your life. First girlfriend, first car. Sometimes I get confused between the two, all I know is one was rusty and expensive to run.

But I was in London, and about to start a breakfast show in one of the greatest cities in the world and on a radio station that was awesome.

The next five years on XFM changed our lives, and for the first and possibly only time, I was able to say to my wife, 'I told you so.'

3

Mind your language, Prime Minister

Do you take sugar as well?

SIR ELTON JOHN, MAKING ME A CUP OF TEA IN HIS KITCHEN

At XFM, I got to do the show I wanted to do. I had a great sidekick from day one in a man named Chris Smith and a crazy Spanish producer called Rocky. I'd never had a 'producer' before.

XFM had a lot of terrific people working there back then. I met Karl Pilkington on day one, now a big star himself on TV. At the time he was the guy who made the jingles and daily promo for my show. A hugely smart, funny and grumpy Northerner, Karl said in the pub before I started, having only just met him two beers earlier, 'You better be funny.'

Now, Karl, Ricky Gervais and Stephen Merchant have made podcasting history and some ground-breaking TV shows together. Ricky and Steve, around the time *The Office* started in 2001, also joined the station on a Saturday afternoon show. Their show was edgy and at times unbelievable.

We were *the* radio station everyone was talking about, but not many people were listening to. Even though we had little or no budget, we had this underground, outsider attitude that was perfect for me. For the first time on the radio, I really felt at home on the station I was on. I wasn't playing Top 40 chart music, I was playing music I loved. Rock and roll and indie. I could do anything, and I did.

I did a feature for a while where, live on air, I called other bigger radio shows, trying to call them *live* on my show to win the competitions they were doing, and then gave those prizes away on my show: we called the feature 'Robbing Hood'.

There was 'Sex Line Rodeo' where every week I called a sex line and would chat away about all kinds of improvised nonsense, and the moment they mentioned anything to do with sex I would stop the call. Listeners had to guess how long the calls would last. They could last more than twenty minutes, as the longer the call the more money the sex line made.

I would create these fantastical stories about who I was, from an undercover police officer working on a deli counter of a supermarket trying to take down an international cheese-smuggling ring, to an inventor called Ralph whose wife had left him but he was on the verge of perfecting the world's first pillow that cut your hair as you slept. The women on the other end of the line would just be happy to chat about anything other than grubby sex acts.

We also conducted my producer Rocky's vasectomy, assisting in this procedure live on air. I wish I hadn't. I'm all for team bonding but getting to see a team member's member is too much. I remember that once it was done, we played a song by Black Grape.

The show started getting celebrity fans, Simon Pegg and Nick Frost would be regulars, and I read in a newspaper that Dr Who himself, David Tennant, listened.

We were the show guests and bands wanted to come on. The band Darkness, one of the biggest rock bands of the 2000s, launched their debut album live on my show in 2003. We had 1000 listeners there as we broadcast live from one of London's famous music venues and the band played three songs. At 8 a.m. right in the middle of London's school run, I introduced the band on stage and on air. I thought they were going to kick off with 'I Believe in a Thing Called Love', their Number 1 hit. They didn't. They did 'Get Your Hands off My Woman', which has the almost Shakespearian line 'Get your hands off my woman motherfucker' repeated over ten times. Live. Screamed repeatedly into a microphone on the school run.

The album went on to go quadruple platinum. I went on to be banned from live music for a while. The amazing thing about this was we received zero complaints.

Zero.

Which means either my listeners were very cool, or we really did have no listeners.

I really grew out of my early skin on XFM. I think sometimes when you start out as a comedian or radio DJ you wear your influences to begin with; it was XFM where I actually started to listen to my own instincts and ideas.

Some of the stuff I did I shudder at now, like 'Sex Line Rodeo'. I was young, immature and wanting to kick back at stuffy radio conventions and the mainstream. I still hope I have that desire now and an edge.

When I started, we were London's 17th biggest breakfast show. I loved using that underdog, outsider spirit as a motivating energy. So I had merchandise made that proudly declared us London's 17th biggest breakfast show. The marketing team refused at first, worried it could be seen as 'negative'.

We then moved up to 14th, meaning new merchandise, a beanie hat this time. One evening I was watching the news and saw Ricky Gervais being interviewed and he was wearing our new Number 14 beanie. We broke the Top 10 and then headed higher in the charts, taking the station and my show to record numbers.

For a brief, really brief, time, I enjoyed a hazy summer where I was actually *the* DJ of the moment. I was getting magazine profile pieces, TV appearances, hell, even the hard-to-please *Guardian* newspaper called me 'undeniably funny'. I went from never having done TV in my life to suddenly being hired by Chris Evans, one of my radio and TV heroes, to host a daily live evening show, *Live with Christian O'Connell.*

I was doing my morning show, then at 7 p.m. would be live on TV to the whole of the UK. This was my Monday to Friday life. I was in my twenties, married and being paid for work I loved, and living life to the full.

I wish my kids had known me then. They know me now as some sad middle-aged man—they've met me at my worst!

Dad used to be 'cool', kids.

•

In 2005, my last year at XFM, I started to feel like I'd taken the show and myself as far as I could. I was wanting a new challenge, another little mountain to try to get up. A new horizon was beckoning.

My life was changing. The biggest part of this was our first daughter, Ruby, being born in 2004. Everything, every cell of my body, changed the moment I held her.

Then I was offered the best gig you can get in commercial radio in the UK, the Virgin Radio breakfast show.

Live to all of the UK, it was launched as a station by Sir Richard Branson and made famous by one of the UK's very best broadcasters, Chris Evans. Now I was getting to do the show he did. I took my entire brilliant team (Chris, Brian who went from the work experience kid to a producer and Rocky) to the other side of London's Soho and a new radio station.

I was pretty much unknown outside of London, so once again I had to start with some listeners who didn't know me, a new relationship. They really didn't like me at first, but I ended up staying on that station for twelve brilliant years.

So many things happened in my time there: my second daughter, Lois, was born. I now had *two* amazing daughters. While Ruby was two weeks late and had to be dragged out of her mum—no really, with some vacuum thingy, and it's the same now at sixteen getting her up in the morning; I get the Dyson and prise her out of that bed—Lois was born at home and came *flying* out like a bullet. We had this tiny home birthing pool in the kitchen and she arrived so explosively it was as if she leapt out yelling 'SURPRISE!'

The love I felt upon meeting them both for the first time at their births still brings tears of such deep joy to me. Those are the moments when you feel this unimaginable love, like nothing you have ever felt before. It was so powerful I thought I was going to die!

I used to like asking guests what their favourite word is, mine is just three letters long: *Dad*.

I'm going to take a break now because if I start telling you how I felt when they first said the D-word, I might just melt away into this keyboard. I'm going to go put the kettle on, get a Tunnock's tea cake, no, caramel wafer, and return after I get myself back together.

•

Ah, that's better. Thank you.

Back at my new radio home, Virgin Radio. There were numerous management and team changes, even a name change to 'Absolute Radio'; and Richie the Chicken Man—remember him?—he came back on board and we picked it all up again all those years later.

We took that show from its lowest point—after the name change when it was down to 900,000 listeners, which doesn't seem that low but was for a national show across the UK—to more than two and a half million. We did this with little or no marketing but great support from our radio family of listeners, who heard all the changes we were growing through. I was given the freedom by some great mentor bosses, Paul Jackson, David Lloyd and Clive Dickins, to make something that had heart and joy, and we cared about what we were making.

I did so much on that show and interviewed some amazing people. I co-hosted a show with Dave Grohl, who is such a great guy and sport that he did the travel reports for the UK live on air. It was one of many pinch-me-is-this-really-happening moments—a member of Nirvana was doing my travel news—dead bounce my arse.

I interviewed Sir Elton John in his kitchen at home after he made me a cup of tea. I then heard him lose his shit mid-interview (at his dining table) at some aide talking loudly in another room distracting him. It's a real-life moment when you are wearing headphones and one of your musical heroes screams 'SHUT UP YOU C***S' so loudly (and pitch perfect Elton) that it almost shatters your eardrums. He was a dream to interview.

The Duke of Edinburgh (the Queen's husband) invited me to speak at his annual Gold Awards Ceremony. Before my speech to the hundreds of teenagers and their parents, the duke and I had some back and forth at St James Palace in front of everyone.

He had so much high-wattage charisma and was fascinated as to why I'd arrived in a hearse. I explained that I'd said on air what an honour it was to be invited by the duke and a caller offered to take me from my show in Soho to St James Palace in style in one of his limousines. However, on the big day his limo broke down, but he didn't want to worry me on air on my special day, so he simply swapped to one of his other *'executive cars'*. That day I finished the show, put my suit on, walked out of the station and saw a hearse. A hearse!?

As the listener was already upset, I didn't have the heart to say, 'I'll take a cab,' so I arrived at St James Palace in front of all the teenagers and parents and the duke's footmen in a hearse. The duke said this was actually the perfect choice of transport for a breakfast show DJ, as you could lie down for a nap in the back. He had the crowd in stitches.

I did think on the way home that I should buy a hearse—no one is cutting you off in traffic, everyone lets you out, you're gonna get a good deal at your local garage if you need new tyres.

My show even crossed over to politics when the-then prime minister Tony Blair called live from Number 10 Downing Street to enter my big competition 'Who's Calling Christian?'

But it was the appearance on my show of another prime minister, David Cameron, that really caused a furore. What happened became the lead news story on all the news channels that night and made the front pages of the newspapers.

Live on air David Cameron did something that was not only very un-British, but certainly very un–prime ministerial.

He swore.

Twice.

•

Now if this was here in Australia, no big deal. It still amazes me when I hear politicians casually addressing each other as 'mate' in the Australian parliament. In Britain's stuffy parliament with the barely awake and, in some cases, alive members, it's always the 'Honourable' or 'Right Honourable' member.

David Cameron's PR team had selected my radio show to help him be 'more real' and appeal to lapsed voters. So the plan was that I'd have the Prime Minister of Britain sit opposite me in my studio and we'd take live calls and questions. I'd told my listeners that no political questions were allowed, as he wouldn't give you the answers you wanted and that's not my show.

I also barred any of his flunkies from being in the studio. This is my golden rule with big-name guests, it's just you and me in the studio. No handlers making eye contact at questions they want avoided. The PM's team hated this.

His security detail had already scoped out my studio, as we were on the third floor and my studio had these huge windows. They had scanned all the windows and this solid-looking unit with bulges under his armpits asked me, 'Do you have to sit there?' I replied: 'Yes, I do have to sit here unless the prime minister knows how to drive a radio desk.' Then it dawned on me why he wanted me to move, so I could be a human shield for the PM. To take a bullet for him. Now that's your job, mate, not mine as a DJ who, may I add, also has his daughter's sports day this afternoon. (Though to be fair, if any of you have sat through your kid's sports day as they struggle with hula hoop and relay race, a non-lethal bullet might be preferable. You know, just a flesh shot.)

So anyway, suddenly, it's just me and the prime minister in the studio for a few minutes of chat before we are live to the UK. He insisted I call him 'Dave'.

We go live on air and I said: 'Let's find out more about the man with some original questions.'

First caller asked the prime minister which is his favourite member of the A-Team. Bang. Hardball right out of the gates.

Second asked if he and his wife, Sam, have a bath together, which end of the bath would he sit at. 'The tap end like any gentleman should,' replied my Right Honourable guest, Dave to me.

The third caller asked for a surprising fact about Number 10 Downing Street. Great question! The prime minister, Dave to close friends like me, told us the letterbox isn't real. Makes sense. This is one of world politics' most famous doors, which Churchill stood in front of many times during the war. You don't want junk mail or those irritating courier cards ('We tried to deliver your parcel so, screw you, come get it yourself') shoved through the letterbox, let alone bombs.

Then the unthinkable happened.

First, David Cameron said 'pissed off', as in people were 'pissed off with politicians'.

Then he said 'twat'.

Now, to us English people, this is a really rude swear word.

It's vulgar slang for 'vagina', and also used to call someone stupid. His aides behind him in the gallery looking into the studio leapt out of their chairs, throwing iPhones all over the place. We went into a song and I had to warn the actual Prime Minister of Great Britain about his language.

I ushered in one of his team, who looked like he was on the verge of tears. He also told the PM to mind his language.

'Yes, sorry Chris [power move, my name is Christian] about saying piss, just got carried away, but twat's not really a swear word—'

'YES IT IS!' said his PR guy and me at the same time.

Come on, Dave!

To very posh people like David 'Call me Dave' Cameron who went to Oxford University and maybe aren't too familiar with the swear words of us ordinary folk, it's also a word for a 'pregnant fish', according to the man running the country.

'Bullshit,' I replied automatically. Then I apologised for my language and the prime minister actually had the cheek to look upset. I was worried he'd withdraw all 'Call me Dave' privileges.

Above the prime minister in the studio was a TV monitor so we could keep an eye on any news. It was on Sky News, and I suddenly saw my radio station's name flash up under a breaking news alert:

BREAKING: PM Turns Air Waves Blue!

I smiled at my guest, who couldn't see the monitor as it was above him. I'll tell you who could: his team. They came flying into the studio and whispered really loudly to the prime minister to wrap things up. The thing I took from this panicked exchange was, *they aren't allowed to call him Dave.* I'm PM Inner Circle I guess now.

By the time he walked out the station's front door, Sky News had a satellite truck and reporter waiting for him.

In today's soundbite-dominated world, the prime minister had just served the British media two aces. The story just snowballed all day. My mum called me to tell *me* off for swearing on air, she took some persuading when I told her it wasn't me but the prime minister.

The BBC six o'clock news is watched by millions around the UK every night. This was the lead news story. As this was the

BBC, the newsreader intoned solemnly before playing the clip of Cameron on my show swearing (bleeped out, it's the BBC, darling) the words: 'Now before we show you the clip, I should warn you it contains two swear words.'

Count them Davey, *two*. The BBC, one of the world's most trusted news organisations, wasn't buying the pregnant fish line either.

There were complaints. Many complaints. After the show my boss, Clive, called a meeting in his office which he started with:

'Today, this becomes a war cabinet team.' Clive was a brilliant boss and someone who lived for drama like this. He shat Sun Tzu out for breakfast.

He then passed around a print-out and asked everyone to take a good look at it. It was the Ofcom, the UK broadcasting's watchdog, ruling on the Top 10 Most Offensive Swear Words for TV and Radio.

An actual Top 10! Want to know what was on there? I'm not supposed to be sharing this, but I'm on the other side of the world so here goes:

10. Bastard
9. Wanker
8. Bitch
7. Twat
6. Cock
5. Pussy
4. Prick
3. Fuck
2. Cunt
1. Motherfucker

Number 1, said over TEN times on my old show on XFM. I've broken the Number 1 word.

I see the prime minister's 'twat' is a new entry at 7. We could be in trouble, if the complaints are upheld, a large fine could be imposed. What happens then? I didn't swear, do I have to go round to Number 10 asking for him to pay my fine?

Ofcom investigated #twatgate. Fortunately, they ruled in our favour and didn't uphold the complaints. A few days after their ruling, a courier turned up at the station with two framed identical pictures. It was a political cartoon of David Cameron swearing and underneath the Ofcom ruling of the incident. The prime minister had written in ink, 'Phew! What a relief x'.

He wanted me to sign his picture and return it to him. That's a man with a good sense of humour. I mean just look at him thinking that a Brexit referendum was a good idea.

Twat.

•

'What was Elton John like?' asked the therapist raising his eyebrows.

Huh? Wasn't he supposed to ask about my life journey, my struggles, overcoming adversity . . . relationship with my mum?

A few days after the Elton John interview in his kitchen, he was doing a very exclusive show for my station in a former chapel. Just 400 guests. That intimate.

I was invited backstage beforehand to say hello, but when I got there I felt this tension and then I was told Elton would only do three songs. He was having some kind of moment.

By this time, with only twenty minutes to go, the audience had settled in and was expecting a very special, hour-long show and the radio station had an hour allocated for it to be transmitted live. I shuffled out like it was no big deal, and told my boss the situation.

'You'll have to get him to do the full hour,' the boss said.

'He's Elton John, he does what the fuck he wants,' I hissed back. We were like that married couple, trying not to have an argument but having an argument.

'Make him do it.'

'How?'

'This is what we pay you for, fix it, find a way,' he said and walked off.

Oh shit.

Fifteen minutes to showtime, I was given my microphone and told the sequence of lights that would mean we were live across the UK. Then, when it was time to bring Elton John on, the light would turn purple.

All I was thinking was how the hell am I going to get Elton John to sing for an hour when he doesn't want to.

'Time to get in position now,' said the stage manager.

As I was ushered around the back of the stage, I could hear the excited buzz of the audience. These final minutes before a show, like when I'm doing a stand-up gig, are some of my favourite moments. The excitement, expectation, potential.

All I felt now was panic: *What am I going to do?*

An hour ago in a bar around the corner, my wife and I had had a few drinks and we shared in the excitement of what was about to happen, an intimate show with Elton John. Now it looked like this would be a *very short* intimate show.

Once in the wings I looked out from behind the curtain and scanned the crowd. I saw a grand piano on stage, like a pearl glowing white. It looked magical.

But the party boy wasn't feeling it. I got it. To him, it was just a show for some radio competition winners. To me, it was everything.

I whispered to one of Elton's team, 'Probably be okay once he loosens up,' more to comfort myself than him.

He formed a half-smile like this had happened many times before and it never ended okay.

On the other side of the stage in the wings was the ominous figure of my boss. He glared over like, *'Remember, make it happen. This is what we pay you for!'* I could think of nothing to solve this and wanted to be anywhere else but there.

'Two minutes' to go and I saw movement on the other side of the stage. It was Elton John. Shit. I was really nervous now. Should I pray?

'Sixty seconds and you will be live,' the stage manager warned.

The small light on the side of my mic went green, it was now live, the safety catch was off.

What was I going to say to the audience here and at home all over the country? I hadn't even prepared my intro. I knew it needed to mark the moment and be funny, maybe a gag about . . . Blank. Nothing. Blank.

'Walk on now, eight, seven, six,' said the stage manager and he patted me on my back like they do paratroopers when it's time to leap out of a plane.

My feet walked out onto the stage, but part of me was left waiting in the wings. Or back in the bar.

'Good evening!' I bellowed excitedly. Shit-eating grin on display. What a tool.

I took in the crowd, saw that James Corden had somehow got in the front row. And some other faces from TV and film. Oh God.

Then words came out of me, to this day I have no idea where from.

'We are lucky to be here tonight, and listening all over the country to a very rare and special Sir Elton John show. Just him and a piano, live in a chapel.

'Normally, after a show like this, we would be giving Elton a standing ovation, but tonight let's do something different . . . let's give it to him NOW, he deserves it at the start of his show RIGHT NOW!

'Come on, everybody get up, let's start the standing ovation now, show Elton John what he means to us!'

The response of screaming, whistling and applause was huge, it almost blew me back off my feet.

'MORE!' I urged and they gave more. I was buzzing. But would it be enough?

'Ladies and gentlemen, please welcome on stage, the great Elton John!'

Elton John walked *out* to a standing ovation, beaming from all the love he was being shown. I headed off stage and as we passed each other he shook my hand, patted my back warmly and leant in to say, 'Well played, you fucked me.' Then he waved to his standing loving audience

As I left the backstage area, the stage manager was all high-fives and even the boss gave me a silent nod of acknowledgement.

I went and found my wife in the audience and sidled up next to her.

'Everything okay? You looked stressed.'

All I could say over the noise of the crowd as Elton hammered out the intro to 'Crocodile Rock' was, 'I just fucked Elton John.'

4

Halfway dead

Is Dad having some sort of mid-life crisis?

RUBY O'CONNELL

'Push me!'

The man in the shed was standing over me urging me to get up and push him out of the way.

He was serious.

Was picking a physical fight with your patients normal? How was this going to help my anxiety and panic attacks? Right now, it was only making it worse.

I was reasonably sure Dr Sigmund Freud never kicked over the patient's couch and pushed his clients into a UFC-style octagon to beat the demons out of them.

To be honest, I was just embarrassed that I was there at all. Even though I knew I needed help, there is this terrible shame among us men about asking for help. Like it's a sign of 'weakness'. In reality, tremendous courage and strength is needed to admit to yourself you need help and then going and asking for it.

I was in a very scary part in my life where I didn't know where else to turn. Finding a therapist isn't that easy, it turns out. You can't just put something on your friends WhatsApp group. My last message was about the best place to get takeaway pizza, now I'm asking for a therapist? Must've been a really bad pizza they'd have thought.

I've heard many men say they don't need therapy and yet no one needs it more than us. No gender has it easy in life, and as a man I'm fully aware the world is heavily stacked to my advantage. This is something I see with even greater clarity as a father to daughters. I learn from their eyes as they realise this about the world.

I will say that being a guy isn't easy emotionally. We have walls around us we didn't even know we had built.

I envy how my wife can be so emotionally honest with her friends. Men can, but only after about ten beers. And that's after spending three hours debating who would win a fight between James Bond and John Wick (*for the record, John Wick*).

Maybe therapists should open up a room at the back of pubs. You see so many men hugging mates, professing love for each other, all under the influence of beers.

But when we're sober, we say nothing, which is when emotional help could be at its most needed and actually helpful. It would at least be remembered the next morning.

I was thinking about this a lot as I was sitting in a stranger's shed seeking help and realising that none of my friends knew how I was struggling. Unable to work and terrified I was going a bit mad.

That's not a slight on them, I could've called them and told them, and I know they would've been understanding and caring. But for some reason, unknown forces within me prevented this. Like I would have been embarrassed by my 'weakness' in front of them. I feared their imagined judgement. I guess this is why when a man has a severe breakdown, or in extreme cases, takes his own life, everyone says, 'I had no idea.'

Society asks men to be providers, leave home, get a job, try to find meaning in the status that the job and salary gives us, our reward for being so coldly focused. To make matters worse, we constantly compare ourselves to other guys. It's as if, unwittingly, all men have been entered into some kind of competition to be the manliest man the human race has ever produced. Constant auditions and trials await us. There is no endgame, other than death.

When you think about this, it starts at conception when our sperm are in a swimming race against one another. This is the ultimate reality show, *The Amazing Sperm Race*.

Some men create a kind of frozen lake of their emotions in their chests and stomachs that even the toughest of pickaxes can't break through from the outside. I've heard many women say of their husbands that they are good, kind, decent men, but '*He just won't talk to me about what's going on inside him.*'

Over the next few months with the man in the shed, I learnt slowly that the thawing and melting had to come from within.

The very idea of paying a stranger to listen to me whine about my entitled and fortunate life horrified me. And that there is the problem with men. Getting men to open up and talk is the hardest part, we're programmed not to do it. Maybe that's why suicide rates are so high, the feelings of alienation and loneliness. That you can't be helped, you are broken.

It's less a silent killer—it's the silence that's the killer.

In Australia, around 45 men a week take their lives. Forty-five every single week. In the UK, the highest suicide rate is among men 45–49 (Samaritans, 2018) and suicide is the single biggest killer of men under 45. Bigger than cancer or car accidents. What does this say? Why is it so?

I did need help, and some part of me took me to the man in the shed.

It wasn't just the part that needed to save my job to pay the mortgage.

So I was ready to open up, but I wasn't as open to getting into a fight to do it.

•

I reluctantly stood up and moved towards WWE's answer to Carl Jung. 'What's the point in this?' I asked him wearily.

'You need to find your soul's fire,' he smiled at me. There was a mischievous twinkle in his eye, one I would learn to both love and hate over the next few months.

'For fuck's sake,' I said and sighed, from my inner teenager. As if I'd been told to tidy my bedroom. *'There's a three-bar heater in the corner of the shed, crank that up and warm my soul.'*

The man in the shed was white haired, goateed, older and smaller than me. He looked like he could get some work at Christmas as a department store Santa.

Fine, I thought, I'll bowl Father Christmas over and ace this spiritual test.

Only I couldn't.

Deepak Santa was leaning into me like a seasoned pro boxer leans on his opponent on the ropes to wear him out. I was now 100 per cent engaged in moving an old man out of my way.

This felt really wrong. But I was losing. I don't know about my soul's fire, but my ego had woken up.

I tried harder, but nothing. He was really centred, both emotionally and physically, it seemed.

I was starting to feel the old familiar creep of school sports humiliation. Would I be doing burpees next? I was often picked last for team sports, after the kid with one eye and the other hooked up to an iron lung because his asthma was so bad. My only thrill at school sports was sliding down the big rope from the ceiling, but maybe that's too much to share.

'Find your chi, your inner power, not just muscle, but willpower. Come on, move me,' he taunted like a spiritual PE teacher. This was now weird.

I tried to remember the grappling lessons I used to have with a world champion Brazilian jiu jitsu coach. I'd train with him weekly at his house. He'd have gym mats laid out in his garden and we'd grapple with each other, sometimes watched by his six-year-old daughter. Goodness knows what she made of it all. *Dad has men over and rolls around on the ground with them.* When it rained, we moved the mats into his kitchen and wrestled on the floor. I'd think of the *Pink Panther* movies and those amazing fight scenes between Peter Sellers as Inspector Clouseau and Burt Kwouk's Cato. Each week I'd leave covered with scratches and bruises on my back and neck. My wife joked about me having an affair, and then actually asked me if I was.

Recalling those grappling techniques, I controlled my breathing, moved my hands lower down and grabbed Santa around the waist, clasping my hands together in the small of his back. I pushed my body into his upper chest and at the same time pulled my hands towards me and his hips. '*Like pushing a fence post over*' came my old instructor's voice, I don't think either of us thought the lessons would one day come in handy when grappling a counsellor. This really was wrestling with your demons.

It worked and I pushed him over.

We went flying backwards, a twisted two-man pretzel locked together, and crashed into his armchair. I landed on top of him heavily and he was laughing, which made me furious.

'YES! That's it, you found your fire, now SCREAM it all OUT.'

Scream? Now you want me to scream? WTF?

I tried to scream but couldn't. I could hurl an elderly man to the floor, but I couldn't scream.

I felt embarrassed. I couldn't scream. My chest felt frozen. I instantly flashed back to the anxiety attacks at the bin.

One very recent depressing morning I had managed to summon the courage to try and get back to work and into the studio that was once my sacred space, and it happened again. Heart racing and me thinking I was going to die. This time though the bin meltdown was replaced with a toilet one. Just to switch it up a bit you know? I had the horrifying experience of seeing my distorted face in the reflection of the mirrored tap. Sometimes we are surprised by who we find in ourselves in moments of real fear and terror.

I went home early, having missed work again, and saw the kids getting up for school, startling them with my presence. Ruby said in private to my wife, '*So is Dad having some sort of mid-life crisis?*'

How does a twelve-year-old even know what a mid-life crisis is? Do they swap notes on their middle-aged dads in the school playground?

Mine is learning the guitar.

Mine is getting a Chinese tattoo.

Mine is paying an old man to wrestle him in a shed.

I couldn't scream.

My own voice, the thing that I earnt my living from, had deserted me.

The full-bodied charge I felt throwing a 60-something-year-old man into a chair had quickly faded to be replaced by a sense of defeat. I now felt even more despairing than when I walked into this shed of shame. I felt helpless, I found myself saying this quietly to him.

The man in the shed took a full deep belly breath then a longer knowing out-breath. This is a little technique he later showed me, going low and longer on your breath. He nodded and said, 'Yeah, I'm sorry, you must feel very alone.'

Hearing his kindness touched a part of me and I could offer no resistance to his words. I found myself starting to sob.

My tears landed on the terracotta tiles of his shed floor. I mumbled apologies through snotty sobs and also offered my appreciation of his tiles. That's being a grown-up, isn't it? Even in your darkest moment of despair, you can still appreciate a nice terrazzo-style tiling. I wondered how many tears had been spilt on those tasteful tiles. He hadn't gone cheap on those tiles, I guess using the savings made on not having an office.

'You know what a mid-life crisis is really about?' he asked.

I looked up saying nothing but my face said it all.

Not that tired old cliché, men my age screwing the receptionist and buying a Harley-Davidson. When women go through something in middle age, it's 'an awakening'. I loved Elizabeth Gilbert's *Eat, Pray, Love*, rightly a bestseller. But if I leave my wife and go to India and shack up with a hot Brazilian, I'm a douchebag.

'How does it make you feel seeing your kids get older, not needing you to carry them up to bed anymore?'

I flinched at this because in our first session I spoke about how hard it was seeing my kids head into teenhood and disappearing from who they were and my relationship with them changing.

'Nothing ever lasts forever.'

I thought I could trust this guy, now he was using this against me. His own style of therapy jiu jitsu on me.

My dad was right: *Never trust a stranger with your secrets.*

My stomach churned. I tried to remember the last time I carried my kids up to their beds. Feeling their sweet warm breath on the back of my neck. 'Daddy's so strong,' they would say. And the memory of that, it melted me again.

My inner bully was telling me I'm not strong, I've let them down, I'm a shitty dad. I felt anxiety rising. If I can't do my radio show and work, how will I earn money for them?

As Tony Soprano said about his anxiety attack in the opening of *The Sopranos*, it was like 'ginger ale in my brain'. I tried to explain, the man in the shed urged me to take my time and handed me a tissue from a conveniently placed box. He's been here before in the shed of hurt, wrestling tears out of men. That or he uses the shed to jerk off in.

Oh God, I hope they're not related.

How many boxes of tissues does he get through in a week?

Are they tax deductible? I love the idea of a load of therapists all stocking up in bulk at Costco on boxes of tissues, the only profession that goes through that many a day. Other than prostitution. Interestingly, both charge by the hour.

He told me I was in the second half of my life. And I had to confront my own mortality.

'I'm halfway dead?'

'Bluntly speaking, yes.'

Based on the average age of male life expectancy, 58.02 per cent of my life is over. This was going to be a tough chat with the kids at dinnertime tonight:

'Girls, Dad's only got 41.98 per cent of his life left.'

I'd have to break it down in terms they'd understand:

'Imagine Dad is a phone, my battery only has 40 per cent left. I'm all good, but you're not making a long call with me or playing a game. Basically, let's not start any box sets, Dad could be zero per cent by the season finale.'

The therapist told me about the happiness curve. I looked it up later. It's a major and respected study across many countries. My favourite part is they even studied it on apes and chimpanzees. An ape having a mid-life crisis: Is he walking out on his wife at the zoo and taking up with one of the younger flamingos?

It goes like this: Imagine a big 'U'. On the vertical axis (haven't used the word 'axis' since I left school, so I may get confused here) is the happiness rating, and on the horizontal axis is the decades of our ages, from 20 to 100.

Happiness is high, really high, in your twenties, as it should be.

Then it tails off and hits rock bottom at, guess what age? Yeah, your forties. Great!

But once you get out of your toughest decade, you start to get happier again, and wiser. So, going by this well-respected study, if I hit 98, I'm going to be the happiest I've ever been. Thinking about my possible 98-year-old life, would I still be doing a breakfast radio show? I imagine I'd be doing it to the residents of a retirement community: 'Good morning Sunnyview Retirement Home! Bingo with Bev is at lunchtime today, water aerobics with Neil at 10 a.m. Call me this morning if you've ever crapped your pants and not realised.'

Back to the bottom point of your happiness curve, you're my age, where your kids are growing up, don't need you as much, you're more tired, aching, you make noises when bending over, you take small joys in the thread count of bedsheets, your parents are also getting older and frailer. So, my understanding of all of this is, my forties are like my 'Nam.

The man in the shed was on a roll, given his age he was on the rise of his happiness curve, his office was in his garden, he was picking fights with zero-happiness mumblies like me. Possibly jerking off about it. Life was good.

He explained that my panic attacks, the anxiety, is my soul trying to get me to pay attention, listen to myself. To wake up.

'The second half of life is a chance of awakening to your soul, what your soul needs, it's been trying to get your attention, it has now. Sometimes we wake up suddenly in our lives, and see that we've been sleepwalking through it for a while.'

I protested that I was very lucky, had a dream job, a beautiful wife and kids. If the teenage me knew what I had now in my life, he wouldn't believe it was possible. His only thrill was that gym rope, and The Bangles' singer Susanna Hoffs.

The therapist went on and explained that in the second half of our lives, we lose many of the certainties we had. The false status of jobs, income, holiday, mortgage: success in those areas does not always mean it nourishes your soul. The objects and trinkets you've accumulated have no real meaning. You are confronted with your mortality, kids growing up quickly, and all of a sudden a big question arises: *Who really are you?* Your identity as a dad is changing now.

Physically, you are changing, how you look and feel. You are decaying.

He had me at decaying. *You try getting up at 4.12 a.m. for twenty-odd years, you might have a little 'decaying' look about you. Don't be so rude. I pay for these tiles.*

I was starting to get it. First half of life is kind of what the world wants from me; the second half, what does my soul need?

I still felt like a whiny dick moaning about my lot. My mum worked herself to the bone as a nurse and my dad in a car factory. But now I wondered, what would they honestly say about their mid-life years?

The therapist then stood up and put his arms out. 'Can I give you a hug?'

I had nothing in me left to offer resistance, so I replied on behalf of a kinder, tender part of me that actually needed that. We hugged and again, embarrassingly, I started to cry.

'It's a brave path you are now having to make for yourself, but one that could change your life,' he said.

As I left the shed, I wondered what had just happened, having basically paid a man to fight me then hug me. There were places I knew where I could get that done and a happy ending way cheaper.

The way back out onto the main road was around some garages and down a small lane. I emerged right into the path of an oncoming young mum and her baby; she startled when she suddenly saw me. I was sweaty from wrestling and red-eyed from crying, I would've been startled if I saw me. My shirt was also hanging out from the grapplefest. And I'd snuck out from a lane behind some garages.

'Christian O'Connell?' she asked.

Shit no, not now.

I stopped a few paces on from her and turned around, giving her my best smile. The kid looked scared, to him I must have looked like a sad clown, which I guess I was.

'Listen to your show every morning, any chance of a selfie?'

I happily obliged, as I always do. I'm lucky anyone cares. But sometimes on a good day, I think of what that photo of me and her on her phone must look like, and shudder.

5

Leslie and me

The only men your age with tattoos are criminals and
fun fair workers.

SARAH O'CONNELL

The man in the shed gave me the idea. To get a tattoo.

Not in so many words, but he started me thinking about how I
would remember day to day what I was learning. I write notes all
the time during the day, ideas for the show and projects, otherwise
you forget. I needed a note, a reminder, and a tattoo could be a
permanent to-do list inked on me. I don't recommend you do this
with your weekly shopping list or bank PIN, or the one password
you use for everything.

Getting a tattoo as a physical reminder of how to help yourself
isn't what everyone who goes to see a therapist does. I'm not sure
those face tatts Mike Tyson has are the wisdom from his therapist:
'It's ancient Hindu for *"Don't bite people"*.'

But I did get a tattoo of a single word; one that kept coming
up in the shed sessions. I got the word translated into one of
the oldest languages, Sanskrit. I did this as I liked the idea

of honouring the age-old wisdom with an age-old language, but also to stop people peering at the inside of my wrist and wondering why I had 'I fucked Elton John' tattooed on it.

No one but myself has any idea what it actually says. It acts as a kind of map to guide me back to a wiser part of me.

Everyone around me was quite shocked when they learnt that I now had a tattoo. To this day, my dad doesn't even know I have one, it's tucked away on the inside of my right wrist. I even turned this into an idea on the show, talking about things your parents still don't know about you.

I feel embarrassed offering any advice on dealing with panic attacks. Not that I think you picked up this book thinking the best advice on panic attacks would come from a guy who talks between songs and tells the time out loud for a living. Forget doctors who've studied medicine and humans for years, no, ask a guy who plays Nickelback.

Yet I did learn a lot about panic attacks and also from them. So much personal crisis, be that tragedy, illness or a job loss, comes sometimes with a lesson and the chance for growth and change.

When you look back at your life, maybe it should feel like you shed many skins, each one coming as a result of a testing threshold in your life. Struggle and resistance do make us stronger. I wish it was different. I'd be the new Tony Robbins if I could sell you a way to personal and spiritual growth from the comfort of your armchair, or while eating pizza. 'Awaken the Pizza Within' would be a bestseller. Less hot-coal walking and more hot-cheese eating.

I still find it hard to talk about the panic attacks, because it reminds me of a time when things were really dark and scary.

It felt life-threatening that my *life* as I knew it was under serious attack. My job, my joy, my livelihood. Over weeks and months, the man in the shed helped me to learn and change in small, sometimes barely noticeable ways. He showed me a lot of patience because many times I was a reluctant visitor.

At first, he helped me notice the 'inner bully', that heckler in our head we all have that tries to keep you small. My heckler was making me feel ashamed of what had happened to me

With the therapist's encouragement, I told the heckler to sit the fuck down—this may be my words born out of dealing with drunken real-life hecklers, but the intention is the same.

Just noticing your critical self-talk is quite confronting at times. If you said out loud all the things you say to yourself in your head, you'd be appalled. Like when you look in the mirror and say, *'Jeez, you look like shit today.'*

You'd never speak to a friend or partner the way you do to yourself; if you did, you'd be really lonely.

We put so much effort in maintaining this version of ourselves we try to present to the world. As if the real us would not be welcome. I learnt that much of our fear is created by our thinking and the body reacts to real and imaginary fear exactly the same. It's amazing how we construct all these imaginary future scenarios that are way more horrific than any horror movie, all done while we can be sitting and having some cake.

You're there, but not really.

I realised that fear is often about what might happen, it's disaster-thinking projected into the future that affects you *right here and now*, tormented by these stories we tell ourselves.

The answer is to try to be more fully present in our lives, aware of what we are thinking and what's going on in our bodies. The man in the shed taught me to use my breath to help me do that.

I loved the breathing techniques so much I even went away to a week-long breathwork retreat in Spain taught by a great man called Alan Dolan.

The kids weren't so sure about my retreat.

'*Who really needs to be taught for a week on how to breathe? It doesn't make any sense. A girl in our class said her dad has been having an affair with his gym instructor,*' my daughter Lois said helpfully to my perpetually suspicious wife.

I later saw my wife had an open browser tab of where I was going to stay. Another one probably had a Google search for 'Easy ways to install a bug on your husband'.

My wife has no real reason to be suspicious, but she is.

Once I was walking home and a lady in a car pulled up and said, 'Hello, I'm going your way, would you like a lift?'

I presumed this was one of my wife's many friends, which shows how much attention I pay to my wife's friends. Seeing as we were only a two-minute drive to my house, I figured she must be local and I didn't want to be rude, so I got in her car, despite, it turned out, having never seen this person before in my life. Leslie was her name, I discovered after asking her. She dropped me off and I thanked her, and as I was fumbling for my front door key, my wife opened the door and spied the car pulling away with her kind friend in it.

'Who was that?' she asked while her eyes narrowed in on me.

'Your mate Leslie, she saw me down the road and gave me a lift.'

'I don't know a Leslie.'

My wife's whole demeanour changed. This meant we were immediately at DEFCON 4.

'I thought she must be your friend.'

She looked at me accusingly. 'I've never seen that woman before. What's going on, Chris?'

I assured her nothing was going on. I mean, if I was having an affair, it's a pretty ballsy move to get my mistress to drop me off right outside my house.

Also, I wouldn't have an affair with someone who drove a car with those beaded car seat covers. It was this second point which made my wife reluctantly accept the truth, probably believing that I would be stupid enough to get my mistress to drop me home but beaded seats would be a deal-breaker for me.

However, an hour later she pulled me aside and looked around to check the kids weren't within earshot. This is a move that terrifies me.

'I've called around everyone I know locally, none of them have ever heard of anyone named Leslie.'

She was doing what the KGB used to do, 'trust but verify', except my wife is scarier than the KGB. The KGB study my wife's techniques, *The Art of Sarah.*

Her eyes bore down into my soul trying to forcibly extract the truth, and all future truths.

'I don't think you're having an affair, I just think it's fucking weird you got in a strange woman's car. I mean, she could've been a deranged stalker.'

On this: Yeah, it is upon reflection odd, really odd, that I got in a stranger's car. As kids we were constantly warned of this, nowadays we do it all the time with Uber.

But 'deranged' stalker? Why deranged? Deranged for wanting to stalk me?

The Spanish breathwork retreat was great, by the way. Leslie and I had a lovely time.

Being more fully present in our lives is something we all struggle with. It takes real discipline to just watch your own thoughts, rather than being them. The benefits are life-changing but if it was that easy, we would all be doing it.

It's all very well to quote Buddha and his wisdom, but he's a guy who left his wife and kids to find enlightenment. I'd be all giggly and serene in my statues if I didn't have to go to sports day and parent–teacher night.

Even Buddha would have struggled with mobile phones that keep us mentally somewhere else almost all the time. If you're a parent, so many arguments will be about phones

We worry about artificial intelligence taking over our lives, but the phones already have.

I feel sorry for my daughters growing up with the constant pull of the phone.

When I was their age, for me it was about my mates and my BMX bike. Hours making jumps and ramps, no idea of the time, I just had to be home before it got dark. I think my mum and dad thought bad people only came out at night. I would just disappear for the day with no real idea whose house I'd be going to, what I'd have for lunch or where. Mum's only condition was that I drank a glass of milk before I went out. Somehow its protective properties would keep me safe and my mum obviously believed all paedophiles were lactose-intolerant. Who knew?

Phones now let my daughters know where and what their friends are up to, all the time.

If I had been excluded by kids and they were off doing something without inviting me, I was blissfully ignorant. Not our kids. They can feel pretty shitty about themselves, all the time, all from the comfort of their own home. Awesome.

After my therapy sessions, I started trying to notice my thoughts, witnessing rather than being consumed by them. I started, and then gave up on, a journal, too concerned about what would happen if something happened to me, my wife and kids finding out my darkest thoughts. Sitting at my funeral angrily thinking, *'He never liked* Peppa Pig? *He said he did. I don't know who my father was.'*

•

Looking back now I can see the anxiety and panic attacks were not as life-threatening as they felt at the time, but they were life-changing. They were a gift. A gift wrapped in an enormous pile of shit. There can be a strange wisdom in anxiety.

Over time I did start to get better. Now I should explain that I say '*get better*' but that's not what I needed to do. Even though that's what I went to the man in the shed for.

It wasn't about '*getting better*'. It was about accepting what was happening to me and to stop hating '*it*'. I needed to bring *compassion* and love to the part of me that was struggling. I was asked how I would treat one of my girls if they came to me struggling like I was.

I needed to make friends with the panic.

This I had a real problem with. Why would I want to make friends with something that was causing me so much pain and terror? No one wants to see in their phone contacts a so-called friend called 'Panic Attack'. Just above your other mates '*Sunday Night Blues that feels exactly like it did when you were at school*' and '*Existential Dread at 3 a.m. when you can't go back to sleep and realise you are all alone in this life*'.

Around this time I read that the word '*courage*', if you trace it back to its origins, means 'full hearted', or 'how big is your heart' (thanks to the great writer David Whyte).

It's not so much about being brave in the traditional sense.

It's about how to keep a full heart, be big-hearted, even as we get angry, let down, heart-broken or scared. Not hardening your heart to life and yourself, or closing it up, is one of the constant challenges we face in life.

Things shifted for me once I had some compassion for myself, I felt myself coming back online. My heart opening back up.

It helped me just feeling the love I had for my life and what I was lucky to do, making things people also loved.

Yes, I was now back to where I belonged, on air.

The relief, gratitude and then joy coming back again was just incredible. As my heart stirred, however, I started noticing something inside me, coming through me. There was a calling.

In the shed I could be honest without fear of judgement. I finally admitted something out loud.

The dirty truth I'd been hiding from myself was that I wanted more, a new horizon. A longing for something more, something unknown, something that would be challenging. We are trained to be risk and resistance-averse. But there is a magic waiting for you when you move towards something that pushes back against you.

I felt like I knew what my year ahead looked like before it happened. What I'd be doing on the show Monday to Friday, ideas I'd be repeating for Valentine's Day, Father's Day, Christmas.

Things had changed, or I had.

I let myself admit the truth, it was time to move on. I was in a comfort zone and it was suffocating me.

It's very hard to accept that sadly nothing lasts forever, life is a continual sense of loss, disappearance and grief. On your best day, you also know it can't last. Ever had that? Being both blissfully happy and simultaneously sad at how fleeting it is? Your heart has room for both, it doesn't prefer one over the other, but your mind does!

Like laughing with your loved ones and knowing it will pass so soon. You just want to live in that moment forever.

I taught both my daughters to ride their bikes. For years after this in my birthday and Father's Day cards, they both mentioned this and *thanked me.* It was that big a deal for them. After learning to walk, which they don't remember having been so young, learning to ride their bikes was another milestone in their freedom. On the first bike ride I took them both on, we packed a lunch and cycled along a river until we came to a bridge. I got them to stop and I showed them how to play 'Pooh sticks' (named after Winnie the Pooh). You get some small sticks and stand next to each other looking over the bridge. After counting down from three, you all let go of your sticks together and they drop into the water and float beneath the bridge. You then rush to the other side to see whose stick came first. The first time we did this, they screamed in the simple joy of it all.

'AGAIN!' they demanded. I wanted for nothing else in my life in that moment.

And I also had a little tear forming, knowing this couldn't last, that it's so precious and that they will grow up.

Then I felt the echo of an old memory, of my dad playing this same game with me. I wondered if he felt the same joy, he must have, and also the heart aching knowing too.

I was beginning to sense a new season of my life was coming. I just wanted desperately to believe my life was a glorious summer, but it had become winter, the kind of winter that *Game of Thrones* loves so much.

There are seasons in life, and within us, I think. Seasons of things passing, dying, then new ideas and offerings 'springing' up, then harvesting new rewards for us.

A spring was following my winter.

At home I could see my kids growing up so quickly and my role as a dad changing. Fatherhood was a job description radically being redefined, without me being consulted. No child-rearing books will tell you this, but I will.

Up until about the age of ten, your kids think you're more golden god than dad. Mine would rush to the door to greet me. They thought I was the funniest comedian in the world. I didn't need a radio studio or stage, I had as good as it was ever going to get. Adulation and encores every night at bedtime. I could make them laugh so hard they farted. They'd get hiccups so loud my wife downstairs would yell at me to 'keep it calm up there'.

But then, as they approached their teens, they saw the golden god's cheap paint flaking off and underneath was just a dull old man. Where I was once getting encores, I was now getting heckles:

'You've told us that story like a million *times* before.*'*

'Jeez, that joke is so unfunny.'

Instead of kisses and hugs there was eye-rolling. So much eye-rolling.

What was I going to do now? I never thought this would happen to me. It was all going by too quickly.

I know this will sound really dumb . . . but that one day, fully realising you are going to die, and getting older, is up there with finding out Santa isn't real.

The two big WAIT, WHATs?

Wait, what? Father Christmas isn't real? It's made up?

And then:

Wait, what? I die?

When you have children, it makes your heart swell, spiritually and physically. It's also terrifying to be that vulnerable because you know that if anything happened to them it would just destroy you.

The life of being a parent is one of having your heart broken, your role is to help them grow up and one day walk out of your door. What's more heartbreaking than that?

This realisation, that life was changing, woke me up to what really mattered—to fully make use of the precious time we had to make our lives what they should be: an adventure.

As a kid I was obsessed, like millions of others, with Evel Knievel. To me it wasn't about how many buses he would jump, it was how brave he was to take the leap, over the buses, the Grand Canyon, into the unknown, that was wild to me.

He leaped for a living. I loved that.

I needed to leap again.

A new frontier was beckoning. Just how wild that frontier was going to be I had no idea.

6

'Every time you open your mouth, people will hate you.'

We could die there.

SARAH O'CONNELL

'I'm thinking about moving to Australia . . .'

The man in the shed spat his coffee out all over his fetching terracotta tiles, such was the impact of what I'd just said.

Did Evel Knievel get this?

He looked at me more stunned than when I first came to see him, unable to walk into my radio station without crippling panic attacks. That was apparently all small-fry compared to this bombshell.

Moving to the other side of the world.

He apologised, saying he had never spat his coffee out before in response to what a client told him.

That didn't exactly soothe me. As a therapist with more than twenty years' experience, he must've heard all manner of dark confessions and troubles.

'Is that wise? Do they even want to hear you over there? Don't they hate us?'

The idea to move to Australia, to do a radio show on the other side of the world, hadn't sprung up completely overnight.

My wife and I had always loved Australia. We went together in 2002 for the first time and loved it, and before I met Sarah she had lived there while travelling around the world. Australia seemed to be such a sunny country, not just in temperature, but outlook and spirit. Over the years I had developed a connection with Australian radio and television superstars Hamish Blake and Andy Lee, who'd always said I should move over.

I didn't just walk out of the shed hurt one day, call my wife and say, '*Pack the bags! We're moving to Australia.*' For quite a while we'd both been talking about our shared sense of frustration, boredom and 'What next?' being a better question than 'Is this it?'

Our lives had gotten smaller.

I remembered saying to Sarah one night over a glass of wine after the kids had gone to bed, 'It can't be that all the really exciting stuff has happened in our lives and we just watch the kids grow up and leave.'

Suddenly, we were both thinking the same thing: not, why we couldn't do it, but, why wouldn't we?

Sometimes in life when you do some work on yourself, whether that's looking after yourself physically, mentally or spiritually, things open up for you. Because you're ready.

I had lunch with an old boss, Richard Park, one of the world's most revered, feared and successful programmers. His son Paul Jackson had hired me for Virgin Radio and was now running a big radio group in Australia. Our lunch was full of tall stories and outrageous gossip. Richard then casually told me about a DJ we both knew who'd just moved to Australia to work for Paul. I was so jealous of this big move. Richard said I should go too:

'They love banter, you'd go great.'

I knew Richard spent Christmas with his son and grandkids every year in Australia and no one knows more about radio than this guy. If he thought it was a good idea, why wouldn't it work?

Immediately after I'd been stung for lunch by this canny Scottish operator, I called my wife.

I updated her on the lunch conversation, and she said the words I will never forget: *'Let's do it, Chris, let's move to Australia.'*

In that moment, the whole thing could've been snuffed out by my wife. The fact she was so keen for something new still amazes me. She had a great circle of friends in London and is very close to her mum.

After receiving Sarah's encouragement, while still in the street walking around London's Trafalgar Square trying to avoid being shat on by the pigeons, I called Andy Lee in Australia. I asked him whether he thought that me going there could work. He said, in what will be widely regarded as the biggest single understatement of my life:

'It will be challenging but you'll be great.'

Challenging.

This was in August 2016 and I'm writing this in late 2020. I guess 'challenging' was an accurate description, if you stretch that word to the absolute limits of its meaning.

When I got home, my wife ushered me into the laundry and stood by the washing machine. This was our place to conduct a serious chat away from the kids. There was safety in the laundry, my children didn't even know it existed, imagining their clothes magically cleaned themselves.

'I can't stop thinking about it,' my wife whispered. Sarah's whisper mode is like a plane taking off. I reminded her that I didn't actually have a job there yet.

'You will, and I have one condition . . .'

In my mind I was trying to work out what her condition would be. I bet it was that I couldn't bring Leslie.

'The dog has to come.'

So, my wife's only condition in blowing up the lives of every member of our family was that our dog came too.

There were no more conditions and with canine matters agreed, I began putting out the feelers.

I spoke to Duncan Campbell, who I'd known when he worked in the UK but now ran another radio group in Australia, and Andy Lee suggested also talking to the group he worked for, which I did.

Andy's group was very excited, and we talked about a few options and it all seemed to be happening. They noticed I was booked as a keynote speaker at a big radio festival being held in Amsterdam and, by coincidence, the boss of the station I could be working on would be there too. It was decided we should meet, and it all seemed like a formality.

All of this was being done without my bosses knowing. The radio industry has the worst gossips and I was worried this could get out. Now I was having late-night phone calls due to the time difference and I was planning a secret meeting in Amsterdam.

Have you ever had a secret meeting? I highly recommend it, especially in Amsterdam.

Before the meeting, I had to give a speech at the conference which sounds grander than it was in reality. Half the audience didn't speak English that well, so my powerful points and jokes bombed, in several European languages. At least, I can always say it was a language problem and not the jokes.

After the speech I headed off to the hotel for my secret meeting. As always, I was early. I got this condition, being early, from my dad and my Irish grandad gave it to him. Being half an hour early, I ordered a beer and positioned myself so I could see the hotel reception. I was like Robert De Niro in *Ronin*. I considered hiding behind a newspaper, with eye holes cut out, but decided against it.

The man I was meeting was a big radio boss in Australia. He was also speaking at the conference, but in a smaller room than me, I noticed. So I casually left my speaker pass in front of me so my guest could see it and take in the 'Main Hall' typed under my name. I figured I needed this power-play as he was very well respected in Australian radio and was a top presenter years ago. Any radio boss who used to be half decent when they were on air is usually very direct and has a swagger. I hoped the 'Main Hall' trick would take some of that swagger out of my Australian secret meeting guest.

But as I waited I got bored. I asked for a notepad and pen. I figured I might as well use the time to start thinking about tomorrow's show. I love just doodling and thinking about shows and seeing what ideas drop out of my two-beer head.

I wrote down a potential show topic: Secret Meetings. I then crossed this out after remembering that the first rule of secret meetings is you don't talk about them to millions of people on the radio. This is why James Bond's radio show would've sucked.

Suddenly, the hotel doors flew open and there he was. He had an annoying swagger. I became doubtful that the conference pass power-play would work.

'Been here long?' he asked.

'No,' I lied.

He noted the two dead beers on my table and a messy notepad. Shit. He seemed to miss the 'Main Hall' pass entirely, and he'd already seen through my first bit of gamesmanship.

He suggested we go somewhere quieter and as we wandered in search of a back bar, I realised my keynote speaker pass had been left behind on the table.

After we found a decent nook in the deserted hotel bar, we took our seats. I glanced at my watch and saw the time: I was supposed to be meeting my current boss and team for dinner in twenty minutes. My guest has ordered a *cheese board*. The balls on this guy.

I was dying a little here, I was being out power-played. The classic charcuterie board play.

'So, you're thinking about coming to Australia,' he opened with.

We were off and running.

'█████████ is a huge fan of yours.'

I'd already had another secret meeting with a colleague of his in London, who almost offered me a job on the spot and said I should meet the guy currently in front of me, as a mere formality.

I feigned awkward modesty. Things were going back my way now, I thought.

No, they weren't.

'I don't get it.'

'Don't get what?'

'You. It's your accent, you're English.'

I'll say this, this guy was very observant. He had more to say in between nonchalantly throwing carved cubes of cheese and cured meats into his mouth, like the mad sun king holding court.

He leant in for his next damning point.

'Every time you open your mouth, people will hate you.'

This was the first time this phrase was uttered to me, and it was one I was going to hear many more times in the future.

'Right, yeah, I get it,' I mumbled, totally deflated.

He was making sense.

I was being fired from a job I never had, so I figured I might as well join the sun king in polishing off the well-curated platter (the cheese was great, by the way), but it turned out he had finished with our meeting.

'I could get you a job in New Zealand,' he said as he got ready to leave.

He was basically telling me to fuck off, right off the edge of the world. And he was enjoying a cheese board while he was doing it.

Andy Lee was right, the move to Australia suddenly was going to be 'challenging'. That was before we even got there.

•

After the disappointment of Amsterdam, I started talking to Duncan Campbell's radio group (ARN) in Australia for a few weeks and they seemed serious about giving me a radio show.

So far, there'd been no secret meetings or cheese boards and no threats to ship me off to New Zealand. There were just lots of phone calls, late at night. I'd creep upstairs to bed at midnight, having told the kids I was chatting to a 'distant cousin' in Australia.

One night Ruby opened her bedroom door, smiled and whispered, 'Are you trying to get a job in Australia?'

She'd done what any teenager would do whose bedroom was above their dad's office, eavesdropping when he's suddenly making a series of calls to some relative he'd never mentioned before.

'Maybe. It's just an offer, darling, you don't need to worry, go to sleep.'

'TAKE IT! It would be so cool to move there; I love *MasterChef Australia*.'

What more justification did we need than a reality TV cooking show?

I got into bed and my wife again reiterated in the darkness, 'The dog has to come.'

The dog? *MasterChef*? The criteria for this move was not what I'd expected.

Then, one Wednesday morning, I was on air and at 7 a.m. while we were in the news, my phone flashed up with a text from my wife.

My wife's random texts interrupt my entire day. In fact, they are so prolific that I've devoted an entire chapter to them. These messages are often sent while I'm live on air, as I point out. To which she'll reply:

'You do not talk constantly, reply during the news'

Hence I regularly receive messages from her before the news.

My wife likes to plan things.

I like to have no plans.

According to my wife, if it wasn't for her, I would've just rotted to death in a chair.

None of our amazing family holidays would've happened without her planning and tireless research.

If it was left to me, we'd just arrive at the airport with only a carrier bag of clothes and I'd book the next available flight to wherever. Then arrive and check into a hotel somewhere. It would be chaos.

But I don't like to have too many things planned or in my diary. If I see an event in my diary, part of me gets irritated at it.

My wife has FOMO, I have JOMO: Joy of Missing Out.

Anyway, this moving to Australia was activating my wife's need to plan and this particular Wednesday morning, her text got my attention.

'Just read this . . . we could die there'

A link to an article, '10 Reasons to Not Go to Australia'.

It's 7 a.m. This is where her mind is?

'We could die there.'

After the show, I read the article. Let me share my pick of five out of the ten 'reasons for not going to Australia':

- There are 1275 animals that could kill you in Australia.
- 21 of the 25 most venomous snakes in the world live there.
- Australia is ranked 57th in the world for broadband speed.
- It is a known fact that wallabies like to break into opium crops, get high and run around in circles to create a 'crop circle'.
- Christmas is low-key.

The one that really leapt out to me was 'Christmas is low-key'. What did that mean—'low-key'?

I started to imagine some Aussie version of Santa arriving in Australia on a giant surfboard pulling surf-sleighs. Casually gliding onto the sandy shore in shorts sporting Oakley sunglasses and a white-haired mullet. He chugs a beer in one, empties a sack of presents onto the beach urging the kids to help themselves while he wanders off to watch the Boxing Day Test in a pub.

I noted that slow internet was now up there with animals that could kill you in terms of threat level.

I'm no expert but *'1275 animals that could kill you'*?

That seemed a bit high to me.

The article mentioned a thing called a stone fish. How's that dangerous?

I googled it. I wish I hadn't. I may never sleep again. This is horrific, a fish that pretends to look like a stone, so you step on it and then, *ha ha surprise!* It fires a prong into the ball of your foot with some really fuck awful venom. I read reports of victims in so much pain they 'begged for death'.

Begged for death! I continued my research and read a first-hand report from an Irish holiday-maker who made the innocent mistake of standing on nature's shitty trapdoor, the stone fish. He said: 'I describe the pain as excruciating because the word comes from crucify, and that's exactly what it was—there was no other way to describe it.'

For balance, I googled 'Deadly Animals in the UK' to get some idea of context.

All I could find was a Top 5 of 'The Most Dangerous Animals and Plants in the UK'.

Not only could we not fill out a decent Top 10, we had to fill the Top 5 out with *plants*. What's in there, stinging nettles?

At Number 5 was 'hairy caterpillars'. Are they taking the piss? No, they weren't.

'Hairy caterpillars can be a real nuisance.'

Nuisance.

It's the greatest horror story Stephen King never told, *The Nuisance.*

In all seriousness, they can 'cause rashes *and* itchiness'. Sure, no one likes an itchy rash but it can hardly be compared to 'begging for death'.

It was clear I could die in Australia.

Either on air, or off air from any of the 1275 deadly animals, or of boredom waiting for a movie to download in a country with the 57th slowest broadband speed in the world.

Duncan Campbell didn't see it that way. When we first started talking I thought I might have to start on a late-night radio show, earn my stripes that way.

We talked, and then talked some more. And then it was on the table: I'd struck Gold. Would I like to move to Australia and the city of Melbourne, and have my own breakfast show on the station with the same name? Not a less high-profile show to ease my way in, but straight into the battlefield that breakfast radio was in Australia.

I remember getting off the phone from that incredible offer. Feeling two things simultaneously. More excited, adrenalised and alive than I had felt in a long time. I couldn't sleep that night I was so . . . buzzed.

Then, seconds later, I was scared of making the wrong call, of not being good enough to make it in Australia. Moving to the other side of the world, knowing no one, being a no one. Sure, Sarah and I had done that before in our lives, but we were younger and without children. This was the single biggest risk of my life. Not just my life, my entire family's.

I said to Sarah it was a huge risk going.

She said it was just as big a risk staying.

•

When I told close friends that I had an offer, and we were taking the plunge—no, plunge is too mild a word for what we were planning, leap, yeah leap—many reacted like the man in the shed. They might not have spat their beverage at me, but they were not exactly supportive. And I'd have done the same.

Some were surprised, like I hadn't fully understood the playbook for this age and stage of life.

Others talked about stability, planning for the future, questioning had I really thought about this?

'You've worked so hard to get where you are, why would you throw all that away?'

The best example was when I resigned from Absolute Radio. My boss, upon learning I was turning down the new multi-year deal they were offering me and heading to Australia, looked aghast and shook his head from side to side, whispering:

'They will *hate* you.'

The whispering made it even more terrifying.

'Hate you,' he mouthed, in case I missed it the first time.

His facial expression was one of concern for me. Like I'd just said I had a terminal illness and would now face a long, slow death.

Then he finished me off with, 'It could really break you emotionally.'

I had flashbacks to *Rocky IV* and Ivan Drago saying, 'If he dies, he dies,' as poor Apollo Creed lay inert on the boxing ring canvas.

My boss then tried to dissuade me from this hugely dramatic decision.

'Name your price,' he said.

I'd never thought I'd hear someone actually say, 'Name your price', but I had to stay strong, even if I wasn't feeling it.

'I'm going to Australia,' I replied.

This would become like a mantra when I was faced with the doubts of the many people who tried to talk me out of the move.

I walked out of the building that had been my radio home for almost a quarter of my life, and thought I was going to be sick on the pavement with the fear that was rising up in me.

I'd just quit.

Name your price? How much could I have said? It would've changed my life. Was I being a big idiot?

I called my wife for reassurance. I relayed what had happened and the phone went very quiet.

Reassurance is normally, you know, audible.

'He actually said name your price? And you didn't?' she finally replied, as if questioning her life choices that had resulted in her being married to a man who when asked to name his price, doesn't.

'We're going to Australia,' I mumbled.

•

Life has firsts and lasts.

Often, you're not even aware you are doing something for the last time. I have a photo of me in my daughters' little fabric indoor tepee and we are playing pretend tea shops. That photo is the last time we did that together.

I didn't know that at the time. If I had, I would have slowed down and enjoyed it more, not looked at my watch and thought of all the jobs I had to get to.

I was right where I should've been. Drinking imaginary tea with my little pinkie in the air.

If I could build a time machine I would go back to that moment in a heartbeat. What I wouldn't give for one more cup of tea at Mrs Scoggins' Tea Shop.

It took months for my visa to be approved. At one point it looked like we wouldn't be going at all—the government suddenly changed the criteria of the one we were applying for, clearly trying to save the Australian public from me. Then we applied for a very rare visa that I might be eligible for, called, and I'm not making this up, a 'Distinguished Talent' visa.

Two days before Christmas I got a very emotional call from Duncan in Australia at 1 a.m. London time, saying my visa had been approved. Now, looking back, I wonder whether he was emotional that I was finally coming after months of work on his behalf, or laughing that an idiot like me was a 'Distinguished Talent'.

It was actually happening.

Shit! This was huge.

Monumental.

The biggest leap ever.

We agreed to say nothing to our families until after Christmas. Then my life, and the family's, became a series of lasts, and we knew it.

Everything felt so poignant, I was aware that each event was the last time.

For my daughters, they had their last days at school, last time seeing their best mates. There's a video of Lois's school friends performing a song they wrote for her. It moved us so much.

I had to say a last goodbye to my mum. That sounds more final than it was, it wasn't the final goodbye, but it felt like a kind of final goodbye, like we both knew life would never quite be the same again.

When I broke the news to my mum, I'd called her to say I needed to talk to her, and I'd go down for the day.

Mum knew something big was up the moment she answered the door, and said, 'Oh no, you haven't got cancer, have you?'

'I'm moving to Australia,' I said.

Her eyes suggested cancer would have been less upsetting. She collapsed into my arms and sobbed.

Then I started crying. I was trying to say sorry. You really don't want to be upsetting your mum like this.

My dad I'd told a few months earlier when I'd got the idea

and he was excited for me. But come time to say goodbye, it was almost too much for both of us to bear. I didn't feel like a grown-up saying goodbye to him, I felt like a little boy.

The day before our last day in England, my sister, Louise, and her husband, Luke, my wife and our kids all had lunch in my mum's garden.

A last lunch.

Spring was in the air and it was a beautiful day. Signs were everywhere in her garden of life coming back.

There was plenty of laugher but then it all came to a stop when it was time for the dreaded goodbyes. It felt like a death.

'I won't come outside to wave you off,' Mum said, 'it will be too much.'

As I held Mum in her little kitchen with the world's most-used kettle, I smelt the top of her head one last time.

I breathed my mum in.

I wanted to somehow burn that smell forever into my senses so I could always remember it as if I'm right there holding her. Even somewhere oceans apart.

As we drove away, none of us, me, Sarah, Ruby or Lois, knew what to say. Tears rolled down my cheeks and Sarah's as I saw my mum's house disappear into the distance.

The next day, we were off to Australia, fleeing the deadly caterpillars of Britain. As the plane took off, one phrase bounced around my brain.

'Every time you open your mouth, people will hate you.'

PART TWO

7

Come fail with me

I've heard the snakes can sleep in your pillow and kill you at night. You'll have to check everyone's just in case.

SARAH O'CONNELL

I'd love to tell you that the moment I left British airspace, the clouds parted, the sun arose anew, and all my earthly problems slipped away as we climbed to 35,000 feet.

But just holding our one-way tickets in my hand made me panic a little.

I'd never been on a one-way flight.

The responsibility I had in making this massive life choice work for my family felt huge. I had this recurring image of me running my family at speed off a huge cliff and then trying to build wings on the way down.

You make such a big decision from a moment's inspiration over a few wines on the couch, that's the easy bit, a spark of an idea igniting months of thinking about it, then comes the admin planning and then you're suddenly leading your family off a plane to start a new life.

It doesn't normally work like this.

Your children are usually joining your already established and settled life. You give them love and security.

I'd flipped that on its head.

Because, as I was about to find out, Australian radio is the most competitive and ruthless in the world.

On every single radio station carpet in Australia is the blood of several breakfast shows. They don't even hose it off, they leave it there as if to say, 'Let this be a reminder to you.'

I had plenty of time to consider what a seismic risk I was taking on the incredibly long flight to Australia. It takes 23 hours to fly from London to Melbourne; it's such a very long time it feels like a trip to another planet.

All I had in my hand luggage were my trusty radio headphones, which I'd had for fifteen years, and the keys to our old house. I have no idea why I kept the keys as we'd sold our family home of more than ten years. The man in the shed would have had a field day exploring the symbolism of keeping the front door keys.

Because there was no going back. I'd burnt the escape boats.

I mean, really taken a flamethrower to them.

Smart guy.

I just couldn't bear to throw them away, it felt too much. Strange, isn't it? Like I couldn't handle the thought of not being able to walk back through that door into my old life. Which now, further away with every hour of flying, suddenly appeared so safe.

•

As we shuffled off the plane, I showed my wife what I'd kept and she did a double-take and hissed, *'I hope this doesn't mean trouble at customs and border security.'*

One of the main preparations I'd insisted the family do in advance of a new life in Australia was watch the TV show *Border Security Australia*. This fly-on-the-wall documentary shows the illegal and illicit items people attempt to bring into Australia through customs. Australia is famous for its very strict laws on bringing in any food or agricultural products. Please dispose of any goats you're travelling with in the bins provided.

The border police are always unfailingly polite and friendly. But their eyes are windows to souls that have seen everything: antelope dick, dried tiger's heads, T-rex eggs. Quite how my entry into this Great Southern Land would be held up with a door key was beyond me. But my wife's tone would have been the same if I'd told her I was carrying a small cannon.

I could sense this rising quiet nervousness started to spread among my family as we got our suitcases and pushed them towards the world-famous Australian customs officers. I looked for the *Border Security* TV cameras, none in sight. My wife waited a good 0.05 seconds before telling them we watched the TV show about them, and then confessed I had a door key to our old home. She was proving to be the weak link in our nascent smuggling operation.

Given the key wasn't made of narwhal tusk, we were ushered through.

It all still felt so surreal.

This was it then.

All the planning over.

It begins . . .

now.

We were met by our driver with my name written in Sharpie on a handheld white board. He was looking for a 'Christain O'Donnell', I was looking for 'Christian O'Connell'.

In every sense.

8

Pets before dads

Are you getting nervous, Dad?

LOIS O'CONNELL

The moment we left the airport was when I really saw just what I had taken on.

They were everywhere—posters of me. Freeway signs, signs on buildings, on the back of a taxi we pulled up behind at some lights. How strange for Melbourne people to have a man that no one has ever seen before on billboards all over town. It's radio, they could've hired a really good-looking model and shoved his face up there.

'Are you getting nervous, Dad?' asked Lois.

I think she saw something for the first time that startled her. Fear in her dad's eyes. I winked at her.

'Nah, all part of the excitement.'

I lied.

My wife and I exchanged looks. She knew how I would be feeling. She gave my hand a squeeze. I glanced at her and forced a smile.

I was going to need more than my lucky headphones to get through this.

I'd asked life for something new and exciting—be careful when you do that, you might just get it.

It was late at night when we arrived, we were jet-lagged, confused and all a little overwhelmed. Everything was unknown and different. The roads, the buildings that weren't as built up and dominating as the ones in London. As we left the airport then passed through the city and headed out to our new home and suburb, a slow creep of 'Seriously, what the fuck have I done?' crept in.

Why would I do this to us? It's all going to be really hard work. All my friends told me I was mad, you're supposed to be settling now in your forties.

The thought of all the *effort* everything would take was dawning on me. Because being a human being takes work and it's tiring, isn't it? There is an inherent messiness to being human and just getting through the day can sometimes take a superhuman effort. Life is basically a never-ending giant to-do list. You groan and moan at just the idea of having to sort out the ceaseless admin of life, like renewing the car insurance. Get some quotes. Try to speak to a human stuck in some dreadful call centre. One of the early disappointments as you enter adult life is just the tedious mundanity involved that no one warned you of. But, you can also have snacks whenever you want.

It had taken so much effort just getting here. The endless planning, researching schools, broadband providers, saying goodbye. I found out it would be hard just getting mobile phones because I had no banking records in Australia—they didn't want Jason Bourne getting a phone here. I did find a network that didn't care about that and it felt good to know I was on the same provider as the pimps and drug dealers of Australia. They should make more of this, put it on adverts:

When you can't afford to lose that deal.

The driver pulled up outside the rental house that was to be our new home for the next twelve months. Four heads like meerkats peered around each other to get a good look at it.

It's hard to find a new family home on the other side of the world online; all I'll say here is, I'm not a guy who easily understands square footage. I just wanted somewhere really nice for our first year and where our extended family could come stay and have their own space. What I'm saying is, I went way too big.

Size and rent wise.

Hell, why not chuck in some more pressure by renting somewhere that was more cruise ship than house. It was located in South Melbourne, Bayside, a few minutes from the beach.

As we entered the faux colonial style house, which would befit a foreign ambassador's residence, the kids' eyes bulged wide open.

'WOW!'

'Don't get used to it,' I muttered, managing their expectations.

In a year's time we'll be in a cheap motel while Dad is forced to dance for strangers at night for cash.

Again.

My wife gave me that look that said, 'Why did you get something so big?'

Two words. Square footage.

You married a DJ, not a real estate developer or mathematician. Did I mention the fact I failed maths at school? Trying to wrap my head around squaring something was beyond me.

The kids were very happy, little did they know Dad had blown their university savings on Jeff Bezos's second home.

Our furniture that we had packed into a giant shipping container three months ago was now here, in a different house. It felt familiar and yet not.

As my wife and I got into bed that night, it felt like our first night as a married couple did. The start of something really new, that hasn't yet been revealed. We naturally observed the cast-iron rule of any relationship that states wherever you are in the world, you automatically go to your familiar sides of the bed. One of you takes the left, the other the right, and that's the way it remains for life.

I had a sleepless night. New sounds and even the new direction I lay in the bed: Australia is called 'Down Under' and I actually felt disoriented like that. My brain was a ferris wheel in a hamster cage, burning smoke from overthinking. Everything was keeping me awake. The posters of me everywhere. Would that just piss people off? Were the kids okay? Would they like it here? Would they make new friends easily? Most of all, I wanted what I couldn't give myself—reassurance that everything was going to be fine.

My wife was fast asleep within seconds, annoyingly, as always.

Hours later once I did get some sleep, after flipping my pillow several times to that sweet cool spot like a burger on a grill, I was rudely awoken early by parrots. Even the birds waking us would now be different; the pleasant morning song of the great British countryside was replaced by angry parakeets having some kind of 5 a.m. fly-by shooting or mating ritual. Maybe both. I woke up and for a few seconds wondered where I was, I had landed but I hadn't. A feeling that would stay with me for quite a while.

This was made worse when I saw our house in daylight. It stood out in the street. And probably on Google Earth: our home and the Great Wall of China both clearly visible from space.

That day was the first in many more of googling everything before setting a foot outside the house.

'Where is . . .'

'How do Australians . . .'

From sorting wi-fi, finding the local doctor and dentist, even how to park your car was different.

My wife became a forensic detective in unearthing clues for our new life via an underground system known as 'The UK Melbourne Mums Group' on Facebook. They become our cultural ambassadors. My wife posted every query on here. I wondered what the other members thought about the new member posting seventeen questions an hour.

'Chris! I really need to find an eyelash lady before it starts to become noticeable.'

I didn't even know my wife had an 'eyelash lady'. I knew she had eyelashes, and that's another thing I love about my wife, her eyes have lashes. I've got no time for lash-less ladies.

But I didn't know she had her 'lady'. Now she needed to find one before it became ominously 'noticeable'. I couldn't help but think what would happen if she didn't find a lady soon: Could we be in a situation where our new neighbours were rushing their children inside at the spectacle of my wife and her foot-long eyelashes?

The problems I'd anticipated were not the ones that were suddenly presenting themselves at speed. Which is why, in the process of finding a new family doctor, I was shaken to the core by an encounter I had.

•

On the first weekend after moving here, we were registering at the local doctor's and the receptionist proudly told me how multicultural Melbourne is. Then she asked what I do for work.

'Radio,' I told her.

She pushed her glasses back up her face and stared, taking me in.

'Not talking though?'

'Yes, I'm here to do a radio show,' I said proudly, grinning the same grin I was wearing on the posters of me everywhere.

'But how will *that* work?' she asked. 'We love *Australian* voices on the radio here.'

I looked around to check that my family hadn't overheard this. They had their noses pressed against their phones.

Every time you open your mouth, people will hate you.

'Thought you said it was multicultural here?' I replied, playfully, but not really.

'Yes, but you know what I mean,' she replied, and rubber-stamped a folder containing my details. For all I know, the stamp said, 'Fired by Christmas'.

So things were starting off well. Even the doctor's receptionist thought I was bound to fail.

•

From the day we landed I had just eleven days until I launched the new show. Before I could go into my new station and say hello and meet the team, there was so much unpacking and figuring out how everything worked.

Aside from our family's number-one priority, locating an eyelash lady for my wife, we needed to pick up our awesome German shepherd dog, Nisha, from the airport. She had flown separate to us—I presume first-class from the amount it cost—and she was in quarantine. (This was before quarantine centres became something us humans would be getting used to.)

Nisha was only supposed to be in quarantine for ten days but had to do two weeks because some American dog at the compound arrived with a bug, so the whole place went into extra lockdown. I imagined a slutty American dog that picked up an STD while joining the canine mile-high club.

We got our dog and had this amazing reunion with her—the noise she made when she saw us! Dogs go nuts when they haven't seen you for a few hours; after two weeks it's a level of ecstasy I'd love to experience every day.

My wife got tearful and said, 'Look, Chris, she's beseeching us!'

I nodded at her joyous whimpering—Nisha's, not my wife's—and secretly wondered what 'beseeching' meant and why I married someone so obviously smarter than me. We were now complete, all the family were here.

I love dogs. We got Nisha after Digby passed away. Let me tell you now, losing your dog breaks your heart. I had no idea. Now, anything happening to my wife or daughters is unthinkable and unbearable, but the level of grief you go through when you lose one of these beautiful souls is bigger than I thought.

For ages I couldn't watch any movie where something happened to the dog. Then I found a great website called DoesTheDogDie. com where you can check if any animals are going to snuff it before watching to stop ruining the rest of your week. Not only that—there's an app. It's a lifesaver.

Years later I can still remember Digby's death vividly, the vet phoning me up to say the chance of Digby dying was 50/50. Which is actually the least useful prognosis. Because I could toss a coin myself without expert medical help. What is 50/50 anyway? Good? Bad?

I remember telling my kids, and them being more worried about how *I* was. Bless them.

And then my wife saying afterwards, 'They took that well, just goes to show, a kid's spirit is strong. Good to know that if anything ever happened to you, that in time, they'd be okay.'

Erm . . . yeah, nice to know that's where I am on the ladder of grief.

Inevitably the call came from the vet to tell me that Digby had died during the night. To be fair, the vet sounded gutted. Because Digby put a *lot* of business his way. From being diagnosed with dog Alzheimer's (it's a real thing, often he'd come into a room wondering where his bone was, then realised he had it in his mouth), to swallowing a knitting needle (that was fun). The vet loved Digby the dog. But he loved owner Christian the cash cow more. Whenever I went in, he always said, 'Mr O'Connell, it's really important to run some tests.' Those tests really being, 'What is the max limit on your credit card?'

So I headed over to the vet clinic to say my final goodbye to Digby and I was really struggling. Then he took me to this little side room. Lying on a blanket there was my dog. Motionless. Dead.

I bent down to stroke him; he still had his smell. My heart was just melting, I was shaking with the effort of holding back my tears, sucking them back down into my soul. Those tears would all come out one day, when you cry for all the times you didn't or couldn't cry and you're watching *Paddington 2* with your kids and it looks like the little fella is about to die but he's saved and you're crying so much the old lady next to you in the cinema actually asks if you're okay as your kids point and laugh at you.

I take Digby's collar off and kiss his cold little doggie head for the last time. I can't believe we won't be going for our Saturday walk today. My weekend begins with that, walking Digby with the girls.

Then the vet says quietly, 'My wife would love a shout out—she listens every morning.'

Wait, what?

Not now, not here, you know I'm saying goodbye to my dead best friend, right?

'I don't listen myself but maybe a U2 song on Monday morning around seven?'

9

520 hours to make it work

I'm hearing you've hired an English DJ, I won't be listening, nor will my hair salon, tell him to go back now before it ends badly.

LISTENER COMPLAINT, BEFORE I EVEN SAID A WORD

Seven days before the new show started, I was to make an appearance at the station, GOLD FM, to be introduced to the team. The day before that, Jack Post, my designated sidekick, and his wife, Bianca, came round to our oversized money pit for Sunday lunch. Shortly before they arrived, my wife, who was already regretting her idea to cook an entire roast dinner just days after landing here, burst into tears over the state of her Yorkshire puddings, which had collapsed. I'm no therapist but I don't think her tears were just about the puddings. It was all too much.

Jack and Bianca arrived, and we did what anyone would do before setting off on a crazy mission—spent the afternoon getting drunk. It felt more like the Last Supper than a beginning.

The next morning, a little hungover, I was met outside the station by my producer, who told me I was to enter via the radio station's fire escape as they had 'something planned'.

Oh no.

As we entered the second floor, I saw them. The entire staff, more than 100 people, grinning like cult members. Born-again Christians, all lined up to give me a very warm welcome. They were cheering and applauding as I walked down the line towards the studio. High-fiving all the way, I started to know what it must feel like to be Tony Robbins. Duncan Campbell, the man who hired me, stood at the top of the steps that led into the studio in front of a giant banner of my face. I'm talking eight feet high. Like I said, cult, and I was the new reluctant leader. (A cult was what some called me when the show started the next week.)

I was urged to 'run' through the banner. Today was not the day for a hangover. What was happening? Part of me felt like doing it, then running all the way back to England. I later learnt it was an Australian pre–football game tradition for each team to run through a banner onto the field.

A microphone was then thrust into my face to say a few words to the gathered wide-eyed staff/cult members. All I wanted to say was, 'Does anyone have any painkillers?', as my hangover was now in a similar state to the shredded banner of my face, which lay on the floor like I'd been torn to pieces. A fitting metaphor for what was going to happen over the next few months.

It was all so surreal. I managed a few pleasantries and thanked them all for their kind welcome, then it turned into a rally as Duncan pumped everyone up even more, saying I was here to get the show to Number 1.

'Christian is going to take this city by STORM! He will be NUMBER ONE!'

'NUMBER ONE! NUMBER ONE!' the cult chanted.

Wait, you think I'm here to get the show to Number 1?

Oh no, I'm not a Number 1 guy.

I'm a guy who made his name at Number 17.

What had I done?

•

Yet again, I found myself wondering if moving to Australia was my best response to having panic attacks. Put myself under even more extreme pressure. Like an alcoholic taking a job in a pub.

I started to feel the enormity of what I had taken on as a physical pain in my chest, it felt as if someone was tightening a band around me. The weight of it all, the huge expectations, the posters all over the city. No boss in the UK had ever done anything like this or declared such a war cry. It was more, 'Do your best, that's all you can do, better luck next time.'

The stakes here were just so much higher.

As I smiled warmly at my new work colleagues, all I could think was, *I'm not sure I can do this, can I do this?*

Everything was amped up. It was like radio on steroids.

The Australian radio market, despite having fewer listeners than the UK, is worth several times more financially. This is why it is so competitive, there are millions of dollars at stake. Why the hell would you risk that by hiring a British guy no one has heard of?

A newspaper here had referred to my hiring as: '*Australian media's biggest gamble ever*'.

The latest ratings had just come out and the show GOLD FM had taken off air and replaced with me was Number 1.

I could only go down!

Industry experts were all querying the decision to hire me, a 'foreign import'. One of the management team told me that my 'first six months would be make or break'.

Six months? That was 130 shows. Which meant I had 520 hours to make it work.

What if it took longer? 550 hours? 672?

Back in London it was only in the last few years of a twelve-year show that we got to Number 1.

Six months? And as an outsider? Forget it. Let's agree this whole thing is a mistake and all go home. Hell, I've still got my door key.

I decided to break away from the crowd and head into the studio. Partly to get away from all the hype and noise, but also to try to ground myself and find some calm. I took a big sigh when I stood behind the studio desk and looked at my new microphone. This is what it all came down to. What I could do from here. Just me and this microphone.

All I have is the microphone, and the words and ideas I have in my head and heart. I loved the pureness and simplicity of that.

I looked out of the studio window onto the streets and an unfamiliar skyline. I calmed myself by thinking that the good people of Melbourne would at least give me a chance.

Right?

10

Nineteen-minute honeymoon

I pledge to help this idiot fail.

ANONYMOUS LISTENER

'Fuck off home'

6.19 a.m.

That was the very first text message sent to my debut show on Australian radio. Nineteen minutes in.

It had taken just nineteen minutes for the abuse and backlash to start.

The honeymoon wasn't over—it had never begun.

Just two weeks earlier I'd been in tears as I felt the love of my two million listeners all over the UK as some of them told me what my show had meant to them over the previous twelve years. Some said they'd followed me across from the show I'd done for five years before that, which meant I'd been part of their mornings for seventeen years. Others said I'd first talked to them when they were teenagers, listening grudgingly on school runs

101

with Mum and Dad, then they'd willingly carried on listening into their own adulthood.

As their lives changed—first homes, marriage, babies—I'd been a constant, like any long-running radio or TV show, the sort of constant that is increasingly rare in our ever-changing world. The show had been a constant in my life, too, bringing me so much joy, being paid to laugh every day, giving my family a great life, and something to lean on in harder times. It had given me the life I'd dreamt of as a teenage radio fanboy, the kind of kid who recorded the Top 40 countdown on cassette in their bedroom. Some of you may have done this, it's not unique to me. Apart from the fact every Sunday I'd hold a tape recorder up to the radio and record that week's Top 40—I'd then play it back and hit pause before the DJ announced the next song and artist, so I could do this myself, giving the chart position and song details.

Most kids pretended to be footballers or rock stars. I pretended to be a DJ.

In my bedroom.

I told my kids this once when they asked where my love of radio began. There was a silence after the bedroom DJ confession.

'Jeez that's just tragic.'

Invariably my Top 40 recordings would be ruined when, just as I was 'back announcing' (technical lingo) the breaking hot news of a big new entry at Number 8 by Wham, my mum would yell up to my bedroom: 'Your dinner's ready, darling! We're having Spam!'

During my last UK show, despite wanting to leave and knowing I had to, I dreaded sitting opposite my wingman Richie for the last time. We were two radio geeks who'd hit the jackpot.

Emails and messages poured in throughout the final show from listeners recalling tough times they'd been through, and how the show had been a little flicker of light in the darkness.

I'd gone from a flicker of light to 'fuck off home' in fourteen days.

Hero to zero.

And I chose this.

•

Starting a new breakfast show is like a social experiment into how much people don't like change. If you're at the centre of that change, they probably won't like you. It isn't just about you. This time, though, it really was about me. My accent, where I came from. Even how I held my arms in the giant posters of me everywhere.

People really care about radio. I know because I benefit from this—I've made a career out of it. I understand that not being liked can be part of the job.

I remember back when I was at the indie station XFM we'd had the Madness lead singer Suggs do a lunchtime show. I loved Madness as a kid, and years later I was blown away by the band playing at Buckingham Palace as part of the incredible London 2012 Olympic opening ceremony. Suggs is a big, charming character and great fun to have a beer with.

Not everyone was happy to hear Suggs on an indie music station, because to them Suggs was a pop star. I have no time for music snobs. Like what you like. But that wasn't the sentiment shared by some of our hardcore listeners, who were aggressive music snobs and also hated the fact we were owned by a large radio group. As far as they were concerned, the 'man' had put Suggs on air.

Things hit a new high when a letter arrived for Suggs at the station. The scrawly handwritten address on the front of the envelope was a thing of joy and beauty and deserves to be in a broadcasting museum so that future generations can see it.

It simply read:

That Cunt Suggs,
London

Nothing else.

To Suggs's credit, when he heard about this, he asked to see the letter, walked up to the huge cork noticeboard (only an indie music station would have a cork noticeboard) and placed it right in the middle. Way to own it, Suggs!

So, I know the depth of feeling for new people is more hostile in radio than in most jobs.

I mean, if you've taken over from Dave in Accounts, you wouldn't expect to be getting emails saying: *'You're not Dave, you suck.'* Or: *'What's happened to Dave? He was better than you. Please die. You dumbfuck. Also, can you hurry up and pay my expenses.'*

Nineteen minutes into my first show in Australia, the truly intimidating nature of what I'd taken on hit me like a gut-punch winding me.

Part of me wanted to walk out, gather my wife and two daughters, take a cab to the airport and fly straight home, hopefully to my mum and a cuddle waiting at the other end.

Could I get my old show back in England? I was still wearing the lucky headphones I'd had for fifteen years: had the luck run out?

Face it, I told myself, moving to the other side of the world to start a radio show was a crazy idea.

No one has heard of me here. I'm an unknown, an outsider. Of the worst kind—British.

Naively, I'd thought the whole world loved us Brits. Our accent and our funny ways. How we are emotionally dead on the inside, how we're lovable, professional alcoholics. We used to own the world. Granted, we're historically the world's worst landlords, but come on . . . We gave the world The Beatles, the Stones, Led Zeppelin, Monty Python . . .

As I was learning, some folk here *really* can't stand us Brits, especially first thing in the morning on their radio.

'Fuck off home'

Three words. And three seconds left on the song that was playing and then I had to act like everything was all good and do my monkey tap dance. I could feel my stomach tightening as I started to think I might have made the biggest mistake of my life.

I turned my microphone on and the red 'MIC LIVE' sign illuminated the studio.

'Good morning, Melbourne!' I said cheerily, albeit unconvincingly in my mind. To me, it sounded more like a question.

When the show finished, I told myself that this was all part of the early teething problems. I'd come for a challenge, hadn't I? To feel alive again.

I reassured myself that things would get better. As I write this I'm smiling to myself, laughing at my naivety, because I had no idea that I was now on a long road of trials and nights of the soul that would test me more than anything in my life so far.

11

Clowns with feelings

I wouldn't listen to this shit if you were the last DJ on earth.

LISTENER EMAIL

Another happy customer.

Any time an email or text came into the show or my studio inbox I'd almost flinch, readying myself for another abusive message. It was all so hard compared to how it was on my old show. It was taking Herculean efforts to appear happy and in control to my new team. I'd come home exhausted, not from the early starts but from the sheer effort of holding myself together, trying to convince my workmates that I was up to the job.

Not a day went by when I didn't get an angry message from a listener about how they hated me, my show. Some would call the station and let my boss know. There were even comments about how I looked in the posters all over Melbourne.

'He just looks like an arrogant Pom.'

'Stood there like some shitty game show host.'

'Looks like he is selling Viagra.'

I really started to wonder if it was ever going to turn around. It seemed unlikely and impossible. I was even starting to doubt the sanity of the guy who hired me, wondering how he could have been so naive. How dare he give me, a job! What was he thinking?

For three days running some guy kept emailing me and eventually one morning I snapped and called him a 'whining dick'. I know, really grown-up, right? After the show the boss asked to see me. The guy had complained and sent her my reply. To be fair, he proved my point. The boss didn't see it like that.

The amount of vitriol was unlike anything I'd ever experienced or even heard of.

The fact my accent said I wasn't even from this country, but from a country Australia has a 'unique relationship' with, intensified everything. I was informed that Melbourne listeners didn't even like hearing from someone from Sydney, let alone the other side of the world.

It felt like the city was against me. I had been reduced to cherishing the smallest of wins, like the end of one week when we had all the phone lines jammed as we couldn't deal with the amount of people calling in to take part in that day's show. I still have the photo I took of that moment.

They were talking to me.

This was huge. My goal was to get them talking to me as soon as possible. Andy Lee warned me this could take months.

It came about after we went on a family outing whale-watching. On the two-hour or so trip out to see the humpback whales, we were offered drinks by the crew. The kids asked if they could have a 'ginger beer', and I nodded my approval. No big deal, the kids love a nice refreshing fizzy ginger beer.

I should've sussed something was up with the giggling as they took big gulps of their drinks. Then a fellow passenger, a well-to-do Australian who was fanning herself with an actual fan, said to me, *'You're a very laid-back dad.'*

I took this as a lovely compliment, sat back, enjoyed my cold beer and gazed out onto the limitless horizon. I looked over at my kids, sipping their drinks, buzzing with the joys of Australia. *Ahh, at last, this is what we came for.*

I then paused and asked why she said that.

'Well, it's not for me to say, really.'

I was now all ears and urged her to carry on. She leant in conspiratorially and said, 'Well maybe it's a European thing, letting your daughters have beer—'

She didn't even need to finish the sentence. No wonder my kids were sniggering and buzzing. They were halfway through downing *ginger-flavoured beer.* Not *ginger beer soft drink* as they'd sold it to their clueless old man. The other passengers all laughed and cheered as I took the beers off my daughters.

I told this story and then asked for stories about the first time you tasted alcohol. We had all kinds of stories about raiding your parents' drinks cabinet, making fake ID, crazy family members who had no problem pouring one listener, at fifteen years of age, a full glass of brandy when he used to cut his nan's lawn every few weeks.

Seeing all the phone lines jammed was a real moment for me. It was working. I was working. Maybe, maybe, it might be okay and last that six months.

It was a little shard of light at the end of a very long tunnel, the kind of tunnel Andy Dufresne crawls through to escape prison in *The Shawshank Redemption.*

But it was quickly drowned out when almost immediately I received an email sent directly to me, from someone informing me that I had managed to annoy 'the entire work factory' and criticising my arrogance and temerity in moving here 'uninvited'.

An 'entire factory' pissed off with me? That's some power I have.

Were they holding emergency board meetings addressing the sudden and alarming drop in productivity? Trying to work out what had happened, then the moment of discovery: 'It was all going great until that English guy turned up on the radio . . . hang on, wait a minute . . . someone hit scan before he ruins this company!'

●

I was told not to go on the station's Facebook account. I did.

Oh, why did I do that? They really hated me.

Gee, that's surprising as most folk are so kind these days on Facebook. It's an open sewer online sometimes, isn't it? You'd never speak to someone in person the way we do online.

My old UK listeners were defending me and getting into Facebook wars with disgruntled Australians. *'If you like him so much, then take him back,'* was one lively exchange I saw.

Since I started in radio in 1998, complaining has changed dramatically because of the internet.

If the world was still on dial-up internet, there would be a lot less online abuse. Think about it, waiting to get 'online' with a landline connection, you'd be waiting for your other half or kid to get off the landline so you could 'dial up' into the brave new frontier of the information superhighway, but by then you're not as outraged as you were because—SPOILER ALERT—our emotions subside and change, and suddenly you can't be bothered.

By the time you're online, do you really want to say how disgusted you are that they are doing an all-female reboot of

Ghostbusters. Or a comedian made a joke about vegetarians that you didn't like.

Before that was an even better system that worked for decades: a letter was the only means you had to complain. This was great because it takes real effort, and time, to write a letter.

You sit down, write the letter, then you have to find the stamps in that special place where you keep things like stamps and batteries, then walk to a post box, again more hassle, energy and time: can you still be bothered?

Complaining is instant now, thanks to the internet. Instant means no pause for thought, or consideration. We live in a world of constant and instant reaction. Rarely is our first reaction our best.

The best thing about the internet and online world is that it's given everyone a voice.

The worst thing is that it's given everyone a voice.

When any of us buys something online, we always want to read the reviews. Which, if you think about it, doesn't make sense because, if you're going to buy an electric tin opener, probably the last person on the planet whose opinion you should give even the smallest respect to is the sort of person who takes time out of their day to write a review on an electric tin opener.

No. I'll tell you why we hunt through online reviews, and it's not to make sure we're not wasting our money—it's because we're secretly excited that we're going to stumble across someone losing their shit over how bad something has been.

Go read Amazon reviews of the widely agreed classics of literature.

The Catcher in the Rye is widely regarded as one of the best coming-of-age stories, but not according to a 1-star review I read: 'Can't understand all the fuzz.' They actually spelt 'fuss' 'fuzz'. They continued, 'No wonder the author's own mother hated it.'

Yeah, that's always how I rate books or movies. What did the author's mum think of this?

My wife, needless to say, loves reviews. In an ideal world she would have checked out reviews of me before dating me. Once on holiday she was shopping, and she sent me to find a restaurant for lunch. I thought I'd just see what looked nice and go in. I found somewhere and ordered a drink and texted my wife where I was.

The following exchange occurred between my wife and me.

'Has it got good reviews?'

'Didn't check, seems lovely'

'How do we know it's any good?'

'We take a chance, like people used to'

A minute passes before I get this: *'It's got terrible reviews, you need to leave there now'*

As I read that, I actually started looking around to check no one could see her message. I smiled at the waiter and summoned the courage to ask for the bill and apologised for leaving so soon. I wondered if he knew. They must hate Tripadvisor.

Tripadvisor is a brilliant idea, by the way. Before spending your money on a holiday or visiting a restaurant, you check to see if it's any good. I could read Tripadvisor reviews for a whole weekend. Laughing at people's entitled whines. And it's always best when it's an overreaction or is just plain unreasonable.

I was looking at reviews for a place in the Thailand jungle as we were thinking about taking the kids there on a big trip. This place looked amazing, I'm scrolling down the glowing 5-star reviews and find what I'm looking for. A 2-star review.

'Only gets 2 as on the lake where we stayed in tents there was no wi-fi and little 4G even.'

Oh, you're kidding! No wi-fi in the jungle, it's an outrage.

•

I say all this to show you the way of the world now. The world I work in. Let me give you some of my favourite complaints I've received. I've kept some of the worst. Some are so rude, odd and bizarre they deserve a wider audience, or if I need a hit of something to wake me up at 5.45 a.m. in the studio.

1. When Robin Williams died in 2014, I mentioned on air that I'd watched his brilliant movie *Mrs Doubtfire* to show my kids his genius. They loved it. I said that for a 90s comedy it had a real grown-up ending, because the couple don't get back together. Williams and director Chris Columbus wanted kids of divorced parents to see that sometimes it's better if Mum and Dad separate but still be friends. Man, I miss Robin Williams.

   Anyway, a guy emails me directly, and his opening line was:

   'Yeah, thanks dickhead'

   He had called me a dickhead.

   'Yeah thanks dickhead for giving away the ending of the movie.'

   Mrs Doubtfire came out in 1993! Hardly a 'spoiler'.
   Has this guy been going, 'Don't tell me don't tell me don't tell me!' for the last 21 years? Thank God I didn't tell him that ET made it home and the *Titanic* sank, I'd be fired.
   I hope he's not reading the Bible, and I ruin it by telling him that Jesus comes back in the end.

2. In my job, I often give away prizes from sponsors and advertisers. Once I was giving away power drills. That's right, I'm in the business of changing people's lives.

So this guy won and immediately started emailing, hassling me for his drill. I told him, 'Hey, you only won a few days ago—with any competition in radio, it's four weeks standard time to get your prize.'

I got seven more emails asking for his drill, three of them in one day! Then one of the craziest emails I have ever received came from him:

My son still hasn't got curtains in his room all because I haven't received the drill.

He's getting quite upset about this and so am I.

I do not want the next Jimmy Savile perving on him whilst he sleeps.

How would you like it if something happened to him and you knew it was down to your actions (or lack of)?

I'm disgusted by you.

Maybe the newspapers would like to hear about all of this, ITS [sic] A SCAM.

Putting to one side the notion that up until then his son had no curtains, and the *only* way he could get curtains was his dad winning a competition to get a power drill from a radio station, this listener thought it was a scam, me conning the good people of Britain into winning tools on my radio show, that I never give away!

Also, Jimmy Savile was a famous TV presenter, and after his death it was made public that he was the country's biggest sex offender. My complainer was suggesting that sex offenders must travel around hoping for a home with no curtains.

I never sent him the drill on purpose.

If you ever hear that I've been murdered, know he finally got that drill and came looking for me. In Australia.

3. I have also been threatened. By clowns. Real clowns.

Just before my birthday, my wife told me the kids wanted to surprise me on the big day by taking me to the circus. Not a treat in any way, shape or form for an adult human being.

Only kids like this stuff and that says kids are mini-psychopaths. Hopefully with good parenting we show them a better path, but only a kiddie psycho would cheer and laugh at an elephant doing a wheelie or a chimp roller-skating or a bear skipping rope.

What kind of a treat is that? Did they have a secret meeting about how to screw up my birthday? What else was on the shortlist? Why not just save the money and let me sit in some lion shit while clowns run at me from the darkness screaming in my face?

Off we went, though, to the circus, on my birthday. Hey! Good times.

I went on air the next day and said a few words about the circus and then after the show the boss called me into his office. He said there had been a complaint. From some circus workers. He urged me not to say anything else about the circus. I asked why, and his words I will take to my grave smiling:

'The clowns are threatening to come down here and cause trouble.'

But, *I really want clown trouble.*

I could be walking down the street one day, then suddenly someone will pull up, shoot at me from a flower in their lapel, or worse, throw a bucket of confetti over my head. A victim of a clown-by. It's got to be worth it for the police report, surely?

'Mr O'Connell, did you catch the numberplate?'
'No, but I did catch the doors, the bonnet . . .'
'How many people were in the car?'
'Twenty-seven.'

If the big change has been the internet, social media has offered a new way for angry people to contact someone they don't like directly . . .

4. I checked Twitter on the way home after a show, thinking I've got the best job in the world, and saw this message to me from an @MrKendal:

'Shut your boring mouth you shit DJ inbred cunt.'

Now, I've got to say, I'm quite in love with this. Shakespeare himself would be envious of this kind of poetic abuse.

If it wasn't for various 'marketing issues', this would have been the name of this book. There is so much in this tweet to admire. Not least of all, that the sender, Mr Kendal, has only ever sent one tweet, and this is it. To me. How special do I feel?

Also, it was sent at one o'clock in the afternoon, more than four hours after I went off air.

Why wait four hours? I think I know why. Let's have a look at Mr Kendal's day, shall we?

Listens to show, or at least enough of it to determine that I am a boring, shit DJ, and that my parents were related.

Hours pass by, he can't let it go. He waits until his lunch break.

'You go ahead without me guys, I've got some things to do,' he says to colleagues heading out for lunch.

He has to create a Twitter account, learn how to tweet, then think about what he wants to say to me. Reads it back, checking it's right, looking for typos. Then he hits send and pushes his chair away from the desk.

'My work here is done.'

He has, to this day, five years later, never posted anything again.

It's like he said all he ever wanted to say on social media.

5. To be fair to the internet, I should tell you that people were willing to go postal to express their disdain for me, too. This one happened here in Australia. Fifteen shows in, the police were called to the station after someone sent me faeces in the post. Yeah, you read that right.

It turned out to be a false alarm. But I loved the fact that when someone reported a package had arrived for me that 'smelt suspicious', my radio station boss immediately thought it had to be shit. Like there was no other possible alternative. 'It's got to be shit. Have you heard his show? It's definitely shit—call the police.'

Also, why do the police have to open up my shitty mail? Are they specially trained for this? 'Our son Derek is doing well in the police, he's just been promoted to the Faeces Force. We're so very proud.'

Despite the false alarm, it seemed I was about as welcome as a bout of chlamydia.

I couldn't help wondering if I should take that initial advice, and you know, just fuck off home.

12

Notes from Down Under

This is a part-time thing, I'm also a paranormal investigator but the money is terrible. Ghostbusters *was unrealistic in that way.*

MELBOURNE UBER DRIVER

While my radio life was going to hell, I was rapidly trying to get to know my new city, despite its population's almost complete rejection of me on a visceral, personal level.

Every article about me when I started stated two things: that I was the 'media's biggest ever gamble', and that my lack of knowledge about Melbourne would hurt me and severely affect my chances of success.

'How can he do well, he's not from round here.'

'He's not one of us.'

'I bet he doesn't even like Tim Tams!'

'I bet he's got a small dick.'

I was warned that Melbourne was a very secular, insular, parochial city and the early reaction to my arrival certainly made it feel that way.

Like any city, Melbourne has a shorthand, a private language shared by its inhabitants that I didn't know, and my accent literally accentuated that. I made it my obsession to learn about the city as quickly as possible. Even the jokes and easy punchlines I could make on air in the UK wouldn't work here. It was like having the wrong currency.

There were so many examples. In-jokes about suburbs that you can tag at the end of a bit that you don't even have to think about, these would have to be learnt and thought about for the first time in my career. Radio is built on intimacy and connection: my accent, I feared, and my lack of shared knowledge could really come between us.

If I wasn't careful, I would be burnt inside a wicker man. The Wicker DJ.

The speed at which I did manage to learn the new language is down to the huge debt of thanks I owe to the Uber drivers of Melbourne. For the first few months I took Ubers everywhere. I would ask the drivers questions and listen to them on every single trip. I'd take notes. Often the same drivers would pick me up, and we became first-name friends. Two are good friends to this day.

Often I'd jump in an Uber with the kids and I'd recognise the driver and it would be, 'Michael, how are you mate?'

'Ah! The English DJ, how's it going?'

These drivers go all over the city and know every suburb. I met some real characters, like the guy who told me with no irony that he was 'training to be a personal trainer and opera singer'.

This was at 5 a.m. as he was taking me to work and chugging a giant can of some fearsome-looking energy drink. My mind imagined he could be the world's first personal training opera singer. Training clients while doing *La Bohème*. Or performing *Phantom of the Opera* while doing bicep curls on stage.

So reliant was I on Uber drivers educating me I became very anxious about my passenger rating. As a professional people-pleaser, I wanted them to give me 5 stars. Surely my back seat conversation must be pretty damn good. Did you know about this, by the way? The drivers rate us? Yeah, for decades we've taken taxis and never given a shit about what they think about us. Not now. We get rated.

When I discovered this, I asked a driver about it. I was in a shitty Japanese hatchback, my knees covering my ears, and I asked him, 'How do you rate us?'

He said, 'By how interesting you are.'

Now I have to be *interesting*?

I chose a Hyundai Getz. I should get 5 stars for anything above and beyond that I do after that. It's the vanilla in the lemon-lime cordial of cars.

My ego couldn't handle the daily abuse from listeners *and* a less than 5-star Uber rating.

What have I got to do back here? A chat show? My own gig? Do I need to bring a PA and lights? A meat raffle?

So I tried even harder with this audience of one than I did on my radio show. I made small talk, asked him how long he'd been driving for Uber, then one driver dropped this bombshell.

'I used to be a rabbi.'

'What?'

'I used to be a rabbi.'

There aren't enough stars in the world to give this man what he deserved. Amazing, he *used to be a rabbi*!

Various thoughts came to me. Used to be? Did he quit? Sacked? Isn't that a job for life?

Rabbis aren't being told, 'Your first six months is make or break, you're one bad sermon from being sacked.' They play to packed houses every night, they don't get rated and reviewed by the worshippers.

Only two and a half yamakas.

As someone raised as a good Irish Catholic boy, I couldn't help but think about out-of-work priests. I mean, Catholic priests aren't generally out of work. They're usually in prison.

At what point while teaching Judaism to people do you think about the career move? Unless this is part of your journey? Maybe being an Uber driver was the logical move? It's a new way to talk to people. Uber Preach?

'Your messiah is seven minutes away.'

•

For those of you unfamiliar with Melbourne, and Australia, here's what my Uber education taught me, coupled with a bit of knowledge I've gleaned while living here. (Apologies to my Australian readers for rehashing, but someone's got to educate us Brits.)

When overseas people think Australia, they think of the outback, a land of red hues, kangaroos and rural towns. They think of the bush, all those gum trees, and they think of the surf beaches, where the tanned locals ride the waves with a casual flair that is breathtaking.

This Australia only really exists in the marketing materials of Tourism Australia.

Australia is less a country and more a federation of city states. Depending how you define it, about 90 per cent of Australians live in major cities along the coasts, the middle of Australia being mainly an uninhabitable desert.

Australians mostly live in the cities of Sydney, Melbourne, Brisbane, Adelaide and Perth. And these are big cities by Western standards. Sydney and Melbourne each have around five million people in them, and Brisbane and Perth more than two million. Both Sydney and Melbourne are bigger cities than any in the UK bar London, and if you dropped them in the United States they would only trail New York City in population.

Aside from the five major cities mentioned, other cities of note include: Darwin, up in the Northern Territory, home of the real dusty red outback that most people associate Australia with; Hobart, the capital of the sparsely populated but beautiful island state of Tasmania; and the national capital, Canberra. All of these are much smaller in size.

Like Athens and Sparta in Ancient Greece, Sydney and Melbourne both dominate the nation's affairs, and have a rivalry that has produced some quite odd outcomes in the short history of Australia since the British set up shop here.

When a national capital had to be established after Australia's individual colonies federated in 1901, the two cities fought so much over being the new capital, a compromise had to be reached to set up another city in a couple of cow fields almost exactly halfway between them, called Canberra.

They had to make a brand-new city!

Given Australia is physically huge, and Melbourne and Sydney are just under 900 kilometres apart, that means Canberra was established in the middle of nowhere, where it remains to this day.

The Sydney–Melbourne rivalry has never really stopped, with the two cities competing for population, money and power. The two are close in all these things. Melbourne is the second largest city in Australia after Sydney. Sydney has a population of 5.31 million while Melbourne's is 5.08 million.

Sydney is seen as a more flashy, conspicuously wealthy and internationally renowned city. Of course, it has a great looking harbour, with the iconic Opera House and Harbour Bridge.

Melbourne has many things, but it cannot rival that harbour. No matter what Melbourne does, Sydney's like, 'We've got a FRIGGIN' HARBOUR, the world's BEST harbour, what have you got Melbourne?'

Sydney people believe their city is similar to LA and London. One patronising Sydney resident described Melbourne as being like 'Detroit', which is unfair.

Melbourne, located further south and therefore a bit colder, is seen as a more cultural city, full of galleries, fashion, top cafes and restaurants, and sport. It regularly wins the title of the 'Most Livable City in The World' and it's easy to see why.

The world's second biggest comedy festival (Edinburgh is Number 1) is in Melbourne. It's the live music capital of Australia and when it comes to sport, it is one of the great cities in the world.

Melbourne is the home of Australia's very own sporting code, Australian rules football, and hosts the grand final. It has one of the four international Grand Slams in tennis, the Australian Open; a Formula One Grand Prix and a MotoGP Grand Prix; cricket's Boxing Day Test; and the internationally renowned horse race, the Melbourne Cup, which is a public holiday in Melbourne. That's right, Melburnians are so mad about sport they get a day off for a horse race.

Melbourne was, like all of Australia, first settled by the Indigenous population a long time ago. How long ago is a bit of a contentious topic. Dates vary from 40,000 to 120,000 years ago. I think we can just agree that the Indigenous population has been here for ages.

Europeans didn't arrive in any permanent sense until 1835 (they'd set up shop in Sydney in 1788) and in the years that followed, Melbourne was established and people of English, Irish and Scottish descent flocked to the new colony of Victoria, boosted by a goldrush beginning in the 1850s that would make Melbourne the wealthiest city in the world by 1880.

Post–World War II immigration saw Europeans of a variety of backgrounds, mainly Italians and Greeks, arrive, changing the ethnic mix of the population, a change that continued with many Vietnamese refugees arriving in the 1970s and then further waves of Middle Eastern and African immigration that continues to this day. The result is that Melbourne is a truly multicultural city, with a high level of social cohesion. This multicultural mix also fuels its outstanding cafe and restaurant scene.

The city has an obsession with dining out for breakfast, lunch and dinner. Nowhere is this more obvious than the city's pride at having the 'world's best coffee'. In 2020 it beat Rome, Vienna and, most importantly for Melbourne, Sydney, to win the coffee crown.

This leads me to wonder why Melbourne, as a great food city, with restaurants of every type you can imagine, became 'famous' for these two dishes:

Number 1: Smashed Avo

This is avocado, smeared on toast. It's lovely, often flavoured with some salt, chilli flakes and lemon juice. But I've often been amazed at the genuine proudness shown for what is essentially the sort of dish a ten-year-old makes on Father's Day when they say they are going to 'treat' you to breakfast in bed.

To be fair, smashed avo on toast has travelled the world. It even took off in America when Gwyneth Paltrow added the recipe to her cookbook. That must've filled a good quarter of a page.

I'm being harsh! What is truly world class in Melbourne is its cafe culture. It's a daily treat to go for breakfast or brunch and to be served a fresh, inventive gorgeous meal. I've not had a bad one since moving here. I take team members to breakfast and you can wander in anywhere and not have to worry about getting a dodgy breakfast. The same cannot be said in London, where the standard varies wildly. You can eat like a king one day then be served cancerous-looking sausages and sweaty mushrooms the next.

Number 2: Chicken Parma

The other food that's an institution in its own right is the chicken parma, short for 'chicken parmigiana'.

It's a chicken schnitzel smeared in melted cheese, tomato sauce and ham. It always comes with chips and a salad that no one ever eats.

It is astoundingly popular. Almost every trip to the pub involves everyone at the table perusing the menu before everyone says, 'I'll just have the parma.'

As you drive around, you'll see banners outside pubs offering 'Parma and a pint $20'.

Importantly, in Melbourne it's called a 'parma', while the majority of the rest of Australia call it a 'parmie'. Such is the venom of the debate over what is the correct name, if a civil war starts in Australia, you can be sure it will be along this fault line.

To us Brits it's the equivalent of the Sunday roast. Which is only pronounced one way, not 'roastie' if you're from London, 'rosta' in Manchester or 'roaster' in Liverpool.

•

I want to wrap up my introduction to Melbourne with what is perhaps one of my favourite bizarre facts about the city. It has a swimming pool named after the late prime minister, Harold Holt. The interesting bit being that poor Harold Holt drowned. Not in this pool, it was at a dangerous surf beach on the Mornington Peninsula.

When I pointed out the strange irony in this to a Melburnian Uber driver—the kind of irony that should send Alanis Morissette back into the recording studio—the guy said, 'Never thought about that until you mentioned it. Yeah, when you think about it, it is odd.'

When. You. Think. About. It.

Naming a swimming pool after a drowned prime minister.

Disappeared without a trace. For some reason that felt familiar.

13

Neighbours

We had a safe-sex talk at school today, we had to bring in a piece of fruit. One boy came in with a tomato.

LOIS O'CONNELL

Learning about my new city was nothing compared to getting to know Australians, not the travellers that visit the UK, but Australians in their own habitat.

Before I'd come to live in Australia, I believed the differences between the two countries could be summarised like this:

Australians
- Laid-back
- National catchphrase 'No worries, mate'
- Love beer
- Don't worry about rules

The English
- Uptight
- National catchphrase 'I'm sorry'

- Love tea
- Rules are for us

I had in my mind a firm idea of what Australians were like and what it would be like to live there.

It would be a country full of laid-back beer-loving folk who would, with open arms, welcome me, a funny charming Brit with my eccentric ways, love of tea and the Queen. Being in a less uptight country would do me and my family the world of good, I thought. More of life spent outdoors and on the beach. Not just the sea air invigorating us but also a fresher air of positivity.

We Brits love forms, rules, regulations, pomp and ceremony. I once had a private tour of the Houses of Parliament and learnt that the distance separating the government and the opposition bench is exactly that of 'two sword lengths apart'.

A trip to any post office in Britain will see all manner of forms required to be filled out and queues of decent people all observing their manners. We like order.

I once almost had a complete mental breakdown at an Italian airport where it was utter chaos, an orgy of misinformation, noise and missing luggage. There were no queues for anything, just people pushing in. My wife shared my dismay and yelled at me, *'How can they live like this?'*

Often, when travelling, I've joined a queue only to find out it wasn't the queue for what I needed. What can I say, we love a queue.

So, life in Australia would be more relaxed, with less admin and pointless bureaucracy. Goodbye to form filling! My opinion of Australians themselves was based on the few I had worked with and the ones I had met in London who seemed to love life, a laugh and a beer.

Within a few weeks of living in Melbourne, I realised some of this was misleading.

Those Australians I met in London were in their twenties, across the globe in one of the world's greatest cities, they should be happy and have no worries. They were single, travelling the world and sowing their seeds.

The catchphrase of 'no worries', I quickly found out, wasn't true of a city with plenty of worries, mainly about having the right permits for just about everything. And regulations that even this uptight Brit couldn't fathom.

For example: There are several bins all with different coloured lids that are only allowed to be collected on certain days. Every Tuesday night I'd have *bin anxiety*. What if you're colour blind? I'd be staring at the bins frantically wondering if it was the food bin with the red lid, or the recycling with the blue lid. It was like knowing which wire to cut on a bomb. I'd be that guy out the front of his house looking down the road at that neighbour every street has, normally retired, who always knows which bins go out in what week.

One day I'll be my street's Bin Leader.

I was also reprimanded for parking my car the wrong way. In 'rule-loving' Britain you park your car on either side of the road, facing whatever direction you like. Not so here. You have to park the car facing the direction of the traffic. What happened to no worries? I was starting to doubt whether Crocodile Dundee was a real person. I bet he had a permit for that knife.

Who knew Australians loved bureaucracy even more than us Brits? How is that even possible? I was stunned that such a seemingly laid-back bunch had so much red tape.

Melburnians are arguably the most orderly Australians, I guess you don't get voted the World's Most Livable City if things aren't organised. Therefore, in Melbourne, there are rules for everything, it's an OH&S officer's dream.

For example, in 1970, Victoria became the first place in the world to enforce seatbelt legislation and, by and large, overnight people just started wearing seatbelts.

In the UK seatbelts were in cars from 1965 but they had to introduce laws to get our parents to actually use them some eighteen years later in 1983. It's a bit like telling motorcyclists, 'Look, you have to have a helmet—but you can keep it in your bag.'

And when they made it the law, people were outraged. My dad was livid!

'I reserve the right to be cannoned through my own windscreen, son.'

This isn't the only example of how Melburnians are more law-abiding than Londoners.

Until 1966, it was illegal for pubs in Melbourne to be open after 6 p.m. This simply wouldn't be tolerated in London. The law was designed in part to encourage men to go home and spend a quiet evening with their families. However, it backfired and resulted in the infamous 'six o'clock swill', when everyone would rush to the pub after work and down as many beers as possible until they were all booted out at 6 p.m., whereupon there was suddenly a horde of drunk people out on the street.

Even dog walking wasn't free from Australian bureaucracy. Not long after I got our dog from quarantine, I took her for a walk in the park near where we were now living. I let her off the lead as I would normally do and as I passed other dog walkers and joggers, I was met with stern looks and double-takes as if I'd just unleashed Hannibal Lecter into the park, and he hadn't eaten in a week.

I was told by some old fella that this was an 'on-leash' park. I didn't even know what that meant. Turns out some parks are 'on leash', some 'off leash', and some no dogs at all. Who wants a park without dogs?

Back in England, walk the dog wherever you want. Just pick up their poop. I must admit I'm a vigilante about this, often chasing after dog owners who've just let their dog curl out a new Banksy on the path and then carried on. Marvel Comics are yet to get back to me about my pitch for a dog shit vigilante. Like Spiderman shooting webs from his wrist, I'd just produce dog poo bags at will.

Now in Melbourne I have to find off-leash parks to be with my tribe, fellow off-leashers (sounds dodgy) and our free-to-roam dogs. I even had to fill out a form for my dog to get a permit to own her. This does not exist in the UK.

When I first got Nisha as a puppy, I was vetted by the breeder (the vetting mainly seemed to check that I could provide bundles of cash to pay for her) and I was given two A4 printed pages. I was told, 'These are the types of different people and social groups you will need to expose her to before she's six months old.'

The list included various ethnic groups and different types of humans, bald people, high-viz-jacket–wearing tradies, people wearing hats. I had to tick off all of these within six months. Like some bizarre real-life version of Guess Who?

'What happens if I can't find certain ones?' I asked the breeder.

'She will react when she sees them.'

Did I get a racist dog?

Us radio DJs are already seen as being a bit suspect. I didn't think I could drive around my neighbourhood inviting groups of Asian kids to 'come look at my puppy'.

•

I really was surprised that it was not the laid-back place that had been sold to me my entire life, in TV and movies, but a byzantine labyrinth of rules and regulations, inhabited by a populace that seemed only too keen to not just follow them but enforce them on others.

Street signs for parking are more elaborate than etchings on an ancient Egyptian tomb.

I became a bit obsessed with the amount of regulations, and discovered there were so many bizarre and outdated laws in Australia. Here are a few:

- *It is an offence to fly a kite 'to the annoyance of any person'.*
  How exactly does one fly a kite 'to the annoyance of any person'? The kite is up in the air.
- *It is an offence to sing an 'obscene song or ballad' in a public place in Melbourne.*
  Wow, harsh. If they banned obscene songs in London, there would be no crowds at football games. Adam Sandler told me he went to watch a football game at Chelsea on a day off from filming and spent more time watching the crowds. He was amazed and entertained at the rude songs and chants. Many of these are improvised around what's just happened on the pitch and somehow, via some strange osmosis, the words are instantly known by thousands of people.
- *It is illegal to correspond or do business with pirates. The maximum penalty is ten years' imprisonment.*
  Imagine your first night in the big house, prison, starting your ten-year stretch. Everyone is hanging around B wing. Big Vern is doing life, he's the 'guvnor' of B wing.
  'What you in for?' you ask him.
  'Held up a bank. You?'

'Emailed a pirate.'

'What?'

'I also did business with him.'

- *It is an offence to make unreasonable noise with a vacuum cleaner after 10 p.m. or before 7 a.m. on weekdays and before 9 a.m. on weekends.*

  Good. Add leaf blowers and only allow them to be used for five minutes a day. Anyone caught contravening these laws is to be punished by death.

- *You can be jailed for up to a year for collecting seabird or bat poo without a licence in Western Australia.*

  We have James Bond with a licence to kill, Western Australians need a licence to collect seabird or bat poo! Why? Aren't they doing everyone a favour?

- *Also in Western Australia, challenging another person to a duel is punishable by a maximum $6000 fine or two years' imprisonment.*

  A duel? Nothing could be more British than some lord challenging some scoundrel to a duel. The fact they have this law means at some point they needed to. That must've been some road rage in Perth that ended up being a duel the next morning.

To be fair, Britain has some very strange laws as well:

- *All beached whales must be offered to the reigning monarch.*

  Is there anything the Queen doesn't want? She owns all the swans, takes our taxes, makes us sing our loyalty to her in the national anthem, lick the back of her head on stamps, and now we have to give her all the beached whales. Come on. I remember we had breaking news on the radio show a few years back about a beached whale on the banks of the River Thames. A marine expert said, 'We think she may have got lost.'

- *It is illegal to jump the queue in the Tube ticket hall.*
  Told you we loved a queue. It's the LAW to respect the queue. I'm 100 per cent with this. Straight to prison for queue jumpers.
- *It is illegal to handle a salmon in suspicious circumstances.*
  How. Do. You. Handle. Salmon. Suspiciously. How? UK prisons are notoriously overcrowded, now we understand why. They are crammed with queue-jumping salmon rustlers. Scum of the earth.

•

While Australia is a thicket of laws, other things were less constricting than back in England, and the most amazing to me was the drive-through bottle shop. This is an invention I've never seen anywhere else in the world. Let me explain.

THEY BRING THE BOOZE TO YOU.

In England we have the 'off licence' and it's an actual shop that sells alcohol. Here, it's called a 'bottle-o'.

Bottle-o. Adding an 'o' to the end of words is very common in Australia. 'Arvo' for afternoon, 'servo' for a service station and 'ambo' for ambulance. I'm not sure why this is, maybe it's the heat meaning it's just too much effort to say those extra consonants.

The bottle-o is a drive-through shop for getting alcohol. Drive. And through.

Now I'm part Irish and therefore a functioning alcoholic but not even Ireland would pull that shit off. Nowhere else in the world has drive-throughs for booze. How much of a hurry are the drunks in? Are Australians such piss heads they can't even park the car?'

I took the hire car to try one of these drive-throughs and was amazed to learn you don't even have to turn the engine off! You can yell from your car what you want, pop the trunk and they'll dump it in the back for you. Swipe to pay and go. No worries. I marvelled at the efficiency. No time-wasting with all that *parking* and *walking* to get your booze, no, that's precious minutes that could be spent *drinking*.

Interestingly, Australia has drive-through bottle shops, but not drive-through chemists. 'Nah, you sick people can get out of your cars, you lazy gits. The walk will do you good.'

But you know what the drive-through bottle-o says? It says this is a country that knows what it wants. Every impediment between you and booze has been removed.

When you pull up, you're not asking for something earthy with hints of stonefruit and aromas of elderberry and ash. No. The only decision is whether to get twelve or eighteen Jim Beam and Colas.

Actually, I should point out that Australia has some wonderful wines and as a lover of the grape, this pleased me. Only an hour away from Melbourne on the Mornington Peninsula are some awesome wineries famous for their pinot noirs. Elsewhere in Australia there are some world-class shiraz estates in Heathcote, Barossa Valley and Clare Valley.

So imagine my joy, and my wife's dismay, when I discovered a great wine shop in our neighbourhood. What I love about Australian wine shops is that they have none of the elitist snobbery I was used to. Here, wine is for everyone, not just for the well-to-do.

In some of the wine shops, they have recommended wines with labels that say, 'I'm good with . . .' and a suggested food for the wine to be paired with. Maybe white fish, chicken or steak.

Then, in a bottle-o, I saw a label that killed me. The label was on a wine carton—yeah that's still going strong here, wine in a box. It's also called 'goonbag', referring to the bag of wine inside the box. The box is often removed for easier drinking. And they said Australia had no culture!

Anyway, the label on the box of gut-rot wine said: 'I'm good with lasagne.'

Lasagne! Not just a meat, a *dish*!

That's getting really specific. But why stop there? Maybe chuck in more in-depth recommendations?

'I'm good with last night's reheated takeaway.'

'I'm good with wondering if anyone really likes you.'

'I'm good with using as a coping mechanism to silence that voice in your head that's your dad reminding you of all the bad decisions you've made.'

Now I think about it, it's strange how food pairings only exist with wine.

You never see beer with, 'I'm good with a kebab at midnight then a blazing row with your wife'.

Tequila: 'I'm good with nothing. No one has a good story about what happened after drinking me.'

14

Embrace the suck

Someone has written 'dick' on your poster outside our school, right across your forehead.

RUBY O'CONNELL

Now, it was time for the ratings, finally some hard data on just how much I was not liked.

The ratings for UK radio come out every three months, in Australia it's every five weeks! The treadmill I had been on just got turned way up. Every five weeks, the pressure just kept getting more intense. Wait, it gets better. The ratings also come out *during* the show. I was used to a nice lunchtime call where I could crack open the champagne or down a pity beer and get myself together before the next day's show. Here, I would be bracing for bad news while I was on air.

Oh great.

Every five weeks I would find out if Australia liked me or not. I had signed a three-year deal, but many had said that if it wasn't working, I'd be gone within a year. Shot out of a cannon back across the world and crashing into the River Thames.

I had no room for failure here. If it didn't work out, I would be a pariah in Australia. No one would touch the shit English DJ who tanked on air. We'd have to go back to the UK and the kids wouldn't know what was happening to them. I couldn't just get my old radio show back as the new one failed. It really was all on me.

I remember once interviewing an SAS soldier who was part of a highly controversial secret mission in Iraq that went haywire, which is putting it as only someone who plays Nickelback for a living can. 'Went haywire' I'm guessing isn't how these heroes felt.

During a mission in the 1991 Gulf War that got 'compromised' behind enemy lines, trying to destroy Scud missiles, three of the eight men were killed, and four were captured and tortured. One managed to escape and has gone into military folklore as the SAS's longest escape and evasion story. He managed to escape into Syria, across the desert on foot, a journey of around 200 kilometres.

Some of the most interesting conversations I've been lucky to be part of have been with former Special Forces soldiers. In no way do they glamorise war, if anything it's the opposite. They are deeply introspective people who have seen hell and also, for Chris Ryan (pseudonym) who escaped capture, heaven.

Chris came on the show a few times to promote his books, but the first time, even though it was a well-known story by then, I asked him to recount what happened. His story was a 'stop the clocks' moment as time stood still. I got emails afterwards from so many listeners who had stayed in their cars until it was over as they couldn't pull themselves away.

The bit I'll always remember was when Chris was starving, having not eaten for days and moving constantly to escape certain torture and death, an entire army tracking him, and his body was breaking down. He was pushing himself beyond pain into an area we will never know. He told me his organs were failing and he knew he was reaching the end. When I asked him what he meant, he stopped for a moment, took a breath, as if drawing that memory back in from somewhere he had sent it away to, then looked deep into my eyes and said, 'Death has a smell, I was dying, I could feel the smell of death.'

What's the point in all this? I hear you ask.

My ratings were so bad in the first year that I could smell the stench of failure.

Sure, it's not the smell of death, but it felt like it.

After so many years of awards and record ratings, to be confronted with your own lack of popularity, it's a big kick in the ego balls.

I had an ongoing diary reminder of the rating results days and after a while I deleted them as I didn't want to see the reminders pop up while I was happy doing something joyous, like walking the dog or enjoying some rare alone time with my wife. I can tell you now, one of the most powerful forms of contraception is a reminder that your stinking latest ratings come out tomorrow at 9 a.m.

Shrinking ratings, shrinking all round.

Sidenote here: I've told you that my wife is a forensic planner, and as such we have a regular-ish diary reminder of a meeting with 'Bob the Accountant'. It's during the week on a school day. It's often a pretty short meeting. I am forbidden from saying any more.

Radio ratings here in Australia are big news, and I mean that, actual news.

Reported in the newspaper and on the evening TV news. Which is really great, as in no way would I want to keep it quiet how badly I was doing. The other thing I had going for me was that I stood out as the only English DJ on the radio in Melbourne. I was like a wanted man—actually, unwanted—with my poster all over town.

A lowlight was being taken by my wife to meet some other husbands and wives who had moved out here over the last few years. A pub playdate, it was going well until one of the guys I was introduced to, a local, said after a few beers, 'You're having a shocker, aren't you? With your ratings,' and clinked his glass into mine as if to say cheers.

Everyone knew.

That was a fun Uber ride home that night for my wife. The driver recognised my voice and said excitedly that he listened to the show. I was so stunned at this revelation I asked him to repeat what he said.

There it was.

Wow.

I actually did have a listener.

Finally came the proof, and after a rotten night I felt some joy. I almost asked him to drive round the block a few times so I could bask a little longer in this moment, like a victory lap.

The sad thing was he only gave me a 4-star rating.

Maybe he could also smell the stench of failure in the back of his Prius.

The ratings just kept coming, every five weeks during the show, and I could tell from the looks on my team members' faces that we'd taken a hit again. I'd never had such ratings in my career; they went up and down but in twenty years on air, they'd never gone down every single time.

I wouldn't be able to sleep the night before the next ratings were coming out, I'd feel so tense and nervous.

I'd lie to Sarah about what days the results were due so she wouldn't be worried as well. Even on a trip back home after a year living in Australia, I wasn't safe from the relentless pressure of the ratings. Due to the time difference I had to get up at 1 a.m. and creep out of the hotel room and go down to reception to wait for my boss to call from Melbourne with the latest. It was another bad one and nowhere in the world was safe from the shitfest.

The show itself, however, was sounding good on air. It was the only thing I had control over. I felt like the show was a buoy in shark-infested waters. I was doing what I do. We did some great stuff. There were bits that didn't work out and looking back I can see I was trying too hard.

'Philipino Collins', anyone? Giving away Phil Collins tickets and a backstage tour, by working out what the Phil Collins song was that our Filipino listener Maria was singing in her native language.

'Psychic crocodile'? I tried to predict the outcome of Australia's opening match against the French in the football World Cup: if there was one thing both Britain and Australia could bond on, it was beating the French at sport. I sent my sidekick Jack down to Melbourne Aquarium to consult Pinjara, the crocodile in residence, live on air.

We got two chickens, both dead (natural causes, we were assured), one wearing the French colours, the other the Socceroos. The croc went for Australia and an upset win was predicted.

Sadly, this wasn't to be and maybe upon reflection, after Australia's 2–1 loss, the crocodile was showing us that the Socceroos were going to be devoured. Either way I fired the match-predicting crocodile and my dumb idea. Next time, I'll go for an emu.

Even doing a good thing would end up going wrong. I said on air how much I appreciated people giving me a go, and anyone who called the show today or texted, I'd call after the show to thank them. I thought no one would care, this small act of genuine gratitude really connected for some reason. So many texted saying kind things and it meant after the show it would take over an hour to call people back to say thank you. We filmed some of this for Facebook and Instagram, and, you're going to judge me, I got the phone number of someone who had called the boss and been awful about me. I left a voicemail thanking them for saying 'I was the funniest DJ they had ever heard and could they have a signed photo?' I knew this would just piss them off so much and *it felt great.* I know that makes me pathetic.

The video goes up online, and in the way of viral video, someone tagged her (as the kids say). She also heard my voicemail. Imagine that, the DJ you called to complain about, saying you *hated him* calling to thank you for your praise. She called the boss back, threatened legal action for 'libel', unless the video was removed. She really didn't like me did she? The thought of a video online saying she did was unbearable.

Imagine me in court for spreading lies about someone saying they liked me.

The case against me, 'This could be damaging for me personally, my family, my business, if people thought I liked that English DJ.' I laugh about it now, but at the time . . .

I'd laughed about it too after I left that voicemail.

The signs were as bad as they could get.

Soon I'd have crows and vultures circling over me like a rotting carcass in the desert.

•

My real fear keeping me awake at night, the monster under the lake, was that if things didn't turn around, they would do something which to me is even worse than getting fired. Getting fired doing work that you care about and believe has value has no shame; getting fired over work that's been diluted and people have interfered with and run by focus groups, that's horrible and soul destroying.

I walked away from all that twenty years ago.

My creative freedom, to make radio my way and run a team, is something of huge importance to me, something I have earned the right to do. I have had some great little teams over the years, they're my E Street Band and I can't make the shows without them. The vision is mine, but I need their input, hearts and souls, ideas, passion, joy.

There are enough radio and TV shows that try to appeal to everyone, cookie-cutter shows. We live in a world of vanilla. They value mass market, one size fits all, using ideas that have been done before because they want familiar and therefore predictable outcomes. You've heard those shows, they are made by producers and handed to presenters.

I like rough edges; I don't always like mine personally, but I'm fascinated by yours. The way I was doing radio here was even more interactive than I'd done before and my listeners have always been a huge part of what I do. I used the listeners as contributors to the show, lots of calls giving me stories, which I just love. My listeners were as much a part of the show as me, Jack and Pats. I wanted them to be part of what I was trying to build here. I insisted they be able to SMS the show, despite being told, 'That won't work.' Okay, so the first message I got was 'Fuck off home', but I pushed on and within the first two weeks we were getting hundreds of messages a show! These little wins kept me going.

Radio, in general, has become very lazy.

In the UK a former producer of mine was hired to look after and rebuild a show hosted by a TV household name. He was asked by the host how I put my show together. The producer said that I'm obsessed with real-life stories that come from my life. Now, as a fellow dad himself, there should've been no shortage of stories to bring to air and use as a springboard to go into a new area to have a conversation about. The TV host said he liked the idea, and then asked the producer to come up with ten personal stories for him.

I had been assured that the show was mine to run. I put the team in place, I made the final calls. But I knew after a while if ratings kept going down, that would be impossible to maintain and I would lose control of the show.

The Secret Sound was lurking in the background . . .

•

I'd like to say that outside of that, things were going well in our new home, but they were not.

Bet you're glad you started to read this book now, aren't you? Suddenly I'm making *The Road* and *Angela's Ashes* look like fun reads.

Truth was, our kids were also struggling with new schools and making friends. Back in England, we could organise playdates to help them make new friends; here, we couldn't. We didn't have any friends and neither did they. Seeing your children struggle in any way is heartbreaking, but added to that was the fact that I felt like I'd dragged them here, uprooted them from friends and at the worst possible age. Right on the cusp of becoming a dreaded species we all know, we came from them: *teenagers*.

15

'Try giving birth.'

Based on your life, I can't see why anyone would want to become a dad.

DAUGHTER, WHO DOESN'T WANT TO BE NAMED, BUT SHE SAID THIS

The first big family event was the girls starting at their new school. Getting uniforms was a nightmare as we arrived in late May in the middle of the Australian school year.

Why are school uniforms so expensive? It's not Hugo Boss or Versace making those boxy blazers.

My wife had given me the job of taking the girls shopping for school shoes, which is a new level in Dante's circle of hell. Everywhere we went, our accents just stood out.

'English, right? What brings you here?'

'A rather intense nervous breakdown.'

'How lovely.'

When I was a kid, school shoe shopping was easy. Because there was no choice. I'm not even sure my feet got measured. I certainly wasn't ever asked things like, 'How are these around the heel?' My school shoes were made of some kind of unbreakable material that they build bridges with and they never showed any sign of wearing until around seven months into the school year. My feet would be bleeding as I walked to school effectively clad in iron diving boots with a bed of nails for soles.

Nowadays their precious feet are measured by 360-degree lasers. There are way more choices of school shoes than we ever had. Lovely soft leather, comfort is a given.

It's as if the shoe manufacturers no longer wish to cripple school children, a major shift from my day. I think the school shoe designers of the 80s didn't get the jobs at Ralph Lauren, Manolo Blahnik or Giorgio Armani in Italy and, jealous of their peers, they took out their revenge on kids' school shoes.

The moment I started buying school shoes for my kids, part of my dad DNA became activated. I suddenly became that dad who, when he sees the school shoes that he forked out a small fortune on only a few weeks ago, yells:

'ARE THOSE SCUFFED AT THE FRONT?'

You don't even know where the words come up from. You have no control over them. You can't stop the dad anger. I'm not proud.

'You need to pick your feet up! I'm not getting you a new pair this year, you'll just have to make do. PICK YOUR FEET UP! In my day I had to wear wooden planks nailed to my feet. It wasn't a shoe fitting, it was a crucifixion.'

During the nineteen-hour shoe-trying session that even the prince's courtiers in Cinderella would've found excessive, I texted my wife saying my human rights were being abused and UNICEF should put an image of me on their new donation campaign.

'Try giving birth.'

This is always her get-out-of-jail-free card to anything I moan about.

'Try giving birth.'

Even if I was injured in a drive-by shooting and phoned her riddled with bullet holes, praying for death's sweet release, saying my last words, all I would hear would be a cold:

'Try giving birth.'

Checkmate. Game over.

Seeing the girls walk off together to their new school was a sight that will always stay with me. I was in silent awe of their bravery and courage. They must've been so scared. They were thirteen and eleven, walking into a big school where they knew no one and were foreigners. Outsiders. Our school years are full of insanity, struggles and dramas. I feared I'd intensified that by moving them to the other side of the world.

I walked with them home from school and offered them a hand each to hold.

'Not anymore Dad, it's just creepy now,' I was told as my hands were swatted away.

As we left the school, we all noticed something . . .

'You've got to be kidding!' the girls moaned in unison.

Oh no. There was a bus shelter right outside the school gates for the school bus. In that shelter was a six-foot-high poster of me advertising the new show. Right outside their new school gates.

I tried to make it okay with a little joke. 'Dad can keep an eye on you.'

'It's just *horrendous!*' they screeched.

In their first few weeks, other kids would walk past my daughters and do the pose I was doing in the poster.

•

Normally the question I ask every day of, 'What did you do today at school?' is met with an overly dramatic sigh or 'not much'. It's the first rule of teenagerhood, you don't talk about school.

But after their third day at school, when I asked Lois how her school day was, she casually said: 'We had terrorism training today.'

Now this is Australia, so this could mean anything. Were they taught how to disarm a terrorist using a teenage girl's most deadly weapon, withering sarcasm?

'You're going to bring down the West, really? You look like your mum dressed you, what are you wearing, some shitty Halloween outfit?'

Or were they being trained to be emo terrorists? As my daughters approached teenagerhood, that felt possible.

Working in central London after a terrorist attack, we were told that our DJ lives mattered to the company and the shareholders, which was a touching message. As a large media outlet, we were placed on high alert. Security would be stepped up, which wasn't hard, as it really couldn't have been any more lax. Every morning when I arrived the overnight security guard would be slumped on the reception desk fast asleep. I would creep past so as not to wake him. One time the fire alarm was going off and a fire crew arrived outside the station, hammering on the door trying to wake sleeping beauty from his slumber.

The station's idea of 'stepping up security' was installing a swipe card entry. Yep. That will do it.

Take that terrorists! You don't train for that in those training camps we see on TV news footage. Sure, we see the barbed wire you crawl under on your belly, the monkey bars, but no swipe card entry doors. Fiendish!

My boss said, 'Our number one worry is they'll take over the airwaves.'

They were concerned that the terrorists would be able to hate-preach, over the internet and FM frequencies, in such a way as to convert thousands of my listeners. It would at least make sense of all that reading of *The Art of War*.

Can I just say, our bosses must think these guys are pretty capable. I've worked in radio for more than twenty years and can't convince the vast majority of our listeners to text us their favourite Christmas present. But that can't compete with a 'National call to Arms! Overthrow the West! Right after the new one from Nickelback.'

One of the attractions of coming to Australia was the kinder, safer, and less confrontational way of life. So to hear Lois come back from school saying she had terrorism training today, I'm like, 'That's nice, and . . . WHAT?!'

She explained, with much eye-rolling, that they were teaching the kids about what to do in the event of a terrorist gaining access to the school. The kids were told at the start of the day that they would be doing this drill but wouldn't be told when.

So Lois was in her smock in her art class making clay animals when halfway through her lesson, they suddenly sounded the alarm. The teacher said, 'Okay children, everyone get down under the windows NOW and don't move. As quickly as possible.'

Lois asked, 'Miss! Shall we take our smocks off?'

And the teacher said, 'No! Every second counts. This is a life-or-death situation. There is no time to take off your smocks.'

Then the teacher added:

'But everyone! Pack away your clay animals first before they harden!'

Because clay—if you didn't know—is quite expensive.

That's right, folks, my kids are ready to deal with the threat of terrorism so long as there's minimal financial impact to the school budget.

I mean, are the terrorists going to sit outside the school in a van, saying to each other, 'Let's wait until the next period so those clay animals are not caught up in what's coming.'

I hate to undermine her teachers, but I said, 'Lois, if that really happens, abandon the clay animal. Or just keep it. Don't queue to pack it away. It's the one situation where I *want* you to be messy. I've seen how you leave your bedroom; there's a good chance that if you don't pack anything away the terrorists will think that room has already been done.'

The image of Australian SWAT teams going: 'Base 2-0—I have the child, and what looks like a hippo but with shit legs.'

'Congratulations Echo 5; we never leave a clay animal behind.'

I do feel safer in Australia and Melbourne. Yes, you have troops in the frontlines, and yes, you've had terrorism. But your terror cells will never be the sprawling organisations threatening to take down Europe. For a few reasons.

Your internet is too slow for people to be successfully groomed. Seriously. Is this by design? Do your national security advisers keep it so slow on purpose? By the time you've downloaded a training video, you're already questioning your life choices.

Also, your security services are excellent. And of course they are: because knowing who the extremists are here is easy. They're the only people not drinking alcohol. ASIO aren't using cutting-edge snooping technologies to root out the worst Islamic extremists; they've basically got a phone book and a till receipt from the bottle-o's. If you don't appear in both lists, you mysteriously disappear later that evening.

•

I think my daughters paid the heaviest price for the move here.

The girls were excited about moving here but how can you really know what it's like, what's really asked of you, as a thirteen- and eleven-year-old.

Those teenage years are hard enough, then having to deal with that, a totally different life, making new friends and being an outsider.

If they were a few years younger, I think it might have been easier. Before my innocent angels were even anywhere near being teenagers, everyone warned me about it: 'Just wait until they're teenagers.'

People would say that to me all the time. I'd be in the park, feeding the ducks with the girls, having a lovely time and someone would say, 'Oh, just wait until they're teenagers.' What other period of our lives comes with such a stark foreboding and warning?

'Just wait until they're fifty and just want you to hurry up and die and leave them some inheritance.'

It's basically saying, *'Don't enjoy this glorious moment, just wait until it's shittier.'*

Do you remember your teenage years? For some, it's like asking, *'Do you remember your time in Vietnam?'*

No one gets out of their teenage years unharmed.

Oh, don't get me wrong. There are moments of wild happiness and experiencing the joys of life that have you feeling sky high. But there's also dealing with incredible physical and hormonal changes, and it's also when you meet the harsh reality of the world.

That it's unfair and that friends will let you down, you will let yourself down, and your parents will let you down. Your dad's face will be on a bus shelter next to your school. Someone will draw a penis on his face.

In some way, through all the dizzying highs and crashing lows, teenagerhood alters all of us. Even if you were the most popular kid in your year, I bet that was exhausting, all that popularity. Worrying it would end at some point, that someone new could arrive to take your crown, that gnawing thought inside that deep down you weren't actually all that special.

Everyone leaves their teenage years with a scar of some kind. Emotionally or physically. All that's really to debate is how big the scar is, and whether as you get older you accept you've got a scar.

You can spot the arseholes in adult life; they haven't accepted they have a scar. Certain experiences or someone saying something shitty and they overreact and go into a negative spiral—often it's because something has touched that scar, still scabby and flaky 30-odd years later.

It was a bit easier for me as I literally got a scar when I was fourteen. In a school hockey match I got hit in the mouth by someone's flailing stick and my upper lip got split wide open. I was taken to the hospital emergency department. This being the 80s my school PE teacher took me in his shitbox of a car. Despite me bleeding profusely, holding my flapping lips together with my fingers and needing urgent medical attention, my sports teacher (name withheld for legal reasons) stopped along the way to get a newspaper and a pack of cigarettes.

I had to have several stitches, I looked a mess, like Rocky at the end of his slugfest. My upper lip was swollen and puffed up on the left side like a botched Botox job. Later that afternoon after school, my girlfriend came to see me, and when I opened the door, she went deathly white at the sight of the teenage elephant boy, and a few seconds later fainted. It's a real self-esteem booster that. My mum heard me call out in panic and being a nurse she came and attended to my girlfriend.

What is it with fainting where people just go all woozy and start mumbling random nonsensical words then just face-plant or do that slow motion stagger around as if they're standing on very choppy seas. 'Ham shoes terrapin,' you'll hear some suddenly translucent person mumble before staggering to the ground.

•

When you're a parent and your kids enter their teenage years, it all comes back. You get to relive it. But now it's harder on two counts.

Firstly, it's harder for them, way harder, because of social media, phones and the way of the world.

Secondly, because you can't save them. That's a tough one to accept. You're hard-wired to keep them alive and safe.

Life for them up until World War Teen is like you're walking through a beautiful meadow with butterflies and magical unicorns, then one day you see it on the horizon, the dark forest. You tell them not to worry about what that is, to just enjoy the unicorns and rainbows and 'let's build a camp'.

But that dark forest moves ever closer. Then, as it approaches, you see it isn't just a forest, there's also an awful stinking swamp. And there are dragons that breathe fire—teenage boys, and other girls.

Your angels start to run excitedly across the meadow towards the trees, you try to keep up but you're so old and knackered you can't, and they run quicker and quicker, away from you and towards the beckoning dark forest.

It's calling them in. As it did you.

They enter the forest, enchanted by its glittering lights they thought they saw. But those aren't glittering lights, those are the lost souls trying to find their way through the darkness. You can hear them crying in there:

'Daddy, Daddy, save me.'

But you can't get in to save them.

You can only shout from the sidelines, outside the forest, and they don't want to hear your crappy advice, you don't know what it's like in the forest of Shitterton. Don't try to tell them you do know what it's like, they will yell back at you:

'*Your forest wasn't like this one!*'

Then teenage boys, predators disguised as fit cool kids, come and pretend to help them. This really pisses you off. Because you know what they really want.

Stay away, you teenage zombies with hard-ons!

And you made this all worse, because you had a panic attack and took your kids to the other side of the world, and the forest there has 1275 animals that could kill them. Not just hairy caterpillars like those English ones.

I think I've made my point . . .

It was awful seeing them come home unhappy after another day of struggling to make friends, trying to understand a totally different way of being taught, trying to fit in as outsiders.

They would have trouble sleeping. Not wanting to go to school. My poor wife bore the brunt of most of these early morning troubles as I was busy dying on my backside on air.

Both our kids started to show signs of anxiety.

The guilt I felt was weighing heavily on me. One night I actually asked my wife if it was too much and I should end their pain and just take us all back home.

Ever the rock that my wife is, she must've thought about it quietly, but in that moment faced with a crumbling husband, she said what I needed to hear: that it will change for the better and to carry on.

The hope I hang on to is that one day our daughters will look back and realise that the struggles and self-reliance they had to find made them stronger. That it showed them just how strong they really are. I have to hang on to that.

Although the other day Lois asked me if I would enrol her in pole-dancing lessons. Is this my fault?

I did something I rarely do, I said no.

I'm not ringing up and asking, can my fourteen-year-old daughter have pole-dancing lessons? Ten years from now she'll be sat in some therapist's office talking about how her dad encouraged her to take up pole dancing.

I hoped they wouldn't get any hassles about how my show was going.

But they did.

In a way that upset me more than them.

16

The biggest decision I had to make

Do the right thing and quit, even our priest was moaning about your show the other day after mass.

LISTENER EMAIL

Every now and again in your life, a decision confronts you that not only has huge ramifications for your life but shapes you as a person.

I was about to learn that, in Melbourne, this was deciding which of the numerous Australian Football League (AFL) teams I was going to support.

The enormity of the decision was to be revealed to me one morning in the place all major bits of news are delivered in my marriage: our laundry.

There is one item in the domestic set-up that intimidates me. Our washing machine, which may as well be an enigma machine to me. As the radio station paid for all our stuff to be shipped over, everything got crammed into the shipping container that came to our house. And I mean everything. To save on the cost of the flights I was tempted to put myself in there too, after all, it had my bed, clothes and microwave.

At one point my wife queried whether we really needed to take my signed framed Evel Knievel picture with us, this while she was packing a spiraliser that hadn't been used in more than three years. The picture means everything to me, it's my spirit animal Evel Knievel jumping at Caesar's Palace, signed by the great man. I'd look at the photo every day, trying to channel what it meant to me. Taking a leap every day and embracing the risk in it all. From my cold dead hands will that not be coming with me, Sarah!

By the way, was there ever a kitchen fad that faded quicker than the spiraliser? Now, I enjoyed those spiralised zucchini as much as anyone, but the hell in cleaning that beast with more moving parts than a steam engine! Let's move on from the spiraliser.

All I will say is that my wife is a sucker for any new kitchen fad. Various gizmos and utensils occupy a pantry graveyard. Juicers, blenders, egg fluffers, I think that, like *Toy Story*, at night they all cry to each other about not being used.

The washing machine was loaded into the shipping container, along with our bed, Evel Knievel and the spiraliser. During transit across the oceans, it got damaged. Maybe by the bitter spiraliser. I got a plumber to come around to try to fix it. I opened the door to the man and introduced myself then took him to the washing machine. As I told him the problem, the back story about us just moving and did five minutes of stand-up-grade material on spiralisers, he listened while looking at the washing machine, running his hand along it and admiring its sleek European design.

Yeah, I don't mess around in the washing machine department, folks.

Then the following exchange took place.

'Before I do a thing, what team have you picked? Because if it's the Pies I'm walking out,' he half joked.

'Oh I haven't been here that long.'

'You need to pick a footy team before you wash your jeans, mate.'

'I'm thinking about which one—'

'I'll walk out of this house right now if you say the Pies.'

'Yeah, I get that. Who the hell are the Pies?'

'Scum is who. Collingwood Football Club, their fans are toothless inbreds. Plus, the chairman is one of your rivals on radio, yeah, I've seen your poster everywhere and clocked your accent. Can't pick Tigers as they just won the flag so people will call you a bandwagon jumper.'

'Right.'

'Best bet is Saints as they're the nearest team to here, but be warned they're a heartbreaker team.'

'What does that mean?'

'Shithouse.'

I told him the team I was considering picking, the Melbourne Football Club, and he tossed his head back in the air as if I'd just crapped my pants and he'd got a whiff of it.

'Pretentious and predictable.'

'Thank you.'

'But not the worst move, hmm, okay, I'll take a look at the machine.'

The washing machine was repaired.

This was just one of many similar conversations I had about Melbourne's fanatical and feverish love of 'footy'.

'Footy' is everything to Melbourne.

It is Melbourne.

All the media interviews I did prior to my first radio show asked about this. Every article about me mentioned it. They were all along the lines of: Melbourne is said to be a very parochial city that's inward looking and how will I deal with that without knowing about footy?

Sport is tribal, and I wasn't from this tribe.

Radio is said to be the most intimate medium, and the glaring fact that my accent said I clearly wasn't from around here and therefore wouldn't know about footy meant a lack of shared experience. I realised how much of my relationship with listeners back in the UK relied on a shorthand shared and known by both parties.

Footy in Melbourne is often described as being like 'religion'. They didn't want an atheist on air.

Everyone wanted to know who I would barrack for (I had no idea what that meant at first, the rest of the world cheers their team, here it's 'barrack'), and they asked with the desperation of zealots trying to convert someone. In Melbourne, the spiritual home of footy, it's discussed by everyone, all the time.

To not have a team is akin to 'not being religious' in the middle of the Spanish Inquisition.

People can't handle it.

They don't care if you actually have any particular interest in the sport or your team, they just want to know you have one. A bit like Catholics only want to know if you're Catholic, they don't care if you go to church every Sunday. They just feel at ease if you at least identify as one of them.

I quickly sensed that my not having a team yet was becoming an issue.

This was further compounded by meetings at the radio station where the topic of who I would choose was becoming the top agenda item. Instead of talking about the abysmal ratings, or the avalanche of vitriol coming my way, senior managers with straight faces would refer to the 'footy problem'.

The discussion would go like this:

'You have to go for a team based in Melbourne, but it can't be Hawthorn or Richmond because they win a lot and it will look like you just jumped on them because they are winning.'

'Okay . . .'

'But it can't be Collingwood, because they are too polarising, everyone hates them, although they do have a massive following.'

'Right, too many fans.'

'You also can't go for North Melbourne because they have too small a following and no one cares about them.'

'Not enough fans, I see.'

Each of the teams is like its own sect with its own stereotype. Collingwood are the working-class team, their followers are seen as inbred and with poor dental hygiene as my plumber implied.

The team I was considering, the Melbourne Demons, are the club of the establishment. Their fans are accused of being rich and going to the snow on weekends instead of watching their team play, which, given the team hasn't won the premiership since 1964, makes sense. There was a photo that went viral around the world of a fan at an AFL game with a cheese board on his lap, sat in the stands. It was a Dees fan.

He was laughed at around the world, all I thought was, could I buy this cheese board in the merch shop?

I was starting to see that selecting a team was like international diplomacy: you were going to annoy some people, but you wanted to minimise by how much, so not offending people became the most important factor.

I couldn't believe this was an issue that my bosses were devoting significant time and thought to.

Before I tell you how I handled all this, I need to firstly share my early thoughts about the game itself.

•

Andy Lee took me to my first game. His team, the Carlton Football Club, known as the Blues, were playing and he would act as my translator for the night's game. Coming in cold, little of what I saw made any sense.

First thing that struck me walking into Marvel Stadium was the size of the pitch, the oval. It was huge. At least one and a half times bigger than a football pitch I was used to. The teams came running out to their club songs then through a banner with some slogan on it. Honestly, it was more like a cult than a sporting code. Being Australia, the banner was huge.

Physically impressive men flooded the oval, some with mullets which I got the feeling hadn't ever gone out of fashion in Australia.

Each team has 22 players, 18 of which are on the pitch at any one time, the rest on the bench.

There is chaos on the pitch, sorry oval, with grown men running at speed at 50/50 balls and clattering into each other. You can kick or punch the ball, grab it, leap for it, tackle, there's no offside, it's mayhem to the untrained eye.

I kept asking my game translator, Andy, about the rules and I got a lot of:

'Don't worry about that, you'll just pick it up.'

What?

And this, 'Oh they just changed that rule last year because it was looking all a bit boring.'

You can't run a sport like that.

Cricket doesn't look back at the season and think, 'This is a bit boring on TV, isn't it?' then add some rule changes like on-field trapdoors. Or sandpapering the balls . . .

Too soon?

I was finding this all very stressful, it looked like drunken quidditch. All of a sudden some mad man from the crowd invaded the pitch, oval, whatever, and started abusing the players verbally.

Nope, my translator explained, this was all perfectly normal and it was a 'runner'.

These guys take orders from the coach to the players. It gets better: the coach sits up in a coach's box looking like a heart attack is imminent, all red faced and thick neck veins throbbing, probably stressed from trying to understand this impenetrable game—and he relays his tactics to the runner via an old-fashioned phone. Haven't they seen an iPhone? Why not just text the runners? Even a fax would be more modern.

With the football I was used to, the managers would yell instructions from the touchline while looking like a heart attack was imminent. Here, they *phoned down the plays on a landline* to a guy who ran onto the pitch with the new instructions. They bring booze to your car, and they get an old rotary phone to call footy instructions.

I've sat near some of the English Premier League coaches and if it was like that, the runner would be jogging out to tell a player, *'He says get off your fucking lazy millionaire arse.'*

Near the end of a game, if I was a player, I'd be calling the runner over and giving him my drink and Uber Eats order.

Let's now address the goals. Like in rugby they have two uprights, but they also have two slightly smaller baby ones either side. This is like the hole on a putting green in golf being inside a larger one.

If you miss kicking the ball between the two big sticks, which is 6 points, you still get 1 point. Which is nice, I guess.

Get it in here, or in here if you can't do that, we'll still give you a little reward.

One thing that was clear to me, it's a really exciting game and it's relentless.

The game was so physical, players grabbing other players by the shirt and this being okay as long as it was 'in the spirit of the game'. The most staggering move was something called a 'speccie'. Let me walk you through this. You can use a rival player's back like a spinal ladder, climbing them with your boots, to launch yourself up to get high balls and catch them. Welcome to Aussie Rules.

The other thing that impressed me was the crowd. You could sit next to rival fans. This was a Friday night and I thought there would be trouble, but there wasn't. The few police I saw were just leaning up against walls chatting away to fans. I loved this.

The next morning, I woke up with a headache, partly from the beers but also from trying to decipher the game. Also my stomach was trying to digest something called a 'party pie' that was served to me at 5000 degrees Celsius.

•

I decided to take all my intimidating decision-making over which team to support on air. I wasn't going to let management focus-group my team choice, and since every Melburnian seemed desperate to convert me to their team, why not let them do that during the show?

Each day I would 'speed date' a club for two minutes. Just like *The Bachelor*. The clubs would have the captain, the coach or a famous player pitch to me why I should support them. It was great fun and every morning that day's team would make a very strong and compelling case: they were by nature hugely competitive with the other teams and I actually got the feeling they really wanted me as the new MVP in town. I guess I was the highest profile new fan of the sport, so who would I choose?

You don't normally get to think about what team you're going to support because the way it normally works is that as a kid you support your dad's or mum's team. You certainly don't get to weigh up all your options. The option is normally, barrack for this team or you'll be living on the streets.

In the end I went for the Dees, Melbourne Football Club, the team of the heart of Melbourne. I thought I could justify this as we'd moved to the most livable city in the world, Melbourne, so I went for a team that represents that. They were playing well at the time, but this I would soon learn wasn't to last, just like my football team back home. Now I have two unpredictable and heartbreaking teams in both hemispheres, oh lucky me!

My decision went over well, I felt like JFK must have felt deflating the Cuban Missile Crisis.

Mostly, I was just relieved that yet another trial here on the seemingly endless road of trials was over. It reminded me of the scene in the Bond movie *Live and Let Die*, Sir Roger Moore's first outing as James Bond. Bond is left for dead at a crocodile farm and using his trademark quick-thinking decides the best course of action is to run to safety across the deadly animals' backs.

As a kid I was blown away by this as Bond bravely and deftly leapt from croc to croc to ensure his survival. This was what my first year here felt like.

17

Meet my new nemesis

You can't wear a leather jacket anymore at your age,
you look like an undercover cop, a bad one.

RUBY O'CONNELL

I came home one afternoon to my wife doing that move where she points with her head and eyebrows. She does this when she wants to tell me something, but not in front of the kids.

My wife has a whole series of covert facial expressions and head movements whose meanings change day to day and are so obvious she might as well sound a horn when she does them and point a giant foam finger at her face. Once, at some awful dinner party, I thought she was having a full-on stroke, but it turned out she was trying to tell me that another couple of attendees were on the verge of getting a divorce. All of this information was relayed to me via a series of facial smoke signals.

This day, her nodding head 'pointed' to the utility room. Oh no. This was serious. The utility room is reserved for our highest-level DEFCON 5 chats. Nothing says 'serious' more than a whispered conversation by the washing machine. I braced myself for the fresh shit that was about to come my way. And I wondered if, in the White House Situation Room where the President of the USA's emergency briefings are held, there is a washing machine.

'Close the door,' my wife said conspiratorially.

Years ago, this might have been an invitation for some mischief. Now it's so the kids won't hear us talk about which fresh part of our lives is falling apart. At these high-level meetings my wife will say, 'What do you think we should do?'

I make the same mistake I always do, and think she actually wants to know my opinion. Then she cuts me off by telling me exactly what we're going to do.

She took a deep breath. Oh no, it's bad—she needs extra oxygen levels just to tell me. I braced myself.

'Don't say anything, but some girls gave Lois a hard time at school today,' my wife said, trying to whisper, something that for her is genetically impossible. (My wife speaks in a very loud voice, which gets louder when she's on the phone, as if she's trying to boost the technology by yelling. They should test noise-cancelling headphones by sitting in a room with my wife while she calls her friends.)

'How do you mean?' I asked tentatively, imagining all kinds of awful possibilities.

'*This girl said . . . and you mustn't get upset . . .*'

'Just tell me, I can handle it,' I urged. Lying.

'*This girl came up to Lois and said, to her face, that no one listens to her dad's radio show.*'

Everything suddenly stopped and went very quiet. Apart from the washing machine, which was on its spin cycle.

'WHAT THE FUCK!?!' said someone.

It was my ego.

'She's okay now, she's more worried that you'll be upset.' Lois was right.

'What's this little shit's name?' I demanded.

'What good's that going to do?' my wife asked.

Good point. What was I going to do? Even Sun Tzu didn't cover this scenario.

In my mind I imagined me going around to her house and yelling up at the thirteen-year-old troll's bedroom window: 'I know you're in there, I heard what you said about my radio show, I'm not yelling, I just want to talk . . . Please don't call the police. Where was I? Yes, the ratings aren't great, but this was to be expected, and year-on-year people who are listening are listening for longer, and this is how the sales team sell radio airtime . . . Could you please come down here? I've got some PowerPoint slides to show you, early signs of growth in core demos of 6–18-month-olds . . . Can I hear sirens? You called the police? YOU LITTLE SHIT!'

I played back what my wife had just said: 'She's okay now, she's more worried that you'll be upset.'

How emotionally fragile do they think their dad is? Are they seriously worried about the damage a thirteen-year-old schoolgirl could do with a few words about his bombing radio show? Sorry, not bombing. Planned, on-track bombing. My boss at one point actually referred to the deserting listeners as 'collateral damage'.

I went to talk to my daughter—partly to check she was okay, partly to assure her that not only was I fine, but my show was too. Surely every radio station dreams of hiring some big shot from abroad who drives listeners away and whose failure is talked about in playgrounds?

I have to admit, talking to my youngest daughter can some-times feel like talking to my wife. They see a matrix when you talk, and then point out errors and contradictions. Little Miss Logic was waiting for me when I stuck my head around her bedroom door.

'What?' she sighed. Always a warm welcome.

'Mum told me what that girl said and . . .'

'It's cool, Dad, I thought it was funny, she's just a bitch.'

'Yeah, she sounds like a bitch—actually, that's not a nice word to call someone. But I just want you to know that my show is going great, it's all okay.' I noticed I was rocking backwards and forwards as I said all this. I may have been weeping too.

'But Mum said you've lost listeners since you started . . . and she told us we mustn't go online and see all the haters and then mention it to you. But I did have a look, and wow, they really don't like you! Some of them are really mean. Are you going to get fired if it stays like that?'

The room seemed to be spinning.

'You've gone quiet Dad, are you okay?'

No, I wasn't.

I'd moved my family to the other side of the world, was bombing in the ratings, my daughters were struggling at school, and now I had somehow picked up a new nemesis, who happened to be a thirteen-year-old girl.

Or was it a rival DJ dressed up as a schoolgirl?

Mindgames.

It's all okay, I thought as I tried to calm myself.

Now kids were trolling me.

As if to compound the whole mess, a few days later we were in a shopping centre and all of a sudden Lois said, 'Oh no! It's ██████! Quick, we need to hide, 'cos she's with ██████

and ██████, and they're awful, really mean. If they see me with you it will be a nightmare.' And so we ducked into the nearest shop.

Let's leave aside the part about it being sad to be seen with your dad in public and focus on the fact that I hid with my daughter from some teenage girl bullies. In an expensive lingerie shop. Another life lesson I've taught that kid: you can't hide very well using negligees as cover. I actually started to get a bit scared as we were cowering behind a rack of flimsy garments. The taunts of the bullies of my own childhood came flooding back. 'No one likes you.' 'You've got no friends.' It was like being back in 1986. I had to remind myself I was a grown man. Not to mention to tell myself to stop stroking the silk negligee covering my head, just because it felt *so smooth.*

While my life had gotten to the 'hiding in lingerie shops from teenage bullies' stage, one member of the household who was forging ahead with a calm confidence that only highlighted how the rest of the family were struggling was my wife.

•

My wife is one of those people who picks up friends easily. Like some Pied Piper. She can go for a dog walk and come back with three new contacts in her phone. On family holidays over the years, it gets bad as she will befriend some fellow mum in the pool and then we will have to have dinner with their family every night for the rest of the holiday and it's awful. I spend the rest of the trip hiding from this family.

We once checked into a holiday resort in the Caribbean and within an *hour* of us arriving, unpacking and getting to the pool, my wife tells me about the receptionist she just met and her daughter's local school. I was barely listening to the director's cut of this receptionist story, instead wondering how she can extract all this life detail when we just needed an extra room key as the kids had immediately 'demagnetised' the swipe card.

By the way, hotels work best with the universally accepted key, a real physical key that turns a lock. How many arguments have there been between dads and kids or couples outside their seventeenth floor room because the swipe card hasn't turned the magic light from red to green. 'You put it next to your phone! How could you do this? It's your turn to go down to reception.'

Suddenly I started very much listening to the receptionist's life story when I heard my wife say: '. . . her daughter's local school . . . never get any guest speakers and I hope you don't mind but I said . . .'

Hope you don't mind? NO. NO. NO. You didn't. I mind very much.

'. . . you would go along and do a talk. Tomorrow morning.'

My kids laughed their backsides off, because it's funny to see your dad's life ruined. Why should I get some rare precious sleep the first morning on my well-earned holiday? Better I go do a talk to a school, which I'll now spend my first few hours of this break working on.

No, you all sleep in, my sweet family.

Countless times my wife has basically pimped me out as a budget TED Talk speaker for hire, quiz host, charity auction host, school disco DJ and, the real low point, a carpark attendant at a pony club competition that my kids were in. This had me in the pissing rain one Sunday morning in a muddy field, sporting a high-viz jacket and marshalling stuck-up moneyed-up yummy-mummies in giant Range Rovers with horse trailers. The great thing about the relentless rain was that it hid my tears.

Now it's all coming back to me, I also remember the time I was *booked* by my agent wife to do stand-up for a third-world charity's fundraiser. A ten-minute harrowing video of the atrocities these poor people have suffered sickened me and everyone else there; there were people sobbing. It was designed to raise money and it worked. The screen froze on a crying mother's face whose daughter had suffered unimaginable horror, and the organiser of the charity quietly addressed the audience.

'I make no apologies for showing you that, it's barely believable, please give generously tonight. Now, let's have some stand-up comedy, you know this man from his breakfast show and TV shows, it's Christian O'Connell!'

I made the universal signal for 'No, no, not now, take a break, later'.

But no, I had to walk out in front of a still shell-shocked and traumatised audience. They didn't want to laugh and I didn't want to be doing my monkey tap dance routine. I arrived to a stunned silence, performed to that and left to that. If they'd filmed my set they could show it next year in black and white and raise millions.

I should just say, the school talk was actually one of the highlights of a great break. The kids were a joy. They lived a simple humble life that some would judge as poor, yet they had a boundless joy for life that most 'rich' people can never attain. They were rich in laughter, love and learning about the wonder of the world. When I came back to my pony club kids, it gave me a chance to conduct another speech at the foot of their sunbeds titled 'You Don't Know How Lucky You Are'. It ended abruptly when I saw they had rested their phones on the new swipe card.

So now in Melbourne, my wife's ability to turn strangers into friends was proving a wonderful thing, sometimes. Like any superpower, it is best when used for good. Every day new friends were being made. Then the big one, a book club was joined. This monthly book club was so exhausting for her, she would come home slurring and mumbling, white wine fumes billowing from her mouth like aeroplane trails in the sky. Just exhausted from all the book 'reviewing'. Is this why Oprah Winfrey started her book club? Just an excuse to get shitfaced with the girls.

I doubt Oprah once came back from book club reeking of prosecco and falling asleep on the couch with one shoe on and a pizza slice in one hand.

I, however, was struggling to make friends and I was starting to get very lonely. The not too well-known truth is that it's hard for men once they get into their thirties to make new friends, and even harder in their forties.

•

If you're a dad you barely have enough time or energy to see your own friends, let alone to develop a new friendship. You're simply not hiring any more. You're not even keeping anyone's details on file if a new vacancy comes up. For me, it was even harder as I was an outsider and I guess they figured I may not be around for long as I had a strong 'dead man walking' vibe.

Women make friends so much easier, men don't. The sisterhood is always looking out for each other. I missed someone to go for a drink with, to watch the UFC with. I even looked for apps for men to hang out with, but soon discovered it's a different kind of hanging out.

One Friday I went to pick up a takeaway curry and for a split second I thought I saw my best friend Jamie. Instinctively I went to wave, I was grinning with happiness like you do when you spot your bestie, then I realised it wasn't, how could it be, I'm on the other side of the world from him. As I walked to my car with my food my eyes actually welled up with tears, such was the heartache of feeling lonely. I dried my eyes with the poppadoms and went home. My wife saw my reddened eyes when I entered the house and asked if I'd had some bad news.

Yeah, I've no listeners and no mates.

My wife, ever practical, said, 'You need to put yourself out there.' Like I was some recently dumped girl. 'Plenty more fish in the sea.'

You go girl.

Later the next week we were in an Uber together and I was getting on roaringly with the driver, an American who'd just also moved here himself a few years earlier. My wife texted me, from the seat next to me:

'Ask him for his number'

I can't ask the Uber driver out on a man date.

But I did.

It was as hideous as you'd expect. There is no way to casually ask a guy whose car you are in, who has just picked you up like a taxi driver, for his number so you could go grab a coffee or beer.

It remains one of the most embarrassing exchanges of my life.

The car pulls up outside my house. Wife gets out, uses a variety of head nods and raised eyebrows to get me to ask the driver 'out'. On a date.

Oh fuck my life right now.

'Thanks mate, er . . . really enjoyed the chat . . . we should er . . . here's my number if you fancy going for a coffee or pizza . . . sometime . . .'

No, I've no idea why I said 'pizza sometime' like we were twelve years of age.

He looked at me slightly awkwardly and surprised, I guess. Oh God, this was awful. It felt like the longest few seconds of my life.

'Sure man, love to,' he said and my heart leapt in joy. We swapped numbers.

Later that day, after an acceptable amount of time, not too soon to appear too keen, I texted him.

I'm waiting for a reply. Two years later.

How could I win over a city on air when I can't even get an Uber driver to meet me for a pizza?

Things looked up again, though, when I got a text from the hairdresser my wife and I had both started going to, a lovely guy who I hit it off with immediately. He was inviting me out for beers that night with some of his mates. I got there and he introduced me to his buddies, who were a good bunch, beers were flowing and the chat was good.

Could he be the one? Oh, be still my beating heart.

During a quiet moment I thanked the hairdresser for inviting me out and introducing me to his friends.

His reply will haunt me forever. 'Oh that's alright, mate, your wife said you were lonely and I should get you out.'

18

Notes from my wife

In a rush and late, the cat has shat all over your pillow,
can you clear it up?

TEXT FROM MY WIFE

In the course of an average day, I get around 16,347 messages
from my wife.

These can take the form of post-it notes, text messages, emails,
signs written in the sky. These missives are symptoms of my wife's
constant need for forward planning in our life, such as:

'What are we doing on the 24th of September 2032?'

'What shall we have for takeaway this Friday night and all
future Friday nights?'

'What day do you think you will die? PM or AM? I need to
know in the next ten minutes'

It all goes into my wife's 'Death Star', her phone calendar.
Unlike the real Death Star, it has no structural weakness.

The power this motherlode holds over my life is impressive.
I cannot enter dates into it, I don't have the requisite security
clearance, only she can. I can only request a date be entered.

I might say, 'I'm playing golf this Sunday at 2 p.m.,' but come Sunday, if it wasn't properly logged in, forget it.

My papers won't be stamped, day release won't be happening.

'Where are you going?' I will hear as I stagger from the garage with my poor abused golf clubs.

'Golf. Remember I said earlier this week, golf Sunday at 2 p.m.'

'Nah, I don't have that, you're taking the kids school shoe shopping. I've got book club.'

My wife doesn't even bother checking the diary, because *it's all in her brain.* Like she's a calendar version of HAL 9000 from *2001: A Space Odyssey.*

Not that we don't communicate well overall, it's just conversation in an established relationship is quite . . . erm . . . efficient. My wife recently rang me and shouted:

'I'm driving past the house in a minute but don't have time to come in. When I toot the horn, can you run out with a glass of water for me?'

There's a very small part of me that thought she was going to wind the window down, grab the water, throw it in my face, and scream, 'Grow some balls!' then drive off.

I just felt grateful she rang. Most marriage chat is by text message. Because this allows couples to communicate despite not actually wanting to talk. Even at home, my wife and I constantly write each other notes. There was a distant time when those would be love notes. Which very soon just became 'notes'.

'Babe, we're out of milk, could you grab some? Can't wait to see you! I've missed you all day.'

Then:

'If it's not too much trouble, can you get some milk while you're out?'

Then:

'*Get some milk while you're out.*'

Then:

'*Get milk.*'

One day it will just be:

'*Get out.*'

Once I was queuing in the post office—sorry to brag about my wild and crazy life—and I received a text message that read:

'*When you get home, I need you to kill the pigeon*'

There was no explanation or context offered. Just, '*When you get home, I need you to kill the pigeon*'

I started wondering what this could mean. Is this a euphemism or code for something? Does she mean sex? 'Kill the pigeon' . . . I had not heard that one before, but I remained hopeful.

So I asked for some clarification.

'*It's injured and dying. You're going to have to kill the pigeon. I'll leave a shovel on the doorstep*'

For the record, I'm not an animal killer. This wasn't under normal tasks that fall to me. Bins out, flat pack assembly, murder things as directed.

And why couldn't I just take the pigeon to get help at the vet? Did this mean if anything happened to me, injured in a car accident or at work, my wife would say to the kids, 'Go get the shovel, we're going to have to kill Dad.'

I got home, and there was an intimidating and foreboding shovel on the front doorstep. I picked it up, the handle was ice cold, like my wife's blood in ordering this pigeon hit.

'Just following orders,' I told myself.

The poor pigeon. A fox had mangled him in a bad way; he couldn't fly or move. The pigeon was looking at me, and the shovel. Our eyes locked, he knew.

You're just following orders.

Then I saw the kids watching from a bedroom window. Noses pressed up against the glass. Front row seats to witness their dad battering a poor sick birdy to death. I suppose I could've used it to my advantage. I could've stood over the pigeon yelling, 'You should tidy your nest properly next time!' and watched the kids spend the next six months cleaning their rooms like they're on amphetamines.

But . . . I couldn't do it. Not in front of my kids. I didn't want them to have nightmares. I didn't want to have nightmares. I doubt you ever forget your first pigeon. And worse still, what if I *didn't* have nightmares? What would that say about me?

So I took him to an animal sanctuary. I put him in a box, and drove him to salvation. I was briefly worried this was part of the pigeon's plan; that he was going to leap up, right as rain, start flying around inside the car, shitting everywhere. Screaming at the pigeons outside, 'I did it, lads! I did it!' He'd get a thumbs-up from pigeons flying alongside: 'You legend!'

•

Top 10 Text Messages My Wife Has Actually Sent Me

1. *We need to have a proper chat tonight about what happens should you die*

We did chat, my wife wanted to increase the life insurance on me 'should I get injured at work'. Looking at the forms she already had, I couldn't help but notice how financially she was way better off with me 'disabled or seriously maimed at work'. Sure, she needed to keep me alive, but only just . . .

I'm a radio DJ, how exactly was I going to get injured at work? And to the point I'm maimed? Crushed by some Nickelback

CDs? We don't even play CDs. I didn't sleep too well that night, worried my wife might be planning on faking an accident with me and claiming on the insurance. Perhaps she'd cut my brake leads. I drove to work the next day but only after using a mirror underneath my car, just to check.

2. *Can you turn the music down? The guinea pigs hate it*

Welcome to my life, where the guinea pigs have more rights than me.

3. *Vet said next time the dog has diarrhoea today we need to get a sample. Can I leave this with you?*

Who knew how hard it was gathering your dog's diarrhoea into a sample bottle? In case you are wondering, I used an old margarine tub. I hope the vets got rid of it after I left it with them, and someone didn't misuse it on toast as Nutella.

4. *You need to make room in our suitcase for my pillow. You KNOW how my neck gets otherwise.*

Yes, my wife takes her own pillow on holiday, meaning less room for my clothes. The guinea pigs travel first class.

5. *I know you've been secretly deleting my shows from tv recorder, it's pathetic*

TV shows these days are recorded on hard drives. I get very uneasy when it says 'Memory 87%'. Then I see more than 87 hours of *Say Yes to the Dress*, and for my shows only three hours of UFC and a few episodes of *Columbo*. Obviously, I'm not a savage, I leave her with two hours of *Say Yes to the Dress*.

6. *I need you to de-nit me tonight. I think they have come back.*

Marriage. This is what it comes to. Date night is set then.

7. *Don't whatever you do use any of the toilets when you get home. Go at the train station*

   i) WHAT has happened since I left the house at 5 a.m.?
   ii) Train station toilets are the very best examples of mankind at its worst. It's not just the human excrement splattered over the toilet doors like Banksy blew out his backside, it's the graffiti. Why do all racists have such terrible bowel problems?

8. *You need to make your writing more elf-like on the presents. An elf wouldn't write in block capitals*

To correct this on the kids' Christmas presents, I used my left hand. It just looked like Papa Elf had suffered a series of strokes.

9. *Can you see if the pet shop does an advent calendar for dogs?*

No, I can't.

10. *You need to dig a hole six foot long and three foot deep. Today*

I get it, time for her to claim on that insurance payout.

19

Home alone

Is Dad going to be okay without supervision? I'm seri-ously worried about him.

LOIS O'CONNELL

I thought things had to get better, I thought they couldn't get any worse.

SPOILER ALERT, they really did.

My life was to become the opposite of a multi-level computer game where you collect tokens as you complete various challenges and levels. If I thought the worst of it was the ratings declining and being publicly humiliated—reporters all loved to use the words 'Struggling British DJ', 'slump' and 'replaced a very popular show with this failure'—I was wrong.

Because through it all, whether it was me or the girls having tough times, my family had one thing keeping it together: my wife, who was the rock we all clung to when we needed to.

Sarah's inner grit, her kick-arse strength should be on the periodic table it's that powerful. All powered by a big heart. Right from the start of our relationship she was kicking me more than nudging me towards going after my radio dreams. As we moved around the UK to the radio stations I was working on and serving my apprenticeship, Sarah made it all happen and made everything okay. She never doubted me.

When I doubted myself, she'd pump my tyres back up.

There were several times when I had a moment of crisis about moving to Australia, when I felt I couldn't guarantee that my show would work, that I could fail.

Sarah looked me in the eye and said unwaveringly, 'I don't care, it won't be because you didn't do a great show, I believe in you.'

There is a horrible old phrase, 'Behind every great man is a great woman.'

For me, it's more truthfully, 'Behind a great woman is Christian.'

I tell you this so you fully understand the tidal effect of what happened just six weeks into us being in Australia.

•

It was a Monday night, and I was on the phone to my mum and Sarah was also on the phone to her mum, Jackie, who she spoke to every day.

Due to the time difference, in my three years here I've really sharpened my arithmetic skills by being able to calculate very quickly the time both in Australia and the UK: it was around 10 a.m. in the UK and 9 p.m. on the same day here. Both of us were chatting to our mums when I heard something awful, but it wasn't just what I heard.

It was something I felt.

Even though my wife was in another room, I heard her crying out down the phone to her mum. It was a terrified cry, not of a woman but a scared little girl.

Sarah's mum had major heart surgery a few years back and a stent was put in to save her life. I feared what must be happening.

Please no, not this, not now. Not to my wife.

Even my mum heard the cry, thousands of miles away on the other end of the phone to me, and stopped mid-sentence. *'What was that? Is Sarah okay?'*

I was already running towards my wife, who was now really crying out to her mum down the phone and she wasn't getting a reply.

Her mum was having a huge heart attack.

She was struggling for her life on the other side of the world and there was nothing her daughter could do about it.

I've done this to them, was the immediate thought I had when I saw my wife's terrified eyes. I've separated a mother and her daughter, I've broken her heart. All because I couldn't keep my shit together.

Jackie had collapsed in a shop in her home city while casually chatting to her daughter on the phone. We needed to speak to the shop urgently, to tell them not to try to move her, as it could make things worse.

I don't think either of us breathed over the next few minutes. I asked Sarah what shop and she fired off where she thought it was. I googled it and called the number; everything seems to take too long in an emergency.

A breezy shop assistant answered the phone in a manner she would've used a thousand times, only this time she was about to get a call she'll never forget.

I breathlessly filled her in on the situation but being British I began with a 'Oh hello, sorry to scare you like this but . . .' while my wife gesticulated violently like a movie director to get the fuck on with it.

The situation was met with silence and then a barely believing, 'You having me on?'

My wife's phone burst into life and she answered it immediately. I went back to explaining everything again but speaking quicker, and the lady in the shop started to walk around the store looking for my mother-in-law on the floor.

'It's not that shop!' my wife yelled.

I'm sorry to say in this desperate moment I shot my wife a petty, angry look like, 'What are you doing? Embarrassing me like this?'

I'm still sorry, Sarah.

I now told the lady I was sorry, again, I had the wrong shop. She also said sorry.

My wife was already calling the right shop and was answered by someone already observing Sarah's stricken mum on the floor. My wife told them her mum mustn't be moved until the paramedics arrived, she would stay on the line and speak to them when they got there.

We later found out from the doctors and surgeons that if Jackie had suffered her heart attack alone, she wouldn't have survived.

The scary and incredible truth was that if Sarah had not been on the phone to her mum, and able to speak to someone on the scene telling them the situation, and not to move her, they couldn't have done what they did.

Which was save her.

My wife had saved her mum's life. Over the phone.

That's no exaggeration.

At one point, the attending paramedics told my wife her mum's blood pressure was really low and seemed okay. My wife guessed that her mum must be bleeding internally, diagnosing her mum over the phone. Sarah was right.

•

By now the kids had come to see what was going on. They saw their mum in a way they never had before. I told them what had happened and that I was booking a flight for them and Sarah to get back to England as quickly as possible, though I couldn't bring myself to say the words none of us wanted to hear.

I told them to pack as quickly as they could, which meant they would get it done in under nine hours. My kids' idea of packing is shocking—99.8 per cent of the time is spent sitting on their beds staring at their phones, snapping chats or whatever they do.

Then as they hear my footsteps approaching and yelling, 'Taxi's here, let's go,' random shit is thrown in their suitcase, none of it suitable for where we are going. On a family trip to the Caribbean, I saw a ski jacket being thrown in. When I asked what the hell they had packed that for to go to a country with an average temperature of 31 degrees (that's 87 for you Fahrenheit fans), I was told, 'For the evening, if the temperature drops.' I pointed out that if they needed a ski jacket for sub-zero temperatures in Barbados, the world was about to end and a ski jacket would be the least of their worries.

Like in any family, various tasks are allocated to each of the parents. My wife decides these with no consultation with me, it's like our marriage vows are constantly being updated like terms and conditions, less 'I do', more 'Accept' or 'Okay'.

What I'm saying is, I get jobs I never applied for or attended the interview for. Checking the kids' suitcases was recently given to me after the Caribbean ski jacket incident.

'It's better if you check their suitcases from now on, because I'm a nervous flyer and I don't need the stress.'

Bullshit. You just don't want this shitty job.

So I told the kids to pack really quickly and also hugged them, telling them it was going to be okay. I'm not entirely sure if I was trying to reassure them or myself. I went to see how Sarah was doing and my phone rang, it was the hospital where Jackie had been rushed to. They needed to speak to my wife.

Sarah was told she could speak to her mum for a few minutes before she underwent emergency lifesaving surgery. Due to the severity of Jackie's heart attack and the incredibly complicated eleven-hour operation, she was also told to say goodbye to her mum, in case she didn't make it.

Can you even imagine that?

I held my wife as she struggled through tears to tell her mum how much she loved her, I could hear Jackie doing what a mum would do, trying to reassure her daughter it was all going to be okay.

I was quietly in awe of Jackie saying she wasn't scared; she was at peace with everything due to her faith as a born-again Christian.

A mother and daughter said emotional goodbyes that they hoped were not actually that.

As long as I live, I'll never forget that moment. I couldn't believe this was happening. It felt like a sudden violent assault. It shattered this fairytale we'd imagined about moving to Australia.

Sarah then tried to focus on packing, and I said I'd do it while she sorted her toiletries. This was a mistake, because when my wife landed in London and tried to get changed before picking up a hire car, she had no underwear. I had one job and stuffed that up. But on the plus side, I'd packed a bikini for her. Quite when I thought she would be lounging by a pool or beach I had no idea. At least she had that ski jacket I chucked in.

I couldn't process I was going to say goodbye to Sarah and the girls not knowing if Sarah's mum would even be alive when they landed. I wanted to go, too, as I knew my wife would need me and I am very close to my mother-in-law, but Sarah's deep inner strength was still there.

'No, you need to stay here and do the show. If Mum dies, I don't want to go back home and live there, you need to stay here and dig in, that's what I need you to do. Make it work here.'

I admired her limitless strength and secretly wondered how I would cope now being here all alone, away from my wife and kids. No idea when I'd see them all again or what was going to happen to Jackie.

I helped them into an Uber and we all said teary goodbyes full of uncertainty.

My wife uncertain if she would see her mum alive again. My daughters uncertain what was going to happen to their nan, and their mum, when they would be seeing me again, and worrying about their school life as they'd been through so much already in their time here.

I felt like I'd let them down, what was this all doing to them? I felt like I had let them down as a dad, failed to provide stability, failed to make them feel protected, safe.

Everything was now in freefall. For me, it was how I was going to deal with myself, the relentless pressure and the show, and now this.

Was my wife's heart about to be broken as her mum was struggling?

I wouldn't be there when I should be. I felt so guilty and responsible for all of this.

Then I noticed that with all the drama, my wife was still in her pyjamas.

Twenty-three hours flying lay ahead of her, agonising and worrying about her mum.

I say nothing about the pyjamas.

•

As I walked back into the house it was 11 p.m. I closed the door behind me and immediately threw up onto the dangerously over-polished wooden floor. The dog came over and started to eat it. I got down on my knees to clean it all up.

Living the dream!

What now for that dream? A new life in the sun was right now a living nightmare.

This is not how it was all supposed to be.

The house felt so quiet. I felt lonelier than at any time in my life.

I went into the kitchen and I don't know if the dog had picked up on all the stress in the house over the last couple of hours, but she had done a huge poo in the corner. It was a pretty powerful metaphor for everything right now. I was half tempted to do the same.

I took the next day off. No one wants to hear a sad clown. Though they'd made it very clear they didn't want to hear a happy one either. The part of me that does the job I'm lucky to do just couldn't step forward.

My head was all over the place and I hardly slept the rest of the night, worrying about my wife, the kids, Jackie, my decision to come here, and what was that noise in the house? Had the listeners hired an assassin to kill me? Was the dog taking another mega dump in the kitchen? Did I pack underwear for my wife?

In the morning I felt a kind of hangover. Jackie was still in surgery. How do these surgeons do what they do?

My boss at Gold FM, Sue Carter, did such a generous, caring thing: she turned up on my doorstep with a coffee and left it there. She lived half an hour away and texted telling me there was a hot drink and bacon sarnie on my doorstep. At first, when

I saw gifts, now fully aware how ruthless radio was here, I feared she was going to leap out, bundle me into a van and make me do that day's show at gunpoint.

'Dance, monkey! Dance!'

I took the dog for a walk and looked out across the bay and a limitless horizon. Wondering when I would see my wife and kids again, or if I should get on the next plane. Was it wrong for me to carry on here?

Brad, my producer, called but I ignored it. I couldn't bear the thought of trying to talk to anyone about this without breaking down. Tomorrow's show was going to be interesting. I looked at my watch to see how long it was until showtime. Then I caught a glimpse of my tattoo and remembered my friend in the shed. What would he say? Other than, *'Fight me.'*

I called producer Brad back. This was the first conversation I was going to have about what had happened. After a few words I realised just how hard this all was as the emotion of it overtook me. Sitting in my car, the tears came. He then did something remarkable in that moment all men secretly dread, the unedifying loss of control in front of . . . another man!

He started to cry too, with me.

That's empathy, that's compassion. It was just what I needed in that moment. The team that blubs together stays together.

Brad and Jack took me out for pizza and a few beers that night. I knew this was because they are lovely big-hearted men, but also checking to see that I was alright in myself, and for the radio show. Which was only a few weeks old.

The first six months is everything.

I spoke to my wife before she got on her second flight to continue on to London. The amazing news was the eleven-hour operation had gone well. Her mum was alive, but in a critical condition and would remain in the ICU for a while. I assured her I was okay, the kids moaned about some argument they had at 35,000 feet in the sky, a welcome blast of normality.

But the next morning, moments before I went live on air, I was back on the phone to my wife, who was at the ICU with her mum and it seemed like Jackie wasn't going to make it. Sarah explained the full details of her mum's condition, which were bad, and apologised for dumping all this on me, which was ridiculous, because what else could she do? I'm her husband.

I could hear the sports news ending on air, no doubt burying any story where England had beaten an Australian team in sport, and my wife knew I had to go. I looked at the new clock at the radio station.

6.03 a.m.

Her voice sounded so uncharacteristically fragile as we said our goodbyes. Her back to Jackie's bedside, me about to start another show and trying to find that part of me that does this—you know, the grinning guy on the posters.

I looked at the clock again with its panic-inducing hand counting down, just like the one I had above the bin not so long ago. Old familiar fears started to rise again. I felt so separated from my family, who are the centre of my world. My entire support system in a time I'd never needed them more. I felt adrift. And I had a show to do.

It was showtime.

I took a breath, gave my team an 'I'M FINE!' smile and opened the mics. With a rasp and tight voice, I began the show.

Our voices reveal more about us than we think, they become constricted when we are stressed, choking on our own inner turmoil. Then when we are speaking from a deeper, more truthful place, they have a different resonance and frequency.

That morning for my opening link, I sounded like I was a fifteen-year-old boy entering the midst of puberty.

•

The next few weeks of being here alone, with my wife and kids half the world away, were really tough. I'd lost my rock, I'd lost my girls. My entire gravitational system and what keeps me grounded had gone.

I would dread the weekend. I had no friends yet to hang out with, to ask for help.

Now, I don't want to turn this book into one of those misery-fests my wife loves to read. You know the ones, black-and-white cover, about some poor orphaned boy whose only friend is a one-eyed dog and halfway through the book the dog loses the other eye, then gets run over by a rich businessman who doesn't stop. It's the same businessman who also ran over his mum. And his nan. My wife loves this kind of misery-porn.

Often, I'll find her sobbing in the bath, pouring over the latest buzz-kill bestseller. She will text me asking for a glass of wine, she needs it reading these books. I'll dutifully take it in like a butler in *Downton Abbey* and I'm met with a 'You should read this, it's brilliant,' while her mascara drips down her face from the tears. The biggest sobs came while reading *The Time Traveler's Wife*. In between sobs my wife sold it to me as 'a woman's husband time travels unpredictably'. My laughter was met with the book being thrown at me. I'm sorry, but if I disappeared for a while and blamed it on a time portal to 1592, I'd be accused of being an alcoholic.

'I wasn't still in the pub, I fell over and woke up in the court of King Arthur.'

It was the he 'time travels unpredictably' that had me. Yeah, that's a tough one, isn't it? I mean, no relationship is perfect.

You're on your way to the parents evening at school and your husband suddenly, nay, unpredictably, disappears to Woodstock, I'd be pissed off.

Back to the world's loneliest DJ, I'll keep this all light for both of us. It was shit.

End of chapter.

Too brief? Okay.

My mother-in-law was still in a critical condition and my wife was spending every hour at the ICU ward. My life revolved around speaking to my wife at various parts of the day when she could grab a few minutes and the time difference allowed it; sometimes I'd get an update before the radio show, sometimes the other end of the day late at night.

Not being with my wife while she went through this, in her darkest hours, felt so wrong after everything we'd been through together. I was on the other side of the world carrying on like everything was fine. Not knowing if, at any minute, our life was about to implode if Sarah's mum didn't make it.

I didn't want to burden her that I was struggling as she had enough on her plate.

Truth was, I couldn't sleep at night with the stress so I used a tried and tested ancient yogic tradition—I self-medicated with wine. It got so bad that if I'd been involved in an accident and was asked for my blood type, I'd have said, 'shiraz'.

They got to know me on a first-name basis at the local wine shop. I think they presumed I ran a local Italian restaurant.

I can joke about it now, but actually there is nothing sadder than drinking alone, patting your dog on the head while looking at photos of your kids when they were younger. I caught my own reflection in the patio doors and raised a glass to this clichéd scene in movies.

One morning the dread was so high before the show, I remember getting out of the Uber outside the station and throwing up into the flowerbox on the wall of someone's front garden. I'd like to formally apologise here to that resident of Goodwood Street.

The radio show was still being met with a backlash. The thing about backlashes is they're not that much fun. It takes a bit of ego to do a radio show, it takes some more to move to the other side of the world and think they might like to hear you too.

So projecting a sense of calm to my wife was proving difficult. Once again, it was the laundry that did me in.

In our washing machine there are three compartments in that mystery drawer up top. I've no idea what they mean or correspond to. Let's also agree the 39 types of washing options offered around the dial are way too many.

I wanted to wash my bed sheets, like I said, domestic god, and didn't know what compartment to put the fabric conditioner in, as I always forget. I love that smell of freshly laundered sheets. I'd happily put it on as an aftershave. So I texted my wife a photo of the mystery drawer in the washing machine.

'Which one for softener?'

Timing is everything. At that moment, unknown to me, my mother-in-law had taken another turn for the worse and my wife, with little sleep, was struggling with the ups and downs of the last few days at her mum's ICU ward. Now with some underwear, fortunately. Then she gets a message from me and a photo about the washing machine. Bad timing. Which she let me know.

Such is the power of my wife, I could just about tell that she wasn't happy with me from the sub-text of her reply:

'Are you fucking kidding me? My mum is in ICU and you want advice on fabric conditioner.'

Nope, not happy. Or maybe she just didn't know the answer to the great mystery of the washing machine drawer. In any case, her words struck fear into me. Just like Darth Vader, who could choke his colleagues who had displeased him from many light years away, my wife also possessed equally devastating telekinetic powers even when she wasn't next to me.

It was another low point in a cavalcade of lows.

As I sat in my new house, empty of people I loved and who loved me, surrounded by a city not interested in having me, I saw an email arrive and read it:

'Why did you come here uninvited?

PART THREE

20

Life lessons in a boxing ring

I'm not angry at you, its the fuckwit that hired you.

LISTENER EMAIL, NOT ANGRY AT ME

The first sense I got that my life wasn't on a permanent down-ward trajectory was when my mother-in-law began to make a miraculous recovery.

One of the most amazing things about Britain is the NHS, our public healthcare. The nurses, doctors and frontline workers should be on more money than the bankers of the country—what's more important than saving our loved ones' lives? The COVID pandemic has shown us all this.

The doctors and nurses of the NHS had somehow saved Jackie's life. However, after so long in the bright lights of a constantly supervised ICU, she started to have 'ICU fever'. Whereby they go a little bit crazy. Jackie had started to get very irritable and would only communicate via notepad with her assembled family.

A method I've since considered implementing with my family.

To try to combat this, my wife somehow persuaded the doctors and nurses to let her wheel her mum out of the ward and outside into the sun for a bit of fresh air. Again, this is the power of my wife. What on paper appears to be a polite request is delivered in a tone that sounds like a threat made by Don Corleone: 'You can say no, doctor, but wouldn't it be a real shame if you found yourself at the bottom of a hospital lift shaft.'

Once outside with her mum, my wife had organised some light relief to provide some 'entertainment': me. This was to be my penance for the washing machine question.

It was a tough gig. A woman who'd had a massive heart attack, survived an eleven-hour heart surgery and had been in ICU for a few weeks was thrust a phone with her son-in-law on it—the very one who took her beloved daughter and her grandkids away from her to the other side of the world—and told he was about to 'cheer you up'.

There'd be many mothers-in-law who at that moment would wish the operation hadn't been a success.

Luckily for me, Jackie loves me. In any argument with my wife, she will always side with me. I FaceTimed in and the previously mute Jackie lit up and started speaking to me. I got a little tearful just seeing her alive, to be honest. It was nothing short of a miracle.

I then walked her on my phone into the utility room and opened the washing machine drawer and asked her if she knew the mystery of the three compartments. The phone suddenly was grabbed by someone and my wife's angry face filled the screen.

The next thing I knew, I fell to my knees as I was being Death Choked by Darth Sarah.

It seemed the mystery of the three compartments would continue to elude me for the foreseeable future.

With Jackie on the mend, I turned my attention to healing myself. It turns out constant stress, loneliness and single-handedly propping up the Australian alcohol industry takes its toll on you.

In a blow to my local wine merchant's plan to purchase a second home and possibly a third, I cut down on the booze and decided to get some acupuncture. As recommended to me by a naked guy.

Getting ready for a workout one day, a sprightly elderly gentleman who had just got out of the shower and was towelling himself dry struck up a conversation with me. We ended up having a really intimate conversation, and I don't just mean because of his nudity. Sometimes you can share such personal information with a stranger. So many times encounters like these started to show me the real heart of Australia. He suggested some acupuncture 'to help with the stress of everything'.

This gym seems to have an abundance of naked old dudes who seem to hang around the locker rooms chatting to anyone. I guess at their age you don't give a shit about certain things anymore, like clothing. Sometimes I think they are all part of some mystical fellowship, existing to help and advise struggling men in gym locker rooms, a naked brotherhood. (Which is a good name for a jazz band.)

At one point he was vigorously rubbing some cream into his backside while asking me what team I supported.

•

Naturally, finding someone to stick sharp needles in you is best done over the internet, so I found someone we shall simply refer to as 'Mrs Woo'.

I went to see her, and she asked how she could help. I started to tell her my life story and she simply stared at me so blankly

I thought she was wearing a mask. That dead stare is usually something reserved for my children.

When I paused, she quietly said, 'You aren't grounded into yourself.'

When I asked what that meant, she said, 'You are running on vapours.'

I wasn't sure if she meant wine, adrenalin or both. She then said the immortal words:

'Do you trust me?'

Do you know what? I did. What did I have to lose?

Mrs Woo told me she was going to ground me with only 'one needle' and it would be very 'intense and powerful'.

I was getting nervous now. I was told to take off all my clothes from the waist down. I replied, 'Naked?' and she nodded.

So I lay on a bed, naked from the waist down, and Mrs Woo took out a long and very thin needle. I was just putting it all together at this point, the half nudity, the long, lone needle. Oh God . . .

'Relaaaax.'

Impossible.

She then grabbed my ankles and pushed them up and back towards my head, like you would to wipe a baby's bottom. Is this being filmed?

'Breathe in, then out for five.'

I took a deep breath in, bracing myself for the needle, got as far as three on my out-breath and Mrs Woo put a needle somewhere in my southern hemisphere.

I was told it would be intense, but that doesn't describe what I felt.

You know that on some dolls there is a factory reset button that when pressed, the doll's eyes roll backwards and it's reset?

That was me on this bed with my legs in the air and a skewer sticking out of my bum.

Tears were streaming out of my eyes from the intensity of it all. I felt light-headed and was overcome by this sudden internal heat so intense I started sweating.

Perhaps this works by making the rest of your life seem good because you don't have an enormous needle plunged into an area not spoken of in polite company.

'Stay lying down for thirty minutes,' said Mrs Woo sternly as she set a timer on her watch and put a blanket over me.

I thought I'd give it a few minutes then hop off the bed and *nrrrrgghhhhhhhhhzzzzzzzz.*

The next thing I knew I was being gently woken with a delicious green tea. I felt so groggy, a mixture of cosmic jet-lag and like I'd been drugged.

When I got home, I went to bed at 2 p.m. and slept a deep honeyed sleep better than I'd ever had since I was a baby. When I updated my wife on my day, she said, 'You didn't get an erection, did you?'

Like this was a standard concern.

I reassured her that a woman moving me like I was on a baby's changing table and shoving a needle into my butt wasn't in any way a turn-on. For some maybe it is. I feared my wife was worried that I enjoyed the experience so much I would want it again, daily. Next thing she'd be asking why all the knitting needles have disappeared.

•

While the needle jabbing had done wonders, I needed something longer term to keep me fit physically. I know whenever I exercise, I'm better resourced mentally. I still didn't know when my family would be returning, although in good news it now seemed like they would. Fridays were the worst at this point, the show would end, and the weekend would lie ahead of me like a vast desert of loneliness I had to cross; I needed to fill it.

In my old life, I trained twice a week with a great boxing trainer, Jon, who was a world champion kickboxer. Once I saw him three weeks out from a world title defence and after our session he ate half a sandwich and binned the rest, then drank half a can of Coke, which I didn't think fighters did before a big fight, and poured the rest away. When I questioned all this, he said, 'This is my secret regime when I'm getting ready for a fight, fifty per cent diet. Basically, I eat what I want, but only half of it.'

He won his title fight. There might be a new diet craze in his 50/50 regime.

So now in Melbourne, I set about finding a new boxing gym and trainer. With my trainer Jon, it was part boxing and part therapy, so I took a while researching different gyms and Hamish Blake recommended someone, saying they were 'a gun'. I thought this was a text typo at first, then remembered I'd heard that word a few times. I asked one of my team what it meant. It's now one of my favourite sayings I've learnt in Australia: 'gun', the Australian way of saying someone is 'great'. I had a new trainer, a *gun*, Leo, and we became good friends over our time in his boxing ring in between rounds talking about life. He'd just moved with his young family to Melbourne from New Zealand, so we had something in common.

After the show every Monday and Friday, I would go for a training session. Maybe there is something about the intimacy in a boxing ring but our chats would often go deep about life. Makes sense when I think about my old mate the man in the shed enjoying a rumble mixed in with therapy. Why not a boxing coach doing some soul conversations? One session I was having my gloves put on by Leo and he sensed I was physically there but mentally I was elsewhere. Then it got weird.

I made it weird.

He looked really deep into me, deeper than Mrs Woo had gone, placed a hand on my shoulder and said, 'I can't imagine how hard this must be, brother.'

He only ever called me 'brother' and I loved that.

Being alone in a strange city, *'uninvited'* and having to pretend everything's okay on a new radio show. I can't stand being away from my kids for a night. Yeah, this was hard.

Sometimes you can't control when you just let yourself go, and I did, in that boxing ring. When someone takes the time to see despair in you and shows you compassion, you can offer no resistance. Despite wearing boxing gloves.

I started to well up a bit in my eyes. In the boxing ring. This is at the start of our session. What is happening to me?

The posters encouraging people to move to Australia for a new life of adventure show images of gorgeous beaches, Sydney Harbour, the outback; they should also have that image of me, eyes filled with tears, standing in a boxing ring being consoled by a very big man.

It's actually harder than you think to wipe your eyes wearing sixteen-ounce boxing gloves.

It was 11 a.m. on a Friday and I was in the heart of Melbourne's financial district and there were traders pummelling punchbags who had stopped to take in the spectacle of a crying man in the boxing ring in the middle of the gym.

My trainer gave me a hug, part of me wondered whether that was all part of the lesson. We could've looked like I'd just lost a gruelling twelve-round world title slugfest. But really, I was a 40-something DJ who was missing his family, failing in the ratings and a long way from home.

There is a scene in most *Rocky* movies where the guy is down and out on the canvas, he's taken so much, surely it's over. But no . . . Rocky puts his hand on the lower rope, no he can't be?

He's taken so much punishment, he's given just about everything he can, then he reaches for the next rope up, how is he doing this? He gets himself up onto one knee now, he can barely summon the energy to get to this point, let alone any more, then he reaches, from some deeper reserve he didn't even know he had, for the top rope, he's trying to get up!

I was down, pretty down, but . . .

21

Fudge Man save me

You're scared of Mum, aren't you, and it's kinda sad.

LOIS O'CONNELL

My family's return was a joyful experience. Big hugs at the airport as I met them at the gate. The first day back and we were reunited I couldn't stop hugging them. The days following their return were full of happiness. The house had noise, chaos, laughter, shouting, basically life back in it. I would still wake up, dreading another long day until I could speak to them again, then remember we were all back together.

This didn't last forever, and the return of my wife meant the serious business of settling into Melbourne was to recommence at breakneck speed. Her return saw an even greater intention of making our new life here work.

While finding a book club and building up a sisterhood (Sarah runs her friendship group like a cult) were key milestones in my wife settling here in Australia, there was no clearer sign that she was really settling than her wanting us to head out on the weekend to a craft fair.

My ideal weekend is nothing planned and see what happens.

This does not sit well with my wife. There is always a plan, sometimes a plan to get a plan. The news of my wife wanting to go to a craft fair chilled me to the core.

My wife loves a craft fair. *Loves* a craft fair. And a farmers' market. They are the same thing really. Stallholders with the homemade 'wares'. If there are stalls and *wares*, my wife is all in. Which means we have to be all in as well.

Her ideal time at a craft fair is several hours. Mine is 23 minutes. And that includes parking the car in a field.

She wanders around a craft fair like she is the Queen on some Royal Walkabout. Talking to all the stallholders and forensically examining their wares. I'm like her royal bodyguard (a budget one she's maybe hired off Airtasker or Gumtree) a few hundred yards ahead, but instead of looking for signs of trouble, I'm acting like a pacemaker trying to get her round in a new personal best.

My wife's DNA material actively changes when at a craft fair or when she plays any board game.

If we'd have played Pictionary on our first date and I saw how it changed her as if some terrifying host parasite had overtaken her former sweet self, we would never have got married. She brings a seriousness and intensity to a game usually reserved for emergency surgery or storming an enemy's fortified position.

I think potential prime ministers should have to play Pictionary live on TV, just so the voting public can see who they are really electing. I'm moving on but for the record I drew a perfectly gettable fire engine . . .

'I'm not shouting, you're shouting.'

While board games are not a safe space for me, craft fairs are positively terrifying.

Our family unit still hasn't fully recovered from the incident known as #thefrancemeltdown. A pleasant holiday in the south of France was marred, yes marred, by a screaming row at a craft fair between Sarah and Ruby. With me in the middle like some UN peacekeeper. I've not seen a UFC fight more vicious than this. And right in front of the homemade candle stall. All because Ruby had asked how much longer would we be here as she was bored.

France is beautiful with stunning countryside, villages and amazing wines and cheeses, but a craft fair is still le crap, even in France.

Now I feared another family holiday was about to be wrecked. We were in Byron Bay, in New South Wales. Byron Bay is a lovely place, home also to a few big-name celebrities, its most famous resident being Thor. Not the mythological God of Thunder and Rain (and also according to Wikipedia 'hallowing and fertility'), but the actor Chris Hemsworth, who plays the well-known Norse god of hallowing. You'd overhear snippets of conversations of reported sightings of Thor Hemsworth surfing or walking on water. And hallowing.

My wife breathlessly announced in bed on Saturday night, 'Someone told me earlier that Australia's Biggest Craft Fair is here, so I thought it would be great fun to get up early and go, we'll need to set the alarm.'

Part of me died upon hearing all this.

So many thoughts. The early Sunday alarm; I live by an early alarm call but I was on holidays. Also what idiot told her?

We were just in a local Italian restaurant called, ingeniously, 'The Italian Restaurant'. Apparently, her confidante was 'a lady in the toilets'. The hidden secret world of the ladies' loo is a mystery and should remain so, but my mind spins at how my wife, gone no more than a few minutes, could befriend a total stranger and extract valuable craft fair information. And there was me thinking you just lent each other lipstick. If I walked up to a bloke in the toilets and asked about craft fairs, it's hard to imagine the approach would be met with enthusiasm.

Maybe this was some clandestine pre-arranged meeting, part of some secret underground cabal of fellow craft fair fanatics. Craft Fair Club, where the first rule of Craft Fair Club is you don't talk about Craft Fair Club. They greet one another in the toilets of restaurants by showing the secret Craft Fair Club sign, a crappy fish made out of metal on some string.

The real horror that kept me awake all night was the word 'biggest'. Pray for me.

The alarm went off and I groaned the groan of a man on execution day, while my wife urged me not to 'come with that attitude'. The teenagers weren't any better. A 45-minute car ride through some beautiful scenery and we were there. My execution site.

Now, Australians like to make everything bigger and better. There is a shopping centre in Melbourne called Chadstone. No idea why they never called it 'The Megamall'. When we moved here, Andy Lee said it was one of the 'things to do'. *So forget the Twelve Apostles and Great Ocean Road, go to a mall, you say?* I've just moved from London, where there are a couple of shops.

Andy boasted as any proud Australian would that 'Chaddy, mate! Amazing. Biggest shopping mall in the southern hemisphere.'

The way he and many others talked about it as a MUST see, it was as if you have one of the wonders of the modern world: 'Sydney might have that farkin bridge but we've got Chaddy. I see your harbour and raise you the Chaddy Food Court.'

And that sounds impressive, doesn't it? The biggest; in half of the whole planet. Wow. Just WOW. And then you have a look at a globe. Or a map. Or Google. And find that the southern hemisphere might be half the planet, but it's not half of the world. Oh no.

The southern hemisphere is 80 per cent sea and ocean.

We wouldn't have spent a fortune looking for that Malaysian jet in the northern hemisphere. We would have asked around, 'Has anyone seen a Malaysian jet that crash-landed last week?'

And statistically one bloke would have been able to go, 'Yeah, it's just over there.'

Because 90 per cent of the world live in the northern hemisphere.

The competition for Australia is most of South America, a bit of Africa and Antarctica.

•

Anyway, back to Australia's Biggest Craft Fair. Craft fairs the world over, and believe me, I've had to see them the world over—England, France, Spain, Italy and now Australia—are exactly the same. Let's tick the characters and stalls you see at the craft fair:

The Fudge Man—It's not a craft fair without this guy smugly standing behind his bars of overpriced homemade fudge. Why is the street value of fudge so expensive? It's more expensive per kilo in weight than gold or printer ink. The Fudge Man always has a big white beard, and probably has a Porsche hidden around the corner he paid for in fudge.

The Dream Catcher Lady—Dream catchers scare me. Why the need to capture dreams? This lady or witch also sells wind chimes. They are like the twins we had at school who even scared the teachers and whose parents dressed them the same. In serial killer movies, there will always be a scene involving a dream catcher or wind chime. I say no more.

Artisan Bread the Size of Your Head—Artisan is shorthand for overpriced. Anything with the word 'artisan' or 'locally sourced' means hand over your wallet. Talking of which, you can buy a new wallet made from repurposed roadkill from the Skulls, Pelts and Belts Guy.

A Knackered Shitbox of a Van Selling Type 2 Diabetes–inducing Donuts—With so much sugar on the donuts, it looks like Tony Montana from *Scarface* sneezed on them.

White Guy with Dreads Doing a Back Massage—Often looks like the guy who drives a panel van with curtains that your parents warned you to watch out for.

Scented Candles—Smell great on the table at the stall, but the moment you light them they smell like a fire in a dumpster.

The Olive Oil Couple—Always run by a married couple, one of them put all their savings into this and they look so miserable like they aren't talking to each other and haven't had sex in three years.

As sure as night follows day, Byron Bay got rocked harder than Thor's hammer being smashed onto Clarkes Beach, with a traditional O'Connell craft fair family meltdown. I LOVE seeing an entire family having a row in public, it's a great event to witness. But when it's your public family row, it's hell. Like reality TV, a guilty pleasure to watch but you never want to be in the show.

The teenagers had mounted a rebellion against my wife, this was foolish.

BECAUSE MY WIFE NEVER

EVER

NEVER

EVER

BACKS

DOWN

This was a scene from Tarantino's *Reservoir Dogs*, where at the end of the movie there is a Mexican stand-off between the main characters.

That's exactly what it's like when my wife and daughters get into it. I'm left with the role of a quivering bystander scared witless of taking a side. That's often made easy for me by my wife yelling, '*Chris, back me up here!*'

My kids look with disgust as they witness their own father and his ball-less spineless rabbit-in-the-headlights response to his wife's oncoming truck of righteous fury. I'm either trying to jump onto that truck, or I'm under the wheels of it. Then reversed over. Then driven over again. Then reversed over again.

I look back at my judging kids and attempt telekinesis to explain they'll understand one day that relationships are complicated.

At Australia's Biggest Craft Fair, the reason for the fight was because the kids had dropped the big bomb.

'*How long are we going to be here?*'

Oh, dear Buddha, no. Asking my wife a question like this, in her craft fair heaven, is like seeing the Sistine Chapel and saying it's a bit crap to the Pope.

Shit's about to get real.

And right by olive oil couple, just before the homemade fudge stall.

As soon as the words hit the ether of the craft fair, and the waft of patchouli oil and broken dreams, I found myself saying quietly under my breath: 'Why would you do that?'

My wife froze on the spot. Crows and birds flew from trees. Thunder cracked overhead. Stallholders packed away their wares, mothers gathered up their children.

The universe prepared itself. Thor hallowed.

'We've only just got here,' growled my wife.

My insides fell out of my backside.

'It's so *boringggggg*,' said the teens.

Oh no. Neither side was backing down.

My wife never backs down.

She has also taught her protégés to *never back down*.

I realised I hadn't even dared to draw a breath in case it brought attention to me.

'Chris, back me up here!'

'Craft fairs are fun, kids, I think you will enjoy it here,' I said with the enthusiasm of a prisoner on death row promoting the benefits of the electric chair.

'Is that the best you can manage?' sneered my wife, and my kids spat at my cowardly feet.

My abiding image is of my wife storming off and dramatically throwing a bag of recently purchased overpriced homemade soaps to the ground.

Once a peace deal had been brokered by me, and it wasn't easy getting all sides back to the table to talk, we continued our time at the craft fair.

My wife sulking, the teenagers sulking.

The car ride back to the hotel was frosty, sometimes silence is really loud. I don't know what came over me, but I thought the best thing everyone needed was a game of 'I Spy'. Because that's what teenagers *love* to play in the car—how can their smartphones compete with that? Everyone became united in turning on me.

'Stupid game, just leave it, Chris,' hissed my wife.

'*No one cares!*' from the teenagers.

The three warring ladies all joined together in taking the mickey out of me.

This is one of my patented dad moves, known as the 'dadcrifice'.

Because sometimes a dad must be sacrificed for the greater good.

It was great to have them back in Australia.

22

A disgusting man

What's Dad got to do with how I was made?

LOIS, BEFORE 'THE CHAT'

Since my family had returned from Britain, I'd noticed a subtle shift. We were all starting to find our feet in this new land.

Sometimes this made me more worried rather than less.

With my daughters, I found myself struggling sometimes to find them. I don't mean physically. It's easy to find your teenage children, just follow the teenage smell, made up of:

- 67 per cent unwashed sports kit
- 13 per cent the mould spores from bedside drinks and food
- 20 per cent 'fug'.

No, my kids have always been easy to find since the days of hide and seek. A five-year-old's idea of 'hiding' is putting their hands over their face and crouching next to the sofa in plain view. My wife was surprised at their crude hiding skills, after being exposed to hours of *Baby Einstein* when they were born. My wife bought this DVD series called *Baby Einstein* on eBay. Which is exactly where the next Einstein will be grown from, eBay.

For the unaware, *Baby Einstein* was meant to stimulate your newborn's brain. You plonked your baby in front of the TV guilt-free so you could go hide by the washing machine, crying and having a drink, telling yourself it was five o'clock somewhere in the world. Believing that after a few episodes a day you'll be raising a child genius who will cure the common cold at dinner one night just by rearranging their spaghetti hoops into a double helix.

What I mean by trying to find them, is finding out who they were becoming while grieving the loss of the child they were but aren't anymore.

One minute you can be glowing in the awe of seeing them smash the school play, the next minute you're being yelled at to '*Go away!*' from the other side of a slammed bedroom door. You ask what's wrong and they can't tell you, because they don't even really know themselves.

Lois came back from shopping one day and placed a new sign on the front of her bedroom door: *Keep Calm and Piss Off.*

This was what I was dealing with.

Piss Off.

I got this treatment from my listeners; I didn't need it at home.

Next thing was our daughters wanted to 'decorate' their own bedrooms. Lois wanted to paint her room black. *Black!* I thought this only happened in the movies, the classic scene of the emo teenager with a giant Sia-esque fringe in a black bedroom with Cure posters and a pentagram bedspread.

Luckily this passed the moment I said I had a black bedroom when I was younger.

I didn't, I've just learnt that things you say you've done suddenly lose their appeal for your kids: it's the dad kiss of death.

'You know what else I didn't do, I didn't study hard and respect my parents. You should do that.'

Instead, Lois opted for strip LED lights and a disco ball. Every night at bedtime it was like going into a Berlin nightclub. It was cool and very Lois.

Ruby got me to paint her bedroom orange, like some Tuscan villa, which was very Ruby. Perfect colour tones for her to make out with her boyfriend.

Then new posters went up on their walls. This I loved. Your teenage bedroom walls were everything. It's where you said to the world, 'This is who I am now.'

I did this, we all did it. Do you remember what posters you had on your bedroom walls?

Rocky, Marilyn Monroe, and the England and Manchester United legend football player Bryan Robson were all on my wall, along with Prince and Bruce Lee. Bryan Robson was wearing a pair of 80s denim jeans and had a bare chest. One day my dad came into my bedroom and basically used my poster of my football hero, Bryan 'Shirtless' Robson, as evidence that gay me was trying to come out. He was gently trying to tell me it was okay. I said, 'Thanks, but I'm not gay, just thought it was a cool poster.'

The moment Dad left my bedroom, that poster came down and Bryan looked at me all shirtless and crumpled in the bin. That weekend some more posters of scantily clad women got put up; my dad must've just taken this as more evidence I was trying too hard.

Some days I felt bad I couldn't give him what his enlightened self was obviously craving, a chance to be supportive to his un-gay son. He was so ready, and I ruined it for him. I have toyed with the idea of calling him up and telling him I'm gay.

I think he'd high-five his girlfriend, put his hand over the phone and whisper, 'I called this in 86 . . . two words . . . shirtless Bryan.'

Seeing my kids take down the bedroom posters of their childhood was like a snake shedding skin that was no longer needed. It's a small thing, but big too.

Harry Styles went up. All ripped and with his 'V' on his six-pack showing. Easy to be ripped in your twenties Harry, come see me in your forties in your cheese years.

There were other noticeable changes, disappearances. Things we'd normally done just weren't an option anymore. No more going for dog walks: 'Boring, that's what old people do.' No more going to the local tip (don't laugh, they used to love this): 'Boring, just dropping off rubbish.' The real heartbreaker was the day holding hands in public was now sadly 'odd'. That really crushed me.

You never knew when you'd just done something for the last time.

I surprised my daughters one day at school pick-up. There was a time this would be met at the school gates with wide eyes and squeals of delight, running into my arms. Not anymore. I got this horrified reaction, hissed through clenched teeth: *'What are you doing here?'*

As if I was a suspected serial killer. I was told to *'never do that again'* unless I'm asked and then to 'park down the road and *stay in the car'*.

I had to pick one of them up recently after a school camp they'd been on for a few days. I was sent this text:

'Please stay in the car, I'm serious it would be so embarrassing'
I replied:
'But I've made a banner'

Met with:

'*Not funny*'

•

To try to get some time with them without any agenda ('Has Mum, like, told you to talk to me about this? It's just so obvious'), I did what I used to love doing with my dad, going for a drive in his car. I don't know whether it's the fact you're side by side, rather than in front of each other, that makes it easier sometimes to open up and chat. It's okay to have silence too, because you're just going for a drive. Maybe therapists should also try this, having sessions where they pick clients up and you go for a drive and chat.

Some London taxi drivers do this but the wrong way round, bearing their souls to you, then charging you for the pleasure of hearing their troubles. Which reminds me of the unnamed place in Australia where I was picked up from the airport by a man who started to moan about his lot all just in the time we had pulled out of the airport carpark. I asked what he wanted to do in life, and he said, 'Funny you ask, I'm trying to become a country and western singer.'

Good on him. Why not? I asked his name, he told me it was 'Gary', but he had recently changed it to 'Garry' with two 'r's to make him stand out. As I took in Garry, the artist formerly known as Gary, his neck ensconced in one of those long-distance flight, inflatable neck pillows and his back against a beaded seat cover (these could have been mere affectations along with the additional 'r' to stand out), I realised I'd never wanted anyone to achieve their dream more than Garry.

It was on one of our car trips while dropping into the car wash that my dad ruined our bonding time by deciding this was the perfect opportunity to tell me about the *facts of life*. Sitting in his car, at the car wash, as the foaming wet brushes came down onto the car (I've no idea if this reminded him of intercourse), he suddenly said, 'You know about the birds and the bees right?'

'*Oh no, Dad, not now, not here!*'

And that's where my dad told me about the facts of life. By the time we drove out of the car wash, I was fully informed. His timing was way off because, six months before he decided to have the chat, I'd already aggressively started puberty. Key word: *aggressively*.

That means for guys, you awake one day as a teenager and you look at the damage done to your sheets, those snail trails, and you think, *I'm going to do my own washing from now on*. And just getting those sheets into the washing machine is really hard when you're a teenage boy. It's the equivalent of trying to get a pizza box into the kitchen bin without breaking it up first. That's what it was like with those sheets and me.

I'm glad I'm not a teenage boy nowadays. All that instant access to high-definition pornography, on your phone, in your palm. I fear I would've caused myself irreparable harm.

Just before we moved to Australia, we had to have the chat with our youngest daughter. You know the chat. The birds and the bees. But not in a car wash.

My wife said, 'Look, there's this book, a lot of the mums who have daughters have been going through this book with them, that's the best way to do it.' This book is called *Let's Talk About Where Babies Come From*. And that's a really nice mother–daughter book title, isn't it? *Let's Talk About Where Babies Come From*. Lovely.

I think the father–son equivalent would be: *Let's Not Talk About Where Babies Come From*. 'Here's a tenner, tell your mum we had the chat, help yourself to my laptop, it's all on there.'

So I had to order this book on Amazon. It turned up, and was 88 pages long. 88 pages? I was still trying to teach the kid that if you stand in front of a swing you'll get smashed in the face. Three years I'd been trying to teach her that. She was going to understand this book of 88 pages of incredibly physiological detail? No way.

I started reading it, otherwise you're going to go in for that chat and you're going to sound like a biology supply teacher.

BTW! Side note: Should some of you find yourselves in this very situation, don't use their favourite cuddly toy as a visual aid. No. Otherwise you'll have your wife going, 'Any idea why she doesn't want Mr Smiley in her bed anymore?'

And as I'm going through this book I'm starting to learn stuff I didn't even know. SPOILER ALERT! Did you know women have a finite number of eggs? Did you know that?

I did not!

I went up to my wife with the book and confronted her. 'Do you know you've only got a finite number of eggs?'

She said, 'Er, yeah right, well done Einstein.'

Us men, we can go on endlessly producing our stuff. Women have a finite number of eggs. Women are like a warehouse and men are like an Amazon factory.

Does anyone else agree with me and think it would be a far better idea if it was the other way around and men only had a limited amount of sperm? I think we'd be a lot more careful with our stuff if we knew one day it was going to run out.

We'd invent some kind of gauge so men would know where supplies were at. Dating adverts would all change. 'Hi, my name's Julian, I'm an accountant in my early 30s. Ladies, hurry up, only eleven per cent left.'

If you were a child of the 80s, the only hope you had of seeing any images of naked ladies was if the porn pixies had worked their magic. Yeah, the porn pixies were the little people who would leave bits of adult reading material in hedges for horny teenage boys.

So I said to my wife, 'Look, okay, I'm not happy that we're doing this when she's this young but let's do it, let's have the chat.'

She said, 'No, I already told her that we're going to have the chat with her and she's requested that you're not in the room.'

I said, 'Okay, yeah, it's going to be awkward if Dad's there, I understand. I'll go upstairs and you can tell me when you've had the chat and I'll come down.'

'No, she doesn't want you in the house.'

I had to go away to the pub while they had the chat and then I got the saddest text from my wife ever. It just said, '*You can come home now*'

When I went back into my house, everything had changed.

You know when your dad used to make one of those spot visits to your bedroom, just walk in and go, 'Hey, what's going on here then, huh?'

So there I was, in her bedroom trying to be cool, making small talk, then Lois said to me, she actually said these words:

'Mum told me what you did to her . . . and you're disgusting.'

I felt like saying if I'd done what I wanted to, you wouldn't even be here.

23

New besties

Mum! Dad's putting aftershave on to go meet his new friend, it's so cute.

RUBY O'CONNELL

While my wife had made friends the moment she stepped off the plane in Australia, my kids had been a little slower in forming a friendship group, but they now had a whole crew they could roll their eyes in front of whenever I said something.

Their success meant I knew it was time for the world's saddest DJ to start making friends, too.

I had resisted my wife's urging for me to 'join a cycling club'. Screw that. I have friends back in England who shave their legs and squeeze into a lycra cycling onesie that no man ever looks good in. Even if you saw Brad Pitt pull up on his bike in a lycra cycling outfit, he's gonna look like a fool.

I respect you if this is your hobby and thing, but some of your fellow MAMILs (Middle Aged Men In Lyrca; women have MILFs, we get MAMILs) annoy everyone on the roads by riding five across having a catch-up while a row of cars six kilometres

222

long stares at your lycra-clad backsides. Then the lycra brigade go berserk if we dare to try to overtake them, threatening us and wearing more high-tech body cameras than a SWAT officer. If your hobby involves you having to film all your encounters with members of the public, it's too stressful for me.

Plus, it wouldn't be a good look as I'm trying to win people over to be also attacking listeners with my bike lock.

Full disclosure, I did take up an equally clichéd hobby. Golf. What a terrible mistake. I should've just got the lycra on. It's not golf I play, it's crap golf. I'm having lessons and it's so hard, no one should start golf at my age. This isn't the age to learn something that requires fine motor control and relies on small precise movements all working together as one. Your grip, body weight, hip, head, arm. That's why Tiger Woods's old man got him working on that swing the moment he came out of the womb. One lesson was so bad, it made me question not just my decision to learn golf, but also who I am as a person. I threw my golf club in the bin in the carpark. Drove home screaming and vowed to never try the game again.

My life was making me have meltdowns regularly enough, I didn't need to pay good money for the privilege.

I had briefly started golf lessons in the UK. There was one lesson that was interrupted by a police helicopter landing on the course and two officers, one armed, running towards us. I seriously thought I was going to be arrested for crimes against golf.

They said an escaped criminal was on the run. Must have been the world's dumbest criminal if he thought a wide-open golf course was the place to hide. Escobar wasn't discovered at the sixteenth hole by the Narcs.

A new home in Australia, combined with far better weather and abject loneliness, lured me out of my retirement. I tried a few very patient coaches when I got here then met my Golf Yoda, a big cheery man who looks like a giant happy baby called Zac. This guy is my kind of coach: our lessons are punctuated between micro techniques with him reading his phone out with horse-racing tips I should back or global bad news while I'm trying to hit the ball. I get angry with my crappiness very quickly as yet another ball leaves my club at an impossible angle and bends time, space and the laws of physics. Then Zac Golf Yoda will say calmly, 'Don't hit *at* the ball, hit *through* the ball . . . oh there's a great each-way bet at 3.30 today at Flemington.'

I'm still a rookie and one Friday me and my new mate Brett were playing nine holes and a young kid came to join us. Yeah, a new mate. Brett I'm talking about, not the kid. Okay, I'll admit our wives are in the same book club and once again the hands of our wives were involved in us becoming friends.

Anyway, at public courses you can often be playing with another one or two when it's just the pair of you. This fourteen-year-old boy had a day off school so booked to play golf. Embarrassingly, this child was some kind of Tiger Woods protégé and brilliant, putting us both to shame.

Now the thing I've discovered about golf is, it's a great way to catch up with your mates, in between being a long way from them while you rummage around in the outback looking for your stray ball. Brett and I talked about our wives, kids, work, gossiping, swore a fair bit. I was confiding that I was trying to poach a rival breakfast show's producer, when this young kid piped up for the first time with some advice for me. My ego got hit harder than my ball. His advice was taken, though, and my next shot was the best of the afternoon.

There was a group up ahead of us taking ages and I offered this kid cash if he could hit his ball near to them to scare them along, but not hurt them. He refused. Rightly so. Of course, I was just testing the morals of this young man and I'm pleased to say he passed. After the game—that he won, a boy, morally he should've allowed us grown-ups to win, but despite this we shook hands and thanked our little playing mate—he said all of a sudden: 'My mum and I listen to your show every morning.'

At no point had he said anything about me even having a radio show. He had overheard all of what we'd just been saying, including my cash offer for him to try to intimidate other players, stealing a rival show's producer, and various gossip including some about an A-lister and a sex toy.

I went bright red and gladly accepted his invitation of a selfie, that happened to be outside a men's toilet. Not the best look. Suddenly the chilled-out bliss of a cheeky round of nine was replaced by replaying everything I'd said that he overheard. I promised that I'd say hi to him and his mum on Monday, and I did. Last thing I need is a kid bringing the show down like a house of cards. And Charlie, if you're reading this, I let you win.

•

So finally, I've got a group of guys—Al, Dan, Andy, William, Matt and Adam—that I go for beers with or play nine holes with. I'd love to say I put this group together, but the truth is . . . our wives did.

The sad truth is that often men have friends that they got from their wives. Our wives are friends and that's how we got put together. I try not to think about this too often. We are so poorly organised compared to our wives' group. They've managed to sort a weekend away and three nights out, and all we've managed in that time was to share barely amusing gifs in our WhatsApp group. It's pathetic. Anytime I see a group of guys out I just see the matrix of a load of wives who put them together.

When I see that iconic image of the Last Supper, now all I think is those disciples Jesus had, Peter, John, Matthew and the boys, their wives all must've been in a book club together.

Through a friendship with footy legend Shane Crawford—who has kind of adopted me since moving here and I ended up hiring him as my show's AFL guy, though most of our chats are three per cent footy and the rest whatever we want to talk about—I got to meet a friend of his called 'Big John'.

Now, in every group of men there exists a Big John. The alpha. They get shit planned and done. Organise. Book things. The grey wolf of the group. I had to bide my time with Big John, he was feeling me out, then one day out of the blue, I got the invite.

Years ago, maybe it would have been a smoke signal and where to head towards for a new initiation. This was a text message simply saying: *'Fancy a man walk? Walk, chat. Few k's'*.

No hello. Grey wolves don't do hellos. Note also, this wasn't an invite to go on a walk, oh no, this was to go on a *man walk*. This is 100 per cent the great Australian male.

Man walk

Walk, chat

Few k's

Like a vow being offered, I accepted.

We walked, we talked. It was great, and we did this every weekend. I loved it. But sadly, something hurt Man Walk recently.

One weekend our daughters, who are friends, joined us and enjoyed roasting the pair of us about how excited we got on the morning of our Man Walk. It warmed my heart to hear that Big John had a favoured baseball cap he wore for Man Walk. Ruby teased me about how stressed I got about not ever being late for my man date. Both of us Man Walkers laughed uneasily, our hidden vulnerabilities exposed. Man Walk never happened again after that, suddenly weekends had 'too much on'. But deep down, two men weren't walking and talking anymore.

And that's a sad thing. I think of Big John looking at the lonely old cap. Sharing this has prompted me to invite Big John out for a Man Walk. No reply yet, it's tough sometimes being a man.

24

I bought a house drunk

Just look around, smile, but do not speak, I'll do all of that.

SARAH O'CONNELL

It all started one Saturday.

My wife was only supposed to be walking the dog, I was supposed to be going to the game.

But by the end of this Saturday, we had bought a house.

I had been invited to the footy to see my new team, Melbourne, the Dees, play Adelaide. I was a guest at the chairman's lunch, basically a free piss-up while you watch the game. A free bar. Bad idea.

Previously I always turned down hospitality offers as I thought it wasn't the best way to enjoy the game. I'd rather be in the stands having a beer and a steaming pie so hot it could melt your face. But I thought, why not? Treat myself.

Sarah said she was going to walk the dog and near the park there was an auction she would watch with her real estate agent friend Amanda. She wanted to get a feel for something we don't have in the UK where there is no bidding on a house at a public auction. If you like the house, you make an offer. You don't gather outside the house frantically bidding for it.

I arrived at the game just before midday and as I'm queuing to get into the Melbourne Cricket Ground (MCG) to watch the footy, it starts. Not the game.

The texts from my wife.

Here we go . . .

'Have a quick look at this place, can you? Enjoy the day'

Who can make a decision based on looking at a house for sale on your phone? Forget it. Plus, I don't want to be on my phone at this pre-game lunch. It's rude. Us Dees fans are ridiculed for being middle class and I'm living up to that by looking at property on my phone and drinking champagne at midday.

I was in one of the most famous and incredible sporting venues in the world, the MCG. It's a modern-day colosseum, but on this day more likely to witness another low-wattage outing from my new team. The 'G' can hold 100,000 people and has hosted some incredible Ashes cricket games between England and Australia at the Boxing Day Test. When my dad came to Australia for the first time for a holiday and to see my new life, he insisted I take him there.

As a sport lover and cricket superfan, he was blown away by its size and beauty. Some buildings have energy, and this place is one of them. We went on a guided tour and I was so stressed all the way round as I knew my hard-to-please dad would make an odd comment.

He did. Right as we were out at the edge of the famous oval, my dad, wearing a fleece zip-up in the blazing heat ('It deflects the heat,' he said when I queried why he had even packed it to come here in the summer), told our tour guide the grass was illegal and possibly contravening the world governing body for cricket rules. Just what a group of cricket-mad Aussies want to hear, some old English geezer accusing them of cheating at the cricket . . . again.

I smiled awkwardly and tried to use my facial expressions to make out that he was elderly and confused. I was hoping they would think I was on this tour as his carer, or fleece dealer.

One Friday I was there in the cheap seats, literally, the top row right up at the back, and had a great night. Friday night at the 'G' is an institution in itself, under the floodlights with a beer. On this Saturday I was with my mate Adam (are you keeping score, that's two mates now if you add Adam) as a guest at the chairman's lunch, it was as much about the game as it was about drinking. I was looking forward to both. I tucked into the free drinks as soon as I arrived. It would've been rude not to.

A former Dees captain came over and introduced himself and said he loved the show. These little moments of small blessings meant the world to me. It was going to be a good day.

Then my phone rang, no surprise who. You can tell who a guy is talking to on the phone if it's his wife, his body almost folds in half as if a giant thumb has come out of the heavens pressing him down into the earth. Bracing for the impact of fresh orders or something he's done wrong or, worse, hasn't done at all.

'Chris, I'm watching this auction . . .' What I heard in my wife's voice chilled me, dangerous intent.

'Yes I know, you said,' I replied, feigning interest and nodding. I needed a top-up for my drink, and for my nerves now that my wife was homing in on something.

'Well, I think I may well put in an offer, apparently it's at a great price.'

'What house? We haven't even seen it.'

'I'll send you the details now.'

I'm sure my wife has special sensors that detect if for some precious fleeting moment I'm having fun without her and she gets activated and acts accordingly.

The text arrived and admittedly it was a nice-looking house, but I was at the game and we hadn't even seen or been into this house. *Why is this happening now?*

She called back. Fuck me.

'Yep.'

'I can tell you're getting irritated, Chris.'

Well done. The senses are working. 'What do you think?'

'I'm gonna go for the aged beef and pinot, chocolate mousse for pudding.'

'THE HOUSE!'

I told her it seemed nice and if the price was right, and it was in our range, put in an offer.

On a house I hadn't seen. I just wanted all the interruptions to stop, to be honest, and I didn't care if this meant we would be living under a fly-over in a skip.

The game started and normal service resumed. We were shit.

The drinks were now making me feel nicely alight. The sun was out, the Dees were really poor, all was well for a moment in my universe.

I then met the man who did a very funny speech at the lunch, a sportswriter whose work I liked. Like most comedy writers I know, he also liked not only a laugh but a drink. We hit it off and at half-time carried on at the bar watching our team fall apart.

One thing I will say about Australians is they value conversation, and I've had some of the most surprising and interesting chats of my life since moving here. Over drinks, they are great company.

Shattering this high-spirited chat was my phone, again.

'WE OWN A HOUSE!!!'

To me, the last few hours felt like my wife telling me she was pregnant then calling me two hours later saying she'd given birth. Selfishly, I just wanted to be left alone to enjoy the buzz at the bar. It had been a long while since I'd had fun like this. Tall stories and outrageous gossip were now flowing like the free drinks.

'Great! Well done.'

I hang up on my wife and carry on.

A few drinks later, another call came. FFS!

'Problem.'

'It's fallen through? Oh, not to worry, not meant to be—'

'No, they're insisting you see it as well before we sign the papers, they're worried you won't like it and we will pull out.'

'Okay, let's have a look tomorrow.'

'No, it has to be today.'

Of course, it does. How dare I have a good time for a few hours? Why couldn't she have walked the dog somewhere else?

'How drunk are you?'

'Oh, I'm fine, only had one or two.'

It was now 4 p.m. and I'd been drinking steadily since midday.

'You can't meet the lady selling it drunk, she's very emotional about selling, plus the estate agent will be there, and the kids.'

'What's the latest we can see it?'

'6 p.m.'

I carried on and, I'll be honest, I may have put on an extra bit of pace to enjoy it before Cinderella had to leave this ball.

I told everyone we'd just bought our first home in Australia. I was informed this was what a true Melbourne supporter would do after watching their team lose.

Fresh drinks were given to me, toasts made, then questions about where this new house was. I actually didn't know, but I was going to find out at 6 p.m., I assured them.

I could tell people were impressed by this wild and exotic new Englishman in town who lived life like this, buying a house from the bar, and with a few drops of beef gravy spilt down the front of his crisp white shirt. Playa.

•

I had a quick power snooze (Churchill swore by them) in the back of a taxi (Churchill didn't have his in the back of a stinking taxi). At my new house, I got out of the taxi and walked towards my wife's parked car. She had been waiting for me. Staking out the new place. I was doing that impression we've all done that says, 'Yeah I've been drinking but I'm fine, just look at me walk . . . see?'

I banged her car bonnet loudly enough to startle the kids.

The game was up, it was clear I was buzzing, I'd actually had some fun with people, I may have even made some new friends.

'Oh boy Chris! Someone's had a good day! Is that gravy all down your shirt? Do your jacket up so it doesn't show. Just go in, have a look round and don't say anything, don't speak if you can help it, be polite, then pretend you have to make a call and walk around the corner.'

I do the classic tipsy slow nod and blink.

We went up to the house and it was lovely. 'It's great, let's do it!' I said excitedly.

'Don't you want to have a proper look round?' asked the real estate agent, as we had only just entered.

I headed upstairs with the kids, who hadn't seen the place either. As I was walking up behind them, I did something that's still talked about now. I fell over. Walking up the stairs.

The real estate agent called out, 'Everything okay?'

'Yeah, sorry, one of the kids fell over, gangly teenagers.'

I looked at them to back me up. They respect me and know my word rules.

'Mum, Dad just fell over.' Little shits.

My wife peered around the wall, looking up the stairs. I gestured at what must've been some shoddy workmanship on the carpet. 'Better get some money off for that,' I whispered.

It really was a lovely house. I nodded to my wife and the next thing I knew I was signing the documents, drunk.

The next morning, I woke up in a little pain. My wife did the classic, 'Sore head? Good afternoon, was it?'

I assured her I was all good. We got talking about the house and I said, 'It's lovely.'

'Can you remember it?'

'Of course,' I replied and said again how nice it was and what a change it would be to live in a single-storey house.

'It has an upstairs and you fell over going up it.'

'Oh yeah!' I lie. I did not remember there being an upstairs. Or tripping up them.

It was agreed I should, erm, maybe go see it again. What must they think of me now?

I went to see the house again, and my drunken instincts were right, it was a great house.

Looking back on our lives, it's sometimes easier to see the pattern. The bigger picture. Buying the house ushered in a whole new part of our lives here. I had felt like we had lost our grounding since arriving, now we were 'laying down roots' and saying to ourselves, this is home now, this is our life and this is where we belong.

25

Replaced

Dad, I'm not a little girl anymore and you need to accept that.

RUBY O'CONNELL

Undoubtedly moving to Australia had a huge effect on my daughters. In the classic Spiderman story, Peter Parker is bitten by a radioactive spider and his DNA is changed forever. With all the deadly animals that hang out in this country, I think my daughters were bitten by some rare spider that activated their teenage DNA. Taking a mega-dose that would kill a normal teenage girl. Moving here seemed to act like a catalyst for them.

They became teenage girls on Lance Armstrong levels of hormones. Their new powers became too strong for me. Just the other day I was told by my tormentors that I was, and I quote, a 'basic white dad'.

This observation was delivered as I was struggling with approximately 32 kilos of beach equipment that my wife thought we needed for a few hours in the sun on the sand. The kind of equipment US Navy Seals might carry for an assault on some heavily guarded terrorist compound.

Strapped around my body, like a human mule, I had:

- two beach umbrellas
- two beach chairs
- one giant beach tent that an entire Bedouin tribe could have lived under
- four × one-litre bottles of water
- one beach mat.

I was coated in sunscreen lotion, or as I believe you call it in Australia 'slip slop'. Many words here sound like a group of ten-year-olds were rounded up, given too many sweets and fizzy drinks, then shown a flip chart, handed crayons and asked to name things. Like slip slop.

Another example: one of the deadliest snakes in the world, the *Pseudonaja textilis*, resides in Australia. Or, as the Aussies call it, the brown snake. Because it's brown. And a snake.

There is a cheese here, a popular variety, called 'Tasty' cheese. In the 90s Australia was told they couldn't call it 'cheddar cheese' anymore (like the French did with champagne that wasn't from the region in France), so cheddar became known as 'Tasty'. How long did that marketing meeting take? What other names did they go through before landing on their eureka moment? 'Yummy' cheese? 'Yellowy' cheese? 'Edible' cheese? 'Cheesy' cheese?

I don't know who named the sperm whale, but I'd wager money it was an Australian.

So I struggled for at least a kilometre in a temperature that was above 35 degrees Celsius, like some contestant on a bizarre

Japanese game show. Lugging all our gear from the only parking spot I could find, which was in another suburb. 'You drop us here at the beach, then go find a spot for the car and come join us,' my wife said casually, as if addressing a footman on *Downton Abbey*.

Thanks, M'Lady, for letting me join you on the beach. I kindly agree and accept, once I've displaced a few vertebrae carrying all this shit for my so-called family. Only to have my teenagers, on seeing me arrive soaked in sweat, greet me with, *'You're such a basic white dad.'*

I had been reduced to this, and no longer worthy of their respect. However, the biggest change in my girls was in the area of . . . boys.

•

Let me tell you this: nothing in life prepares you for the first time you see your daughter making out with her first boyfriend. Nothing.

This was always going to happen. But nothing prepares you.

One day I came home and found Ruby, who had turned fifteen, and a young man lying down—lying down!—together on my couch!

It was all too much. We'd gone from no interest in boys to lying down on the couch with them. WTF! Don't you work up, or down, to that? Did I mention they were lying down?

I had to take a knee just to catch my breath. Life had hit me hard. I know she was fifteen, and this was what she should be doing, and enjoying, and . . . but . . . She had her first boyfriend.

Firsts and lasts—like those lasts that you didn't know you will remember forever and the firsts you will never forget too.

I remember my first girlfriend—there are certain 'firsts' in life you never forget.

The girl's dad was a plumber, and whenever I visited he would deliberately make a point of carrying around some bit of plumbing equipment, no doubt essential for his job, but a mean-looking thing that resembled a medieval torture device. All while looking at me right in the eye and bashing the hurty-tool in his big, meaty palm. An ancient part of me knew this was a warning. His hands looked like a baseball catcher's mitt.

My hands, by the way, are very delicate: at a recent photo shoot the photographer remarked on what 'lovely slender hands' I had. The photographer then made me cover about 99.2 per cent of my face with these 'lovely slender hands'. Am I to assume if this radio lark goes bad, maybe there is a future for me as a hand model? *Australia's Next Top Hand Model*?

Anyway, my first girlfriend's dad was so scary he told me I wasn't allowed in the house with his daughter alone after school, which was prime make-out time. I could talk to her *on the doorstep*. This was in the 80s, not Victorian-era Britain where pornography was black-and-white images of a lady's bare ankle. Neither of her parents were home after school, but I obeyed this rule, for fear of those massive baseball catcher's hands and his hurty-tools twisting me into a human U-bend.

Fast forward, and everything changes when you're a dad to daughters. You see the world through a different lens. A telescopic lens on a rifle.

I always wanted to be one of those cool dads. I thought I would be, because my job is pretty cool. I was interviewing U2 frontman Bono, and we were talking about being dads. I put it to him that he'd actually be that rare thing—a cool dad.

'You'd think so,' he said. Then he told a story about Jay-Z and Beyoncé staying at his home in Dublin. Pretty cool, right? Two of the world's hottest stars, staying at yours! The bragging rights over your mates would be huge.

'Your kids must've been blown away,' I said to Bono.

He continued his story, saying that at one point during the night, he went to get some more wine. I'm guessing that when Bono goes to get more wine, it's not to see if there's anything decent left among the crap stuff people have left from a previous gathering. You can always spot the shit wine because a guy will dump it and run, but any good drop they turn up with, they give it the big, 'Might want to open this now, it's a front-facing shiraz that needs some air.' Whatever, Marc with a C. Never trust Marcs with a C, or Stephens with a 'ph'.

Where were we? Bono! The U2 frontman! Bono went to get some more wine, and on the way he happened to overhear his fifteen-year-old daughter on the phone. And word for word, this is what she was saying: 'Yeah, Dad's in there now, boring the arse off them about third-world debt.'

Then Bono told me: 'The thing was, Christian, I *was* boring the arse off them about third-world debt.' Those nights round at Bono's must really fly.

Anyway, this just shows that no dad is cool. Don't even waste your time trying.

We also like to think we're laid-back dads, but no. Since bringing my girls halfway around the world to follow my dream, I'm sure they will want to go travelling and follow theirs. And before they do that, I'll sit them down in front of the movie *Taken* and tell them it's a documentary.

I was once asked to DJ at my daughter's school disco. Did I take the job because it would make me a cool dad? No, I did it so I could *follow her every move with spotlights from an elevated position.* If any boy went within the same postcode—pregnancy test.

'Would you like to dance with me?'

'I can't, the strange DJ's turned the music off and put on a documentary about teenage single parents.'

Megaphone voice 'SLOWLY MOVE AWAY FROM THE GIRL.'

'But Daddy, he was just trying to give me a gobstopper.'

'That's clearly a euphemism. Take two steps left, I can't get a clean shot.'

A modern dad is a terrified half-man. Scared of screwing up his kid's self-esteem, and scared he's being a terrible parent. Pretending to understand TikTok.

Us modern dads are caring and sensitive. We read blogs on sugar intake and know that gluten is the most dangerous gateway drug in the world. Our parents weren't like this. I don't think I had a glass of water until I was 32.

My kids aren't really that scared of me. They shouldn't be. Well, maybe just a little bit. But the only thing I have over them is turning off the wi-fi. What a lame threat: 'Don't make me turn the router off!' It's nothing compared to the hours imagining what my dad might do when he got home from work.

Back in my day, Dad was basically the Supreme Court. Unless you got arrested for blowing up a rescue dogs' home, there was very little justice he had to dispense. You were never going to get in big enough trouble for your offence to be referred by your mum to the higher court of your dad.

Your mum was the County Court, doling out punishments for petty offences day after day. Small claims shit. You weren't quite sure what you would have to do to get your dad involved in the justice process, but just like wondering what an alien invasion or a nuclear winter would be like, you really didn't want to find out.

The phrase 'wait until your dad gets home' was Mum's County Court passing the responsibility to Dad's Supreme Court.

Our dads were more like dictators or semi-mythical beings. A nod of the head or the odd mumble passed for communication. For years, I thought my dad had low motor functions. But no, he was just a 1970s dad.

•

All of which explains why, when I met my daughter's boyfriend for the first time, he wasn't quaking in my presence. Which upset me.

For years, I'd thought about this moment. Meeting the first boyfriend. I'd be finishing digging a shallow grave and casually mumble 'Hi' as I asked him to help me carry something.

It would be a body bag with a mannequin in it, but he wouldn't know that. We'd carry it to that grave in the garden and I'd simply say, Clint Eastwood–style, 'I don't much care for folk who lie to me.' Then I'd casually start whistling, like it was no biggie. Like this wasn't the first time I'd had to do this.

But that's not what I did.

I said 'Hello' and 'Nice to meet you.' And then I did something really sad. Any time the kids have a friend over, I, as a hard-wired professional people-pleaser, start to do some schtick so they'll like me.

Yes, I'm saying I wanted my daughter's boyfriend to like me. I actually went giddy when Ruby told me after he'd left, 'He said your dad's funny.' Which was nice, although part of me would have preferred, 'He actually shat his pants when he met you.'

I knew she had a 'boyfriend' but seeing him, in my own home, *lying down on my couch*, was something else. I was happy for her—it's an amazing time in our lives, those first flushes of young love.

Just maybe don't have that amazing time in my house, or on my couch.

Nothing prepares you for its dizzying highs and its can't-get-out-of-bed lows. All of it. It marks the first time your heart is cracked wide open to a previously unknown joy. Then at some point, that same tender heart, so fresh and vulnerable, is truly broken, by a disappointment so painful it feels physical. And it is.

My first girlfriend dumped me. In life, someone has to be the dumper and someone the dumpee. Adele really should write a smash hit called that, 'Someone Has To Be the Dumper, Someone Has To Be the Dumpee'. I was the dumpee. It crushed me. I sought solace in listening to miserable music played at very high volume in my bedroom.

My dad, not a patient man, would storm in, smelling of talcum powder and Old Spice aftershave, and say, 'Open the curtains in here, son! It's a beautiful day out there and you're listening to this miserable bollocks.' He really would've made a great music critic for *The Guardian*, my dad.

After he walked out, The Cure would get cranked back up as Robert Smith spoke for me when he sang 'Boys Don't Cry'. It's a great song about a young boy (me) who wants the girl back but can't break out of his imposed shell of rigid masculinity. Or to my dad it was 'miserable bollocks'.

Oh Leanne Harris, why did you dump me?

You get over it, though. It's not like you secretly track them down on Facebook 35 years later and see they're a childless, twice-divorced, part-time vet's assistant who's living alone in a caravan, and think, 'Bet you regret dumping me now, Leanne!' I mean, who would do that?

So, my daughter, my angel, the little girl whose tiny little cute shoes I used to put on her tiny little cute feet, is on the couch before me, interlocked with a boy. And while she was high on the rush, I'd hit a new low.

My life as a dad, as I'd known it, was suddenly over. I felt like a fading football coach, sacked from the job I'd held successfully for years. Now I had to reapply as some kind of dad consultant.

Thanks, Australia, for your super dose of teenage hormones, and for boys keen on my girl.

As her boyfriend was leaving, Ruby, having waved him off with her face flushed with joy, turned to me, who was staring silently and taking in the scene, and said:

'This must be hard for you, Dad, it must feel like you've been replaced.'

Thanks, daughter, for helping me identify just what that searing aching pain in my heart is. I had been replaced. Nothing had prepared me. Parenthood is a constant cycle of arrivals and departures. My little girl was arriving in a new place in her life. And I was departing.

Replaced.

•

While being replaced by a boyfriend hurt, another replacement really stung.

Lois, my youngest daughter, played football, or soccer as it's incorrectly often called in Australia. It was a real bond between us, our shared love of the game. But that bond was dropped for Australian rules football.

This was at the insistence of an AFL legend, Shane Crawford. We were around at his place one Sunday afternoon for a barbecue, that I ended up cooking, otherwise Shane would've killed us all with a chicken cooked so lightly its heart was still beating.

Lois, who can handle her own, was getting in among his four boys fighting with inflatables in the pool. She was more than giving as good as she got and Crawf loved her fighting spirit and talent and begged her to change codes to Australian rules football.

I was horrified as in my mind I had a *Bend It Like Beckham* future for her mapped out. She would play for Manchester United and be my pension. And my beloved code was being replaced by a game that I understood about as well as I understood theoretical physics.

But being a parent means putting your needs second and their best interests first. So we encouraged her to give it a go.

And she loved footy.

She played for the school team and then joined the local team, Hampton Rovers. Which at least sounded British. I went to watch her first game and seeing as they were kids and girls, and being a basic white dad, I just presumed it would be touch football.

How wrong I was. This was Australia. This was footy.

As I gasped from the boundary at the full contact on the pitch—and I'm a UFC fan who has sat cage-side at some truly brutal fights—a fellow local dad leant over and, noticing the look of shock on my face, cheerfully told me, 'The girls are actually rougher than the boys.'

I saw hair being pulled, boobs upper-cutted, faces smashed into the ground: it was like a Tarantino movie. And they all seemed to love every minute of it.

I also saw the camaraderie before and after a game, the coaches fostered a great team spirit with these girls.

Every weekend I'd be a boundary-line dad. It was the best.

During the week I would take Lois into the garage, get my boxing pads out, she would glove up and eagerly box as I showed her the basics and worked on her fighting spirit. My wife would come in and urge me to 'tone it down a bit' after seeing me show our daughter how to elbow and knee. I think I was getting too carried away, to be honest. Liam Neeson in *Taken* is my role model as a dad.

Things came to a head when one game I was cautioned by the umpire after Lois was rough-housed by some opposing team thug, and I yelled, 'Get her back harder! Don't let that go unchecked!' Other dads and mums looked at me horrified. Lois looked embarrassed and did that hand gesture her mum does at me that says, 'Take it easy.'

Later that same game, Lois was tackled way too hard and hit the ground so heavily that I could see she was concussed. That night I rang Shane Crawford as I was monitoring her and wasn't sure what to do. Crawf was kind enough at nine o'clock on a Sunday night to call the team doctor of one of Melbourne's biggest AFL clubs and get their advice. Crawf passed the doctor's advice on to me and also asked, 'Did she smash the kid back that did it?'

The next day I was called to her school as she was feeling unwell. I went to pick her up and as we drove home, she said proudly, 'I got best on field,' and handed me her certificate for this. I also saw it came with a bonus that shows sadly, once again, big money has ruined sport.

A twenty-dollar burger voucher.

Between boyfriends and footy, my daughters had shown me they were fitting in just fine. I was now the only one who certainly wasn't getting any best-on-field awards.

26

Building the treehouse

I wasn't sure at first, but you've bought something different to the radio here, I've almost forgotten your English now, almost.

LISTENER EMAIL

From day one I was different. The accent and being English was only part of it. The way I did radio, the way my show was set up around me, my approach, my love of storytelling and the telling of stories to me, putting the listeners at the centre of what we did. All the rival stations disregarded me, which suited me perfectly.

Before the show started, I told the new team I wouldn't be filling the show with the daily offerings of the latest TV reality show 'stars'. You know, the wannabes from *The Bachelor, Bachelorette, Farmer Wants a Wife, Love Island, The Voice, Tradies Want Handjobs.*

I remember someone looked confused, like I was mad, and said quietly, 'Okay, what will you be doing then?'

Well, not that.

My big thing was to make the show into more of a conversation, and to try wherever possible to be real. This may sound like some dry old guff, but what I'm trying to say is that to me ordinary life is extraordinary: the things we do, who we are pretending to be versus who we really are, those parts of ourselves we try to hide away, the stages of our lives, the thresholds, the transitions, the coming into and out of different seasons of our lives, the joyous, the sad, the firsts, the lasts—what's more interesting than talking about that?

The odd things we do (and checking to see no one saw us doing them), strange rules our families have, crazy relatives, money-making schemes you had as a kid, all of us reflecting, telling stories about it, celebrating it all.

Because even though we call the chat with our kids about how they came into being the 'facts of life', the real fact of life we don't tell them is that it's really hard at times. And sometimes, it's great to make jokes about that.

Laughter is still one of the greatest coping mechanisms to life, connection is the other. That last one I've learnt since moving here.

So I doubled down and set about trying to make something different, not better, an alternative. That flowed from my heart and my team's hearts.

Yeah, on that: you want to make something good, of value in your work, then you need people around you to do that with. I had that in Jack and Pats from day one. Good people.

Jack was recommended to me by the boys Hamish and Andy, he was a sidekick known as 'Cackling Jack' on their show. I'd first met Jack when they all came to London filming *Gap Year*. I seriously thought he was a stoner. When we started working together I learnt he wasn't, but he was clearly very different from me.

A millennial, with a wonderfully naive take on life, which mine wasn't.

He was flown over to London to be interviewed by me for the role of sidekick. I could do a whole show on that, strange job interviews! He insisted he be flown business class because he had a 'bad back'. Years later, I'm yet to see any sign of this condition. That's Jack. Human slinky.

He has a heart of gold and is a very, very funny man. There is a smile in his voice that's happened recently, it's a joy when people you work with grow into their potential and take risks, leaps themselves. He has always put so much faith in me; he said I'm his mentor. Truth is I've also learnt from him. It's a joy working with him.

Then Pats.

She's a game-changer. Women are often narrowcast in radio, in restrictive roles to keep those naughty boys in check: *'Oh, come on you guys!'*

Pats isn't that. She's so much more. When I first met her and worked with her I couldn't believe she hadn't been used more on air. She's world class. When she speaks from her heart, you really listen. She's at her best unfiltered, which is all I've ever asked her to be. I never know what she's going to say, and sometimes she scares me a little. And I need that.

I was blessed to have Jack and Pats.

My producers are a small but kick-arse team. Brad, without whose big-hearted support I don't know if I could have got through some of the harder days. Colette and Rio, stolen from other departments in the station who, although they'd never worked on radio shows before, they seemed like fellow free spirits. All of them believed in me and showed such kindness to me from day one. I know I was a force of nature when we all started, and they'd been used to strict running orders and planning, over-planning.

I'm not really like that. I have ideas, tons of them, but it's more a hazy blueprint with lots of room every day for free-flowing chat to happen, for surprises, to tear the show plan up and chase whatever wind the show picks up. The show must never bore or drag, that's the cardinal sin.

I had no idea whether it would work, but this was all I could do. Good people making good stuff. I'm happy getting sacked if I tried my best to build my own treehouse of joy, hope and laughter. I wanted to do what was in my heart. I genuinely wanted a show that could be a little beacon of light.

The longer I was in Australia, and really starting to love our growing life here, I really wanted the show to do well, not for the ego, but because I wanted to stay here. I didn't want to go back to England.

I realised that if I was to succeed, I had to entertain them so much they'd forgive me my Englishness!

I thought I had to do that, but it wasn't what they wanted. There was something else I needed to learn.

Early on, though, it seemed my Englishness would mean I wouldn't even get a chance.

Then, what felt like small doorways started to present themselves, and with them the invitation to ignore them or take the risk and uncertainty of what was on the other side.

•

The first time I felt I was getting some momentum and connecting with them was when the station was doing 'Pay Your Bills', a giveaway where listeners' bills would be paid off. I've done this in the UK and it's a well-known radio promotion.

I got an email from a listener named Robyn, and this poor woman had just suffered too much. I asked my producer to get her on air as she needed money, more than the amounts we were giving away, for something so simple. We had to help. One of the team said this was maybe 'too dark and heavy' for a breakfast show. They were saying the right thing—we didn't have the ratings that meant we could take a lot of risks.

To me this was a moment where I was really doing what I said I was going to do, that this was more than words. I had values for the show, and unless we turn our values into actions, it's just noise.

It was 7.11 a.m. when I called her up live on air. And she broke the hearts of every single person listening. She wanted money for two headstones, for her sons who had sadly passed away within a few years of each other. When she said that, she slowed down time. Everyone leant in to hear her.

Robyn just wanted money for something to remember them by, something permanent.

In a life that had taken just about everything she had from her.

As I was hearing her and giving her room to talk openly about the real pain of grief and loss, about wanting to end her life at times, all this live on air—and yeah, it was dark and heavy— I hoped we were bringing it out into the light, of course she'd feel like that. There was silence in the studio and from around my team, everyone looked at the ground, I started to shake from the effort of trying not to cry but I couldn't hold back any longer, my voice betrayed me and I started to choke up. On air.

This wasn't good.

I feared everyone judging me, *the weepy English DJ.*

'What's he doing NOW? Where did they find this guy?'

Lovely Robyn started to console me! Like the awesome mum she must've been. I felt so ashamed that I was the one being emotional and that she was trying to make me feel better.

Not that I should be ashamed anymore, I'd cried in the arms of a man in a shed and a boxer.

Then something *truly* remarkable happened.

After our chat ended and I'd said we'd get the headstones, I went into the ad break and swiftly took myself to the toilet to get myself together. As I returned to the studio and walked past my producers I saw something that made me pause to check it was really happening.

All the phone lines were filled up, with callers who had also been moved to tears by Robyn. People wanted to help, even those who didn't have much money. Some thanked me for giving them a wake-up call to how grateful they should be in their lives. All because of Robyn.

My heart swelled again when she sent me a photo of the headstones a few weeks later.

I think Robyn, and the year I'd had full of struggles—how I'd been forced to talk openly about those, to risk being vulnerable, which made me feel so uncomfortable—actually drew the listeners to me more than just me being funny. I didn't know it at the time, but something was happening. It wasn't just about radio. It was about us. People. And life.

And I loved all of that.

•

After this, I became a bit more me and less of an act. I'd always tried to be open and conversational, but the trials of the past year had made me shed another layer in a way.

People started to contact me and they were not saying that they hated me/my accent/poster/the idea of me/me breathing/me talking on their radio.

Wow.

They were reaching out, saying thank you, saying how they were moved. I got messages like this:

I hated you at first, then I heard your call with Robyn and I'm emailing to say I'm sorry for judging you so harshly. Thank you for coming here. I hear empathy and compassion coming from what you are doing.

This was so amazing to be part of. The change.

Robyn's story had opened something up. In me and in the listeners. It influenced how I approached the show from then on and paved the way for what happened a few weeks later, which I think changed forever how the audience felt about the show.

27

The Peter Logan effect

After hearing today's show, that came out of nowhere, I had to pull over. I was crying so much, tears I needed, then I finally went back to dad's grave . . . thank you.

LISTENER EMAIL

'I don't think you should do it, Chris, no one wants to hear about cancer first thing in the morning.'

This isn't an argument with my producer, it's with my Uber Producer.

My wife.

Biggest fan, biggest critic.

Both equally important.

Is there a good time of day to hear about cancer? I thought.

An email had been sent to me from a man called Peter Logan.

Peter was in his fifties and had terminal, stage 4 bowel cancer.

His story was that his condition wouldn't be the way it was if he'd done the test. In Australia, once you hit 50, the government sends you something the locals call *'the poo test'*. Obviously, a medical term.

As the name might suggest, the test is for bowel cancer, and Peter got his, and did what many men do, shoved it in the back of the closet and forgot all about it. If he'd done the test, his life and his family's life would be very different.

Peter wanted to ask if I could use his story as a warning to my listeners. I called Peter and we had a great chat; he'd spent a few years working in London where he used to listen to me every morning, before moving back home to Melbourne. I asked if he would like to come in to be on the show and tell his story himself, no one better than him, rather than second-hand from me. He leapt at the chance.

I now had to tell management as this was unprecedented. I could tell some of my bosses weren't sure, they were worried it could make people tune out, but they seemed to understand my reasons for wanting to have Peter on the show.

I got why some didn't want to devote part of the show to talking about cancer. It's no one's idea of a fan hangout in the morning. Cancer terrifies us, it's robbed so many of us of mums and dads, brothers and sisters, sons and daughters.

It lurks in the shadows, literally showing up as a shadow on X-rays, and I hoped we could bring it out into the light. Peter's message could—would—save people's lives. Why wouldn't I want to give people that?

I was still overthinking everything, fearing one false move or idea could ruin the show. This could be a mistake. It's not a ratings booster. Breakfast radio is supposed to be all about 'keeping it light', and suddenly the English guy on the radio is rolling out cancer corner.

Peter's story was so sad, but it also offered hope. This was bigger than radio. It's about life. I took the leap, my team were with me, and so we turned *The Christian O'Connell Show* into *The Peter Logan Show*. I had jingles made calling it that, T-shirts made for Peter emblazoned with 'The Peter Logan Show' and in tiny letters 'with Christian O'Connell'.

We didn't just get him in for a quick chat, he co-hosted the show for an hour. I got him to introduce the songs. He was a natural. Full of vim and vigour, he blew everyone away with his presence, honesty and refusal to be bowed by his diagnosis.

His last link on air with me was a piece of radio I will always remember. It made the hairs on the back of my neck stand up. He spoke like a preacher on the mount about life, using our brief time here, the regrets he had and not doing the test, how he wouldn't see his daughters get married, walk them down the aisle, or become a grandad.

I carried on with the show, or tried to, after big hugs with Pete and while I was setting up the next hour, mid-sentence I saw him through my studio window, his young daughters hugging him, and I thought of the overwhelming love I have for mine and I lost the power to speak. Which is kinda important on live radio.

I quickly played a song, then another, then another. It took me a while to get myself together. I texted both my daughters and told them how much I loved them. Peter came back into the studio to apologise for making me so upset, we hugged again, and I thought at least he saw the power in what he had done that morning. But it was just the start of it.

•

For days and weeks after we were getting calls from listeners thanking Peter for being so brave in sharing his story. How cathartic and healing it had been to hear cancer talked about on the radio and defiantly so, just like Pete.

I never had any idea at the time just how big the Peter Logan effect would be. Peter told people to do the test, don't end up like him. He told them when they returned the test they should write on the back 'Peter sent me'.

Within the next few weeks, thousands of completed poo tests got sent back. The Peter Logan effect saw a 600 per cent increase in returned kits. What a legend.

Peter became folklore on the show. He saved lives, he changed mine.

After months and hundreds of hours of ideas, stories and jokes, the show finally connected on a deeper level—thanks to Peter, and the pureness of empathy and the power of being courageously vulnerable, of being real. That's a quality in short supply in our world, one full of liars, cheats, fakes and frauds.

Sadly, this story doesn't have a happy ending.

Towards Christmas, Peter started to decline and I went to see him to say goodbye. I was met by a grinning Pete, as always, but in his eyes, I saw a fear in a brave man. His unbelievably strong wife, Sharon, administering the cocktails of drugs that even Keith Richards would think too much.

Despite all of this, Peter said something to me that made me spit out my beer: yeah, we shared beers. Peter was an Arsenal football fan and, like most Arsenal fans, bitter about other clubs' success. Only sports fans will understand this, the pure rampant tribalism sport has, and how all fans have certain rival clubs they *hate*, with a passion maybe even bigger than the love for their own club. They not only hate this one particular club, but they also hate to see it do well.

For Peter, this hated club was Liverpool. And they were a resurrected team under Jürgen Klopp, heading to win the English Premier League. As I was getting ready to say the words neither of us wanted to say, goodbye, Peter sighed and said, smiling: 'I just hope I'm gone before I have to see Liverpool lift the fucking cup.'

28

Drives with my daughters

I guess you do know some stuff about something after all.

LOIS O'CONNELL

One day you wake up and see with horror your daughters have been replaced. In their place now are zombies who've eaten your sweet, innocent little girls. The little girls are no more, the new version of themselves are just as beautiful, but they now reveal themselves as spies who've been observing you secretly for years.

They know your weak spot.

They have you sussed, more than you know yourself.

Finding ways to still spend time with them becomes challenging, so I did what my dad used to do with me: take them in my car for a drive. It's the best. Without taking them to a car wash and telling them about sex.

When one or both of the girls and I would go for a car ride, I would play songs and tell them about the band, then ask them to play me a song they liked. I started to pick songs I thought could open up some areas of conversation. I'd school them in the classics, The Who (at least once a week I'll hear them cranking out 'Baba O'Riley' from their rooms, the future is looking good, folks), Led Zep, The Pixies, Stevie Nicks, Stones, The Boss.

One trip after a tough week for them I played them The Beatles' 'Let It Be'. Telling the story told to me by Paul McCartney (*klang!* might just wanna pick up that name I dropped) about how he was visited by his mum, who died from cancer when he was just fourteen, in a dream when the band were nearing the end. How it has a kind of hymnal feel to it, and how in life we have to learn when to push, when to paddle and when to *Let Things Be*. I then paired this with 'Here Comes the Sun' (yeah Mr Radio DJ), linking the songs with a little Beatles double play, which to me is a song about how after darkness and tough times the sun always rises over a new horizon, as in life. We sat in silence and reverence as the song worked its magic on us. Feeling it. Sharing a moment. This felt great.

I then asked them to play a song, and they picked 'Papa Don't Preach' by Madonna.

Okay, very funny, girls.

They liked music so much I got them a vinyl turntable each and they learned to love, like I do, the greatest music format in the world, vinyl. I get such a kick hearing them blast Fleetwood Mac out of their bedrooms.

I also took them to their first live music gig. It's a formative experience, your first time seeing live music. It's so exciting, all the people there, the energy, the noise, and for me it was the first time I'd 'seen' someone famous. You weren't as overly familiar with your favourite bands and rock stars then; nowadays you've seen too many Instagram posts from them trying to convince you they are *real* people. I don't want my rock stars to be like me, I want them throwing TVs out of windows and trashing hotel rooms. Before social media and YouTube, the only time you saw your favourite stars was seeing them live.

Which made it extra special. You wouldn't believe your own eyes were seeing actual live-in-the-wild rock stars.

My first gig was INXS. If I close my eyes, I can see it all now. Me and my mate drove up to London in his VW Beetle, it was 1990 and we were seventeen. The Suicide Blonde tour. INXS were amazing, Michael Hutchence was mesmerising in his black leather trousers, swigging from a bottle of vodka. Hutch looking as cool as, and women going wild. Rock and roll right there in front of my very own eyes. You never forget your first.

My daughters were lucky, their old man could get them into just about any live gig in the UK. I've taken them and their mates to see Coldplay at opening nights of huge shows; they've had one of Britain's best rock bands, the Stereophonics, play live in their own kitchen and had school friends come round to watch.

So what's it to be, girls? Let the genie work his magic.

'Can you get us tickets to One Direction?'

No girls, don't blow your first like this!

But they insisted. They loved 1D. Like millions of girls and boys did. As I didn't play that kind of music I couldn't blag tickets, and it was sold out. So I went online to get tickets and sell a kidney to get us good seats.

•

Let me tell you about that show. Twenty thousand screaming fans making a noise that I'd never heard before. When we got there, a security guard recognised me and came over, offering me some ear plugs. I thanked him but said I'd be fine. This isn't my first rodeo, my friend, these ears are hardened.

That was until 1D came out on stage and the screaming, times 20,000, started.

My organs were being eviscerated. I looked around for my new mate and he came running over like a soldier coming to the aid of a fallen comrade pinned down by enemy gunfire. 'Medic! I need a medic here.'

Looking around at all the teenagers there, I kicked myself on a lost opportunity. That I didn't buy a load of booze and sell it to all the under-age kids there at a huge mark-up. Offsetting the cost of the tickets.

Did I mention this gig was at one o'clock in the afternoon? A matinee! Bless them little One Direction fellas back then.

Harry Styles led the band out on stage yelling, 'Hello London, are you ready to rock?'

Not at lunchtime, mate, my lot have just had pizza and ice cream, they're a little bit sluggish. Plus, it's *one o'clock in the afternoon.*

Tell you what though, it's not a bad idea. The matinee gig. What about matinee rock shows for us grown-ups? We're all knackered in the evening, as are the Foo Fighters these days. Dave Grohl is in his fifties. No need for babysitters, go see a concert, then you're back home in time for dinner.

Half an hour into the One Direction show, they'd done the hits. Something extraordinary happened: they stopped singing and it was time for a Q and A! *What?* Not at $200 a ticket it isn't, mate.

Giant screens came down for the audience to text their questions. I was losing the will to live. I tried to text *'Can I have a refund?'* but my kids grabbed my phone off me.

The band had just been asked what they liked to have for their dinner. (For the record, Harry Styles is a lasagne man, Niall a margarita pizza.)

My daughters then did something I'll always be so proud of, they asked if we could go home 'because it's really boring now'.

•

Melbourne is the music capital of Australia. There are some great venues here and the local music scene is brilliant and so many international bands love playing in the city. Over the summer there are many live shows and festivals. The girls have balanced out the 1D since moving here, seeing Elton John, Taylor Swift, Billie Eilish and The 1975.

I used Australians' love of live music for a competition in my first six months. I wanted listeners to reunite their old bands. Maybe a band they used to have with their mates at school. Maybe you were pretty good and starting to get record label interest. Maybe something broke the band up, a woman, a dad telling you to focus on your studies or learn a trade.

I called the competition 'One Last Dream'. I offered a spot on the bill of a big festival playing in front of more than 10,000 people. I had no idea if the listeners would go for this, seeing as it was in my early days of eating poop in the ratings, but I took the leap, and they loved this one.

So many listeners jumped on board to reunite their old bands, and used Facebook to track down former band members they'd lost touch with. I even offered to hire private detectives if you couldn't find your old drummer or keyboard player. More importantly, I was actually asking them to reunite that old you, who had dreams, who was going to be a rock star, with the current you, who worked in sales and didn't like it at all.

Sometimes life isn't fair, it doesn't care for your dreams, you may well have had talent and been your local town's 'band' that everyone knew and said were going to be stars. But it never happened.

Now you're in your forties, fifties, your kids just see you as you are now, old and boring (well, mine see me that way anyway). Not as someone who played to packed pubs, had women fancy them, as someone who had dreams.

This became another little moment in the early days of me on air when the listeners connected to me from a different place. Letting people tell their stories, I wasn't trying to just make them laugh, or do a radio stunt, I was talking about life. I loved how they connected to that.

We had so many entries, old tapes and CDs, it was a battle of the old bands. We met some amazing characters, we shared moments of heartbreak when hearing about band members who had died, we heard exciting raw recordings from bands meeting up in their garages and playing together for the first time in decades and 'the magic was still there'.

We had a tough time getting it down to three bands that were picked to play in a pub live. We then took a song from each and I played them on air the next day to find a winner.

Once we had the winning band, Bungalow, we were ready for the big show. On the Friday before the weekend of the festival, we had the daughter of the lead singer of Bungalow on air. She melted many hearts when she said she had never seen her dad so happy as the last few weeks.

Bringing them on stage after telling the crowd their story and about 'One Last Dream', I was nervous for the guys. I wanted them to enjoy it and to meet the moment. Not to be overwhelmed by it. To step out of themselves and respond to the invitation.

They smashed it. I mean that, they were so good that the headlining bands, who were playing later in the day, stopped what they were doing backstage and joined me at the side of the stage to watch Bungalow. When they came off stage, I saw grown men with eyes filled with tears. I joined them!

The bands that came runners-up thanked me for giving them back that part of them, it had woken something up. I just loved this, and it was better than any ratings wins.

This is what I came here for.

29

'Man Walks into a Radio Station with Ten Thousand Dollars'

Thank you for coming to Australia with your family, i HATED you at first, even posted something on facebook about you, i'd stopped listening to morning radio, but you've got me back, i laugh, i cry, i hear empathy.

P.s can you play Shania Twain tomorrow at 7 o'clock for me?

LISTENER EMAIL

The real thing I fell in love with in Australia wasn't just the amazing outdoors lifestyle, living five minutes from the ocean and way more sunshine, although they're all pretty awesome.

What I grew to love most was the people. And their big golden hearts.

I'm taking you back to my old life for a moment, which I have to say I was lucky to have, just to understand how different things are now.

Before moving here we lived in a very small town with just two streets, but being England it still managed to have six pubs in those two streets. You may already know this, but there are quite a few pubs in England.

Australia has just over 6000 pubs and bars, that's not bad. *England has 53,000!*

In case you are wondering, the Top 5 most common pub names in Australia are:

1. Royal
2. Commercial
3. Club
4. Grand
5. Railway

The Top 5 most common pub names in England are:

1. Red Lion (I know there are more than 500 Red Lion pubs in the UK as one of my listeners, as part of her bucket list, set out to have a drink in every one of them, and she did!)
2. Royal Oak
3. Crown
4. White Hart
5. Plough

In England, by the way, we use our 53,008 (to be precise) pubs as a means of giving directions: 'If you see the Red Lion, you've gone too far . . . turn around at the King's Arms and go past the

Running Horses and the Bishop on the Bridge is on the left . . . opposite The Queen's Head.'

Here in Australia, it's rubbish as a means of directions.

'Turn left at the filing cabinet, right at the old thing master and if you see a Betamax VCR, you've gone too far.'

This was another learning moment for me, people can dump any old crap they don't want out the front of their homes, and the council will come and collect it . . . at some point. It's called 'hard rubbish'. As you drive around the suburbs you see all manner of stuff: ironing boards, desks, exercise bikes. When I first saw a load of stuff out the front of someone's house, I presumed some cheating love rat had been thrown out of his house by his irate wife.

'. . . get out! How could you?! And take your canoe, ski poles and foot spa . . .'

One listener, when I shared on air my surprise at this, told me she'd once seen a taxidermy cheetah.

When Harry and Meghan came to Melbourne on a Royal visit, they were taken to St Kilda beach. All around that area is hard rubbish dumped outside homes. I could imagine Harry and Mego (as they would call her here) suddenly stopping the Royal motorcade: *'Reverse back please, Higgins . . . Megs . . . is that a Soda Stream and trouser press? Yes, it is, hang on, let me get that.'*

Now back to my former home, Dorking. Dorksville. It's a quiet, charming village. Picture thatched cottage houses, vicars walking through the town chatting to everyone. It actually has more antique shops than pubs. One of these antique shops had in its front window for several months a suit of armour for sale. I mean, full body armour of a knight or guardsman at a castle. Then one day it had gone. I went in to ask who bought it, as it was thousands of dollars, and this old man in a three-piece suit doing *The Times* crossword lowered his glasses at me and said, snobbishly, 'Young fellow, fond of tattoos, not from old money, recently won the lottery he told me, well, he took it all.'

I thought of someone winning millions on the lottery and instead of getting the normal speedboat, mansion and Bentley, goes and buys Richard of Lionheart's suit of armour. Getting his mates to fire nerf guns at him while wearing it and swigging on bottles of Bollinger. It's a good time.

Dorking is nice, decent and famed for being a *good place to bring up kids*. Which also means boring.

Ten years we did there and we loved it for a while but the last few years were killing us with its suffocating *loveliness*.

Life is so different now. I walk the dog on a *beach*, and have to allow extra time for the chats I will have with strangers, people are so friendly here. I look out to the ocean every day I drive to work. I'm never not in awe of the ocean drive to and from work. That's a commute I look forward to. It looks different every single day.

I have got into barbecuing, this is my level of cooking. Nuking meats on a grill. I've watched YouTube videos on it, ordered meat rubs, even went on a one-day course to become a 'grill master'. I own several meat thermometers. I've recently bought a smoker after watching the Netflix show *Great American Barbecue Showdown*. I never thought I'd get excited about mates coming round for beers and my brisket. Long way from dinner parties in Dorking and talking about planning for our retirement.

It's the people, though, that are the real stars here. I don't just mean those who listen to me, I mean everyone. I'm talking about real life.

From the day I got here, people just seemed more relaxed than us Brits. Well, only the ones who weren't demanding I be sent back to the UK. And that was, I have to say, a minority (I think, or had to think to survive). People seemed friendly and ready to laugh or chat with you. I remember going to buy a pair of jeans and ended up chatting to the guy behind the counter for almost half an hour. We Brits aren't rude, but we can be reserved and stand-offish at times. Many are the times on a European holiday when you can suddenly feel a sense of national shame as some British sunburnt idiot will ruin everything by yelling, 'Youse got the football on? The Man U game is on, yeah, turn it up lurve for us, we're thirsty, ten beers soon as you can, put the footy on first . . . that's it, no way ref you wanker it's a penalty! . . . those beers coming dahling?'

We don't always travel well.

This Australian openness with each other and the world around you actually changed me. It opened me up. I talk to strangers way more now, I carry myself a bit lighter when I'm out and about.

•

Nothing showed me just how caring Australians can be than what happened with a man called 'Patrick'. This may or may not be his actual name.

This story will always be folklore on my show, referred to in hushed tones as simply 'Man Walks into a Radio Station with Ten Thousand Dollars'.

A grandmother, Janette, had emailed me asking for help with her autistic grandson, Rheagan. This beautiful three-year-old boy needed some special support: poor kid couldn't sleep alone, had separation anxiety, and his family was worried about what would happen in two years' time and how he would cope at school. They wanted to get this gorgeous kid a therapy dog, from a wonderful place called Smart Pups. The dog would give him the loving unconditional support only a dog can, sleep next to him at night, would follow him wherever he went, and if he got lost the dog would be trained to track him down.

The problem was the family needed $20,000 (£11,500) to pay for the training of this wonderdog. They had twelve months to do it, they had worked so hard to get the $700 they had raised and their time was running out. This amazing grandmother was doing two jobs, including Uber driving at night without her daughter even knowing. That's the sacrifice a mum makes when her single-parent daughter is just struggling to get through every day.

I called Janette the night I saw her email. This poor woman was so strong and just wanted the money for her grandson and her daughter. I made no promises but said I'd love to see what we could do. She thought me calling her at 7 p.m. was a 'prank call'. Bit of a cruel one, wouldn't you say? How savage are the wind-up DJs here?

Supergran Janette was on air the next day and people wanted to help. She was embarrassed to be asking for help. We all feel this sometimes, don't we? Some shame about stepping forward with an outstretched hand. Yet we, as humans, as I have been shown time and time again here, have a natural intrinsic hard-wired desire to help each other. It just needs to be reminded to us.

We had kids calling in to donate their pocket money, tradies offering that weekend's beer money, and within 24 hours we were calling Janette and her daughter to say they could get Rheagan his Smart Pup. Rheagan was going to have that puppy he always wanted. Just the best news you could give anyone.

After that show I was riding so high, being humbled by the kindness of strangers I would never meet, I sat down on the studio floor just so I could take it all in.

I was promptly snapped out of my studio sit-in when things got even more unreal: the station receptionist said there was someone to see me. I went down to reception and saw this big tradie in a high-viz vest holding an envelope. I said hi and he handed me the envelope: it was a big fat one, fat like gangsters' envelopes are fat full of cash. I did wonder if this man in high-viz was a very modern mobster who cared about health and safety.

The man, Patrick, was giving me $10,000 in cash to help Rheagan get a Smart Pup. I was stunned and didn't know how to deal with this so I invited him to come into the studio so we could chat privately. I took him into the studio and passed wide-eyed producers wondering who the high-viz steel-capped-boot–wearing guy was and why I was holding a big fat bundle of cash.

I said, 'This is really generous, Patrick, but we have the money for a dog now, please take it back.'

He patted the fat envelope away. 'Give it to someone else who needs a Smart Pup.'

Patrick then told me he had to get back to work quickly or his boss would get angry; he had a good, honest, hard-working job on building sites. Ten thousand dollars is a huge amount of money and I urged him to take it back.

'You really touched my heart hearing about that poor boy. My hobby is gold prospecting and I've cashed in a little lump for this,' he explained, nodding at the envelope.

A little lump?

Did you also say your hobby is gold prospecting?

Hearing this, I pleaded again for him to take his money back, as I guessed it must have been part of his nest egg for him and his wife. This wasn't an option for Patrick. The producers looked on at us, still confused as to what might be going on in the soundproofed studio, seeing me thrust bundles of cash at a guy and him refuse it.

Maybe thinking I was trying to pay folks to listen. And I couldn't even get them to do that.

I asked for a photo so we could share his story the next day, but Patrick was one of those quiet heroes, he didn't want to come on air and have his picture taken. He wanted no publicity for what he'd done. He also said he didn't want his wife to know.

We can all relate to that can't we?

The number of times I've been in the doghouse after giving a nugget of gold away, again!

We shook hands, I thought I saw a little glisten and moisture in his eyes, and he said he needed to do this and didn't want to say anymore. We then upgraded the formal handshakes to my preferred method of saying goodbye, hugging, and off Patrick went back to his building site to swing a hammer having just given me $10,000 in cash to help a child in need.

Australians don't like big heads or big public shows of emotion but I have seen, heard and felt their huge hearts and generosity.

Not long ago, the listeners hated me; now they were opening their hearts, and their gold reserves.

30

'Who's Calling Christian?'

A guy who knows his guitarist reckons Billy Idol is calling
tomorrow. He can't today as he's too busy.

PRODUCER TO ME (THE BIG TAKEAWAY, BILLY IDOL IS BUSY?)

I had started to feel that with Robyn, Jeanette, Patrick and Peter
sharing their stories, and my own life away from radio actually
approaching the outer fringes of normality, the show was really
finding its place. Its heart.

I knew too I had been sharing stories all the time. Now
I realised people *were* listening, but it took three incredible people
to show me the way.

The tipping point was another show idea that both terrified
and excited me. It scared me as it was a hugely different way of
doing radio and was totally driven by the listeners. At the time
there still weren't a lot of listeners connecting to me and this could
be too different, too much and too soon.

It was something I had created and became known for in the UK. A genuinely ground-breaking and game-changing idea. But I had built that up over years and years. None of that mattered here.

The segment was called 'Who's Calling Christian?' and the idea was for listeners to get celebrities to call me. It was a big ask for an audience still getting to know me.

The idea came to me on the way to meet my team in the pub for lunch back on XFM in the early 2000s. Probably a Red Lion. In the street I walked past the actor who played Sergeant Bob Cryer in the long-running police TV show *The Bill*. Not exactly an A-lister but I reacted as if he was when I recounted excitedly to my team who I had just seen, a famous person in the street!

From the impressed reactions I started to wonder if there was an idea in this: ask people to look out for celebrities—whether it's a sports star, musician, TV presenter, someone who was big in the 80s—and if they see them, get them to call me live on air.

We developed this idea and offered a bounty for the winning celebrity you got to call the show. The ice-breaker was that the celebrity who got voted the favourite call in two weeks of running the segment would also win cash for the charity of their choice.

Despite a worryingly slow start it took off, and became something I did many times over the years. Some highlights were Prime Minister Tony Blair calling me live from 10 Downing Street, and Charlize Theron calling from a private jet where the pilot was refusing to take off until she called me. Chris Martin, he of Coldplay, called in, but he was actually entering someone more famous than him—he was around at Steven Spielberg's house!

I wasn't sure if it would work in Australia though, whether it was too soon to ask so much of an audience still getting to know me.

Despite my fears, my team backed me and we went for it and 'Who's Calling Christian?' debuted in Australia in October 2019. The show was just over a year old.

My biggest worry was location. In Britain, we had a bigger pool of celebrities for listeners to contact, forgotten stars of the 70s, 80s and 90s. Many Hollywood stars come to London for press junkets, to live there and to star in West End plays.

For the audience, this was a seismic change. I'm asking them to *not call me*, but to get someone famous to call.

The risk of this backfiring and me being humiliated was high.

To my absolute joy, the listeners made it fly. From the get-go, day one. They contacted celebrities on Instagram, Facebook, emailed their agents. They got celebrities to call me live in Australia from all over the world.

The highlights came thick and fast. Here are some of my favourites:

1. Thor

One of our listeners, John, called saying his son worked for Chris Hemsworth—Thor to you and me. Yeah, him again.

John told us on air that Chris Hemsworth even worked for his glazing business when he was nineteen and was so bad that he had to fire him.

Do Marvel know this is part of Thor's origin story?

John's son Aaron said he would try to get Chris to call in. Then nothing, until the second week.

Just back from doing the school run, Chris called us live. He was brilliant and the joy of this feature is they aren't in interview mode. Chris was at home and talked more about the hell of the school run than a movie he would be plugging on a chat show. He showed us a different side of himself, sharing a funny story about getting the prosthetics department on a movie to put a fake nose and face on him so he could go out unnoticed on the beers with his mates. Imagine if you were in a pub and you saw a guy at the bar sipping his beer and suddenly his nose slipped off and into his drink. You'd think you were so inebriated that it was time to call it a night and head home.

2. James Corden

From 'Carpool Karaoke' to 'Who's Calling Christian?'

One of our listeners contacted James Corden on his Instagram account, and no matter how famous you are, when you're bored you get your phone out and you scroll, scroll, scroll on social media. He saw the message, used to listen to my old show and was on it a few times, so he picked up the phone and called in.

James smashed it, he's naturally a very funny and talented man. As he had risked everything by moving to America to start a late-night chat show, a Brit and outsider, the first few minutes of our chat were us catching up and swapping notes about our similar-ish experiences. Though he wasn't having needles jabbed into his carpool and I wasn't singing with Paul McCartney and Stevie Wonder in my Range Rover.

3. Olivia Newton-John

This was a big deal, Olivia Newton-John calling in. She is royalty to Australians and her struggles with cancer are inspirational. She was funny and full of real presence and joy, she lit everyone up.

For two weeks we had these amazing chats with whoever was calling in from wherever they were in the world. Radio without a safety net. I would have to improvise an interview immediately live on air when I found out who was on the line at the same time as the listeners. I loved it.

As this is flying-by-the-seat-of-your-pants radio, it's going to go wrong sometimes. Lucy Lawless, star of *Xena: Warrior Princess*, called in and as we were chatting I quickly googled her. I mistook her for another actress who she looks like, who is in the big American TV show *Billions*. I started asking Lucy about *Billions*, which she is not in. She's such a pro she answered my dumb questions politely rather than embarrass me on air.

The moment we played a song, my team came in, pointing out my huge clanger. They're not as polite as Lucy. At least I'm boosting team morale.

'Who's Calling Christian?' proved to be a huge success that people loved listening to and being part of. The way it worked so well showed me that the show was now really firing. It had the heart of Robyn, Janette and Peter, but it also had surprise and unpredictability. I could feel momentum.

For me, what excited me so much was that I could feel that people wanted to be a part of what was happening here on the show. I think I was getting better, too. I was more creative than I had been for years, taking more risks and leaps, and the big one— I was more open-hearted. And I really valued the connections I was making with listeners more than any time in over twenty years on the radio.

People seemed to be enjoying what I was doing, putting them and real life at the very centre of the show.

No topic was ever left dead, you could pick up anything we'd talked about whenever you wanted. I made a feature of this called 'Late to the Party', where listeners could email in about anything we'd previously talked about.

My job, as I see it, is to pay attention to life. One day I was driving with the kids after school and I saw a fire engine parked on the street and the firefighters trying to get a cat out of a tree. I pulled over and got out to watch. Being Melbourne, the firefighters were super friendly and as I chatted to one of them, I said I thought it was a myth that they have to get cats out of trees.

He shook his head, 'Nah mate, all the bloody time.'

Next day on air I shared this then asked people for their stories of calling triple zero for a non-emergency reason. All the lines were jammed with callers. My favourite was the lady whose cat got stuck in a tree, as did the firefighter trying to rescue it, and his mate who tried to rescue him, and the cat. She then had to call the fire service again, to get help for her cat and the two very embarrassed firefighters. What a scene!

This to me is what makes my job the best in the world.

One day Jack came in having seen a business advertising 'Burgers and Tax Returns'. We talked about this on air, wondering what came first?

I then asked listeners if they had ever heard of any similar businesses that are amazingly multi-disciplined. Over the next few days, we heard about some brilliant ones:

1. Costume Hire and Dog Grooming
Great, get yourself a pirate fancy-dress outfit while your shitzu gets a haircut.

2. Clothing Alterations and Table Tennis Store
Again, were they sitting around bored one day at the table tennis store and thought, 'Hang on, we could easily take up trousers or a hem line in between selling table tennis gear.'

3. Pet Crematorium and Car Mechanic

As someone who has lost a pet, I wondered if the heartbreak of going to get the ashes of your beloved cat or dog could be lessened by at the same time getting your car serviced or the carburettor fixed.

4. Cafe, Taxidermy and Hair Salon

This place is basically the Swiss Army knife of shops.

5. Fish and Chip Shop and Brothel

Here, extra salty can mean so many things.

Momentum. You could feel it. Suddenly, whatever we tried, the listeners supported. They were smart and funny. I asked them for their 'Weakest Claim to Fame', a really minor encounter with a celebrity. I share a few of these here to show you just how much they were getting it:

'I filled up Tiger Woods's car with petrol, no words were exchanged.'

'I shook hands with a guy who shook hands with Bruce Lee.'

'I sold John Farnham's wife fresh underwear as apparently he likes to wear fresh undies for every show.'

The burning question was, would this momentum be reflected in the ratings?

One month after launching 'Who's Calling Christian?' I was about to find out.

•

I felt less stressed this time ahead of the ratings coming out, the calendar reminder didn't see me grab a blanket and curl up in a dark room. Or a shed. I'd done what I could, if it didn't rate, I'd go out with a show I was proud of. I was doing the best radio I'd done in my career.

I was also not that focused on the ratings because the weekend before they came out it was my wife's fiftieth birthday. After the year we'd had, I decided to throw a big party for her with a load of our new friends, mainly Sarah's. My team were all there as well. They had been my constants.

The theme was 'Dead Famous', come as a dead celebrity. My wife was a stunning Audrey Hepburn, I was supposed to be Prince, but looked more like Captain Hook. I changed midway through the night into Elvis.

It was a big night. I'd over-ordered on booze, the guests all arrived in their awesome outfits, and at one point there were three Freddie Mercurys, which started to confuse guests after a few drinks as to which one you were talking to.

The morning of the party my wife was worried that it wouldn't be a good party, people wouldn't dress up, or it would be awkward, we didn't know everyone well enough. I wanted her to have a great night and to liven everybody up with copious amounts of alcohol. I spent the week before making a killer party playlist. I'd hired music speakers and I would do the music. DJ'ing as Prince/Captain Hook.

I tried to play songs as well for the various outfits, the three Freddies all had a dance-off.

That night there was a buzz in the air, or maybe people were just buzzed from the champagne cocktails I gave them on arrival. Plus, a sangria that had so much rum in it you could get drunk just off the vapours of it. Seriously, your eyes stung if you got within a metre of it.

Then I surprised Sarah with a cake I had made and said a few words. I saw the happy (booze-fuelled) faces all around us, people having a good time and there for Sarah, I was a little emotional, and it wasn't just the Black Sambuca shots. I had found two fellow guests lurking in the utility room like teenagers at a house party about to snag a bottle of Sambuca, and we did something no 40-something should do anymore: shots. By the washing machine. *Rock and roll!*

My wife made a beautiful speech that reflected how both of us were feeling, surrounded by some great new friends in our new home. We caught each other's eyes and we both had tears. Looking out at Margaret Thatcher, three Freddie Mercurys, Johnny Cash and Kurt Cobain, it was like some strange after-life party.

You know when you have those nights that just take off? There is something in the air and it's combustible. They are rare, this was one of them. People danced in our kitchen/dining room as I DJ'd. I'd moved all the couches to the side of the room. House parties are the best. You forget that as you get older.

What really tipped the night over the edge was when my newsreader Pat's husband, Chris, a great guy, Dean Martin tonight, whispered to me, 'Have you got a funnel?'

I had no idea what he was on about. Then he suggested we make a beer bong. Now, this was something I hadn't done since I was nineteen. But, like I said, there was something in the air that night, and why not? But I didn't have a funnel, so like MacGyver, we improvised using a two-litre Coke bottle. We now needed a hose, problem was mine was attached to the wall in our garden, so we got a bread knife and cut a section of it off, in the dark. It took ages. A bread knife is made for cutting bread, not thick garden hose. And friends, this wasn't just any garden hose. This was one I'd just bought and was 'guaranteed 100% kinkless'.

We were like two drunken midwives trying to cut an umbilical cord with a knife that could only handle a loaf of bread. Eventually, we were ready to go.

I turned the music off, my wife glared at me, and I announced it was time for . . . *beer bongs in the garden!* Like it was a traditional special announcement after the cutting of the cake and speeches.

Everyone gathered round, and had a go, even my wife. You've never lived until you've seen Audrey Hepburn chugging a beer bong.

The night ended around 2 a.m. The next morning, we had terrible hangovers. The place was a mess. My kinkless hose was in tatters. It looked like teenagers had wrecked the place while Mum and Dad were out. Not 40- and 50-somethings. I needed to move the furniture back and rather than ask my mate Adam (Fred Astaire) who stayed the night, I rushed around getting it done myself, still having that glow of invincibility from the booze only hours before, and dragged the big couch back over to its place.

As I bent over to lift the deadweight couch, I felt something tear and a searing shocking pain shot into my lower back and spine. The pain was so bad I could hardly breathe. I staggered to the floor, unable to move. Everything jammed up.

I waved goodbye to guests who had stayed the night from the floor, thinking some painkillers would have me up in no time. That didn't work. I really couldn't move. My wife wanted to call for an ambulance; I refused, saying it would be wasting their time. She called a medical helpline and they said if I wasn't able to get up and go to the toilet, then I needed medical help.

I couldn't do that, so I had to pee into a salad bowl while propped up on my elbow on my side. The kids were told not to come into the kitchen, in my wife's usual subtle way:

284

'GIRLS! Your dad is weeing into a salad bowl . . . *Don't come down here but it's really funny!*'

Twenty minutes later two paramedics arrived at our house. They clocked the booze, the mess of the house, and the severed hose and beer bong discarded in the garden. Wasn't hard to put all the clues together. They tried to help me up and couldn't, due to my pain being so severe. I was then introduced to something of an institution in Australia.

The green whistle.

Which was just that, a giant green whistle you sucked on and inhaled sweet pain relief, a strong drug called Penthrox, pretty much giving you instant bliss! Apparently, sports stars when injured ask for the green whistle. I can see why, it's pretty great.

While I sucked away like a kid with a lolly, the paramedics managed to get me into a wheelchair, classy, then outside the house onto a stretcher. It was midday now and the neighbours were really impressed to see me wheeled out of the house sucking on drugs, more than slightly high, waving inanely. I may have also been dribbling.

The paramedics turned out to be listeners of the show and couldn't have taken better care of me.

At the hospital, I got checked out and was diagnosed with a few compressed vertebrae. I needed daily physio and my chiropractor, Simon, my magic man, slowly got me moving. But I could hardly move for the next few days, walking took a lot of time and effort, I'd have to lean on walls and catch my breath back from the searing sickening pain. I ended up missing the radio show for a few days I was in such a bad way.

•

This is why I wasn't on air the day the ratings came out. In fact, the pain had taken my mind very much off them all together.

I was struggling to get out of bed, I had one sock on and was trying to summon the strength and courage to try to get my jeans on when the phone went. I saw it was my boss.

I didn't want to take the call, as I was so fed up with the pain that putting on jeans was causing. I feared my state would be made worse with a ratings drop. Maybe all the pressure had broken my back.

When I answered my phone, I could just tell straight away there was good news from the vibe on the other end.

We must be up, maybe to Number 3 or, dare to dream, even Number 2. Both my boss, Sue, at the station and the man brave enough to risk his career hiring me, Duncan Campbell, were in the office on speaker phone. They could hardly contain themselves, good for them, I thought bitterly, I couldn't even put my jeans on.

'Do you want some good news?' Sue giggled.

Radio bosses *do not giggle.*

I was very close to tears, I was in so much agony. Then I started to think, what if this is *the call*?

No, please, not with me like this. All bent over and nudey.

I'd fantasised about whether this day would ever come, not what it would be like, more would it ever happen to me.

But I was on air in my dream of how it would go down, being carried around the building, not using a salad tong to reach a sock.

But this was the call.

Together they screamed that I was Number 1.

They were both crying they were so happy for me, and after everything me and my family had been through.

They had supported me all the way. I know in private there would've been doubts but I owe them—the big Irish CEO Ciaran Davis and the man in black, the shadowy Phil Dowse (he'd been my consultant for over ten years in the UK, an Australian so blunt and to the point, instrumental in getting me here and a top man)—so much for taking their leaps into the unknown too.

Back to me, getting *the call* I never thought would happen to be honest.

I let out the biggest sigh of my life.

I literally crumpled from some deep, deep release.

I hadn't fully realised until that moment how tightly I'd been holding myself together.

I had no words.

They asked if I was okay and I said I was stunned, and also had no pants on. I thanked them for their belief in me.

Fuck.

We hung up and I sat down, slowly, on my bed and tried to take it in. I remember rubbing the middle of my chest, my heart, and thinking, 'Wow, I've done it.'

I had to tell Sarah.

I called her and I guess she thought I was on the floor again in pain. 'Chris, is it your back? Are you okay?'

As soon as I heard her voice, I wasn't okay. I was a shaking blubbing mess with the sheer heady rush of great news. The relief.

I felt like I breathed in and out fully for the first time since moving here.

'Ratings today . . .' Sniffle, sob.

'Oh dear, I see, oh shit, look, erm, the show is going to take time to—'

'. . . I'm number one.'

'What? WHAT? Number one?'

Then she said, 'Are you sure?'

I think she feared I'd been back on my old friend the green whistle and, in some druggy haze, just hallucinated it all.

'Yeah, it's true.'

Then Sarah started sobbing. We both just let go. Happy tears all round.

After a short while she composed herself and said, 'Can I get you anything? I'm on my way home.'

'Just . . . can you help put my jeans on?'

My team all went to the pub. As they should.

My wife had to dress me and got me a hot water bottle and we toasted the most incredible, unbelievable news over a glass of leftover party champagne. Not from a hose.

I'd thought of a lot more scenarios where I didn't get to Number 1, including a scene where I was tarred and feathered and sent back to England in a shipping container. In all my imagined scenarios, though, I wasn't in crippling pain unable to put on my jeans, which just goes to show you can never predict how life is going to pan out.

Mainly, when it happened, I just felt relief.

I wasn't supposed to survive here.

One of Australia's best and most popular DJs, Marty Sheargold, recently confided to me that the entire industry here thought I had taken on too much, including himself. He said he googled the news that I was coming here and actually felt sorry for me, knowing the hell I would be walking into. Not because he didn't rate me, but because he knew how hard it would be to build a show in a city like Melbourne, as an unknown and weighed down with all my Britishness.

But despite my newfound humility and my gratefulness towards the city that had finally accepted me, I don't want you to think I'd completely changed.

Upon hearing that the show reached Number 1, while still being bent over in pain, I texted Lois at school to tell her. She replied with, *'Well done'*

Then I added:

*'Be sure you tell that little *$# who said no one listens to your dad's show'*

And she said, *'Let it go Dad. It's sad,'* and added an emoji I didn't understand.

Not long after hitting Number 1, the big bosses took me to lunch and offered me a new long-term deal. They also wanted the show to roll out nationally across Australia with a nightly best of.

This may sound like they only did this after I got to Number 1. The truth is they had backed me all the way, took an unprecedented risk in hiring me, and then had the balls to let me do it my way and stay hands off when the ratings weren't good. All of us had been waiting for this moment.

•

Dear Mr Christian O'Connell,

I am writing this email to you to apologise for something I said about you when you first started on air with my favourite radio station – Gold 104.3.

When you first started you sounded quite dull and boring, I rang and spoke to someone on the desk and asked who you were and advised that you were as 'Dull as Bat Shit'.

I would like to take this opportunity to personally apologise to you and anyone else that I may of [sic] offended on the phone that day.

I was wrong, and I have been listening to your show every single day and have grown to love it,

Simon

What happened to me?

As soon as my phone went, I knew what the news was.

Peter Logan had died.

In that moment it made me deeply, instantly, appreciate that I was alive. Death gives us that.

Our lives and being in this world are precious privileges we usually take for granted. Maybe we need to as thinking about this would just be too much to bear all day long. Otherwise we'd be too aware of our fragility. We'd be inside those padded giant protective bubbles people go rolling down mountains in, 'zorbing' I think it's called.

Which in a way we are, in our own bubbles.

In an effort not to take what precious time I have for granted, I once bought something known as 'a death watch'.

Or as it became called by my wife, *'That fucking watch.'*

Basically, it's a watch that counts down to your death.

In real time, how long you have left alive.

In years, months, days. Hours, minutes, seconds.

A visible way to remind us to use our time well. A great idea.

A bad idea for someone like me, though. Who has a tendency to overthink, obsess, and most of the time has a bonfire of thoughts and ideas going on in his head. Imagine throwing a load of fireworks in a bin and shutting the lid, that's my head at times.

I got the watch, entered in my age, weight, exercise levels, etc. and it crunched the numbers and estimated my best-before date. And began counting down. It's terrifying and confronting to see that with your own eyes. The seconds rapidly disappearing.

This death clock lasted three days until my wife broke it. The watch caused me more stress than I had before I strapped its ominous face on my wrist. I'd be in traffic, looking at the death clock and blaming the idiot up ahead for wasting my time and glancing at my rapidly counting down life.

Get out of the way, I am dying!

My wife would be telling me about her day, maybe a dream she had the night before, and sparing no detail, and I mean—Sparing. No. Detail.

And yeah, maybe I'd give a few glances at the old death clock and, you know what, she didn't care for it.

Her foot met my death watch and crushed it. It's bad enough she has my balls, now my own death has been denied.

Make of that what you will, Dr Freud.

When I got the call that Peter had finally succumbed to his cancer, I was standing on the beach on holiday in the new year, slathering on the kid's sunscreen and being told, *'Don't get it in my hair!'*

There were teenage boys on the beach eyeing up my daughters. I had to witness the timeless dance of teenage obsession, all furtive looks, looking away and looking back again. The sheer thrill of being seen by another.

What fun.

I stepped away, waving my phone and nodding to my wife that I needed to take the call. I'm not the guy who takes or makes work calls on holiday, but this was different. It was Sharon Logan, Peter's wife.

His suffering was over, he was at peace. Cancer had taken him, but not his message.

It really moved me when I heard Sharon say that he'd died just a few minutes ago. I rubbed my hand on my chest where Peter had first touched my heart when I needed that in my year zero here.

His email asking for help, to spread his message, made me feel seen and valued. He was inviting me to step forward, or not.

Open, or close.

'*G'day Christian . . . I'm sure you receive many of these emails . . .*'

I looked up at the sun and felt its glow on my face and body. I walked back to my family and Sarah could see from my eyes what the call had been about.

Sarah reassured the kids I'd just had some bad news about my friend Peter. They returned to looking at the boys on the beach, as they should. This itself made me laugh.

Then Lois sighed and said in a matter-of-fact way: 'Dad's never been the same since Bing Bong died.'

This was another 'What's wrong with Dad now?' moment in the darkness of a movie theatre during the life-affirming, beautiful and touching Pixar film *Inside Out*, when Riley, the young girl who the story is about, grows up and Bing Bong, her imaginary friend, dies.

Riley doesn't need Bing Bong anymore, she has to let him go and Bing Bong does this for her by sacrificing himself, allowing Riley to rise up towards joy and . . . *why did they remind me of this heartbreak?*

Oh, Bing Bong . . .

Wait, am I Bing Bong?

I went off for a walk to get some headspace and leave behind my teenage tormentors to plump their feathers at the boys. Once that sweet spot in your heart gets touched, it unlocks all these other thoughts, memories and feelings.

Am I Bing Bong? Or Paddington Bear? I'm so confused right now, maybe it's the heat.

The news of Peter's passing really set me off in deep thoughts as I walked.

•

I found myself at the most easterly point of Australia and ducked under a fence so I could stand on the very edge of this great southern land. The sky above showed two weather patterns at play. There was sunlight in the distance and fierce incoming grey rain clouds. It made me think that in-between transit happening above me was like our life when we moved here. There was one world and a new emerging one, not yet known, and they were in conflict.

As I stood on this eastern tip of the country, under the elemental forces of the sky and above the crashing waves below me, I felt the full force of the journey I had been on. It's only looking back when we make sense of how far we've come and who we are becoming.

I looked out across the south Pacific Ocean, the next bit of land was more than 12,000 kilometres away (Santiago,

Chile, actually), invisible to the human eye. I felt humbled and lucky to be in Australia, to have this life out here.

There was something powerful about looking at the force of the sea and waves, the tidal forces at play that were stirring up everything inside me.

The true life of a parent is to suddenly be filled with a limitless deeper well of love, but with that comes the terrifying knowledge and fear that its loss could devastate you. Every day you have with your children, it's a day closer to them leaving you.

On Ruby's sixteenth birthday I made a video of pictures of her throughout the years and we all watched it together, the kids laughing at various photos, some with teeth missing, some with haircuts that never suited. My wife and I were in bits at the sheer speed of her life, time's arrow accelerating.

I watched the video again later that night with just Ruby and she did something I'll always remember: she could sense Weepy McWeep was about to go off again and she put her hand on mine and said reassuringly, 'It's going to be okay, Dad.'

That's my job! I do the reassuring for *you*.

I've been replaced by your boyfriend, now by you . . .

As I continued on my beach trek, I saw someone unmistakably English. I've come to recognise the type: the pasty pallor, often bewildered, and way too many layers of clothes scream 'I'm not from round here.'

'You okay?' I asked.

'Yes, sorry.'

Told ya, British. Apologising immediately without any reason.

He was lost and I pointed him in the right direction. Technically impossible to get lost along the sea, but that's us Brits. Then he stared at me.

'Christian O'Donnell?'

O'Connell, doesn't matter. Forget it . . .

I nodded, thinking I've never seen this guy before in my life.

'You used to do the breakfast show?'

I answered that yes, I did, then he said: 'I wondered what happened to you.'

What happened to me?

After a quick update to North Face–clad Willy Fog, I carried on and was trying to make sense of it all, death always brings everything into a sharper contrast. As if the director of your life refocuses your lens and the edges that were blurry are suddenly clear.

Someone very wise once said you sometimes meet the new you in the form of a stranger.

Peter came into my life to share his message that saved other people's lives, he also reminded me about what really matters.

We swapped emails right before he passed away. His last to me signed off with:

'. . . *keep up the humour, never forget the human*'.

His power and robust vulnerability made me love him right away. And yet it's the thing I've spent too much of my life seeing as a weakness in myself, fearing it, trying to turn away from it.

It's only when we inhabit our vulnerability that we actually connect so much deeper with each other. It's why sad songs about love stand the test of time, even when sung by Celine Dion. Why we pay good money to see a movie that breaks our heart. Why my wife reads those books with black-and-white covers (maybe I should've gone down that road to shift a few more copies).

It cracks open our hearts.

What happened to me was more like a coming of age than a mid-life crisis (*spits words out*). And my age just happened to be my forties.

You can have many of these in your lifetime. Not just as a teenager like in those great John Hughes movies I love. But at 21, 33, 48, 89, whenever. It happened to my wife, to Ruby and Lois, a coming of age. Life isn't linear.

Throughout your life, you have these events, moments, seasons that you choose yourself: getting married, going for a new job; and those you do not: death of a loved one, depression, anxiety, divorce, getting sacked.

Both can happen at any age, not just your mid life, and they are where life happens. Where we can grow, change, or we turn away from it all and close up.

Bruce Feiler, an expert in the transitions in life, has this great explanation that really struck a chord with me; it might with you.

He talked about the classic fairytales, and how we want our lives to be like this, meet someone, fall in love, have kids, live happily ever after. In every fairytale, a wolf turns up, or something resembling the wolf, and the hero shows up to rescue everybody.

Wolves show up in various forms in our lives. Panic attacks for me, or that thirteen-year-old girl saying no one listened to me . . .

We want to run away from the wolves sometimes, like I did. We want a hero to come and slay the wolf for us, or we can face the wolf and be our own hero.

Change your own story.

Anytime we embrace not knowing, uncertainty, risk failure, rejection, we're being vulnerable. By not leaning into that, you're not living life generously, you're always cutting part of you off from being fully engaged, fully participating, fully alive, with life.

Because we are terrified of what people might think about us. Because we all carry this dirty little secret—*that we're not good enough.*

If I hadn't been stripped of everything I thought would protect me and keep me safe when we moved here—status, security, friends, family—if I hadn't experienced that violent humiliation and humbling that made me so open and raw to the world, if I hadn't accepted my vulnerability, then I wouldn't have the amazing life and joy I am having now.

Without having done all that, then maybe I don't call Peter and invite him onto the show.

Those things we work so hard to accumulate, then hang on to and defend, sometimes actually get in the way of our real path in life. The path back towards who we really are.

When we were unpacking on the first day here in Melbourne, I picked up an old snow globe and shook it up. That's what happened to us all when we moved here.

We shook up *everything*.

Our lives aren't yet fully settled but things have been realigned, remade, reborn. Good and bad.

Not long ago I was asked in an interview when I was sharing the war stories (*Art of War* style) of the move here, 'Why did you stay?'

Why didn't I just quit, and fuck off home?

Good question. This made me look back and, sometimes, what you see all depends on where you are looking from.

We are trained to avoid resistance. We spend much of our lives staying away from it, but finding those areas in our lives, in us, and the fear it stirs in us, often means we are on a new path, and if you take the leap, risk failing, struggling, and choose to be open-hearted, real and vulnerable, there is real magic there.

Those times are when I grew, when I was tested, invited to shut down or open up my heart.

Now I wouldn't take those away.

I'm actually thankful for them. I'm better for them. All we have are our stories.

The ones that keep us too small for this life . . . or make us bigger.

We decided to tear up the script and write a new story.

Why didn't I quit?

I may have been losing listeners but I found myself. By making something new, different, struggling, doing something better, failing, trying again, and again, putting together a new team and inspiring them and firing them up. Connecting every morning with the radio family we were building. Turning haters into, well, more tolerators than lovers.

Every day I got to do it all again. And I loved that.

What would happen today? What might I learn or discover? I was lucky to have that. I'd missed that.

I was doing the radio I'd always wanted to do. I was enjoying it more. I had more gratitude. Thanks to the great team around me on air in Jack and Pats, I felt like I was flying.

When Jack shared his heartbreak one morning that his oldest friend's dad had just died suddenly, we all remembered that one friend we had whose dad was a legend, who gave you beers before you could legally have them.

Or when Pats talked about years of trying IVF and surviving cancer and what all of that meant on her fifth-year anniversary of getting the all-clear, and then having a daughter she never thought she would, we all shared and felt her joy.

If that show didn't work out, then trust me, I'd happily fuck off back home because you don't deserve me!

Keeping your heart open means living with courage. It really does.

As I said earlier in this book, courage means 'full-hearted'. How full-hearted are you?

That's life's big challenge: how do you keep an open heart even when things hurt you, scare you, break your heart?

So many times, in arguments when you hang on dearly to being right, you shrink your heart.

Courage was Ruby.

Courage was Lois.

Courage was Sarah.

Courage meant firstly and mostly accepting the not-knowing-ness of it all.

Not knowing if it was going to be okay. If this school was the right one for our kids. If they'd find friends.

If my wife's mum would survive, and could Sarah make a life here away from her best friends?

Me not knowing if I was going to work out here or find friends and had done the right thing for my family.

We want so much to know the outcomes of all our interactions in life. Like we are outcome dependent. It's not a generous way to live our lives, is it?

We are conditioned to think, *I'll only do this if I know I'll succeed.* I had to think, *I'll do this but I know I could fail.* Not, *What would I do if I knew I wouldn't fail?*

What would I do if I knew I could fail?

I had travelled thousands of miles to move here, but really, my biggest journey, and it's the most important one of a life well lived, was into my heart.

This is my story, it's ongoing and as I say this to you right now, we've just had a really scary time with one of the girls, but we know we can get through it. We've seen the life-changing power of hope and courage.

I hope my girls don't settle in life.

I hope they learn from the move here that sometimes all you can do is keep going and showing up, even if there is no clear path ahead.

That *you* are the path ahead.

Follow your mojo, even if it takes you to the *other side of the world*.

Don't listen to self-proclaimed experts. In bars in Amsterdam, though I'm glad you did say no, Mr Charcuterie board, you tested me and I was better for that.

Listen only to yourself, to what's calling you, not the desperate smaller voice that thinks it needs to know if it's all going to work out.

Throw it all away, throw yourself away, see what comes back. Risk yourself.

When we landed here in Australia at Melbourne airport, we were both arriving and departing in a way.

My life was going to be totally reliant on the help of strangers. How utterly terrifying and amazing.

I learnt from those strangers, who never really were strangers.

We are just each other with a different story.

We are all connected. You feel that when thousands of us all enjoy a music concert or comedy show together. Arriving separately, but then arriving together in that experience.

I learnt that we become truly alive by our connections, and when we share our *humanness* we become bigger, we see we are not alone.

I wish I could go back to me at that bin. The me who felt utterly broken, alone and terrified. To pat him on the back, not to reassure him, but to say, 'Keep going. Keep breaking apart.'

Because sometimes we need to be broken open.

•

I retraced my steps back to my family. My wife wanted to get a photo of the girls to send to our parents, who had missed them so much over Christmas.

The girls *hate this*, despite spending most of their waking hours taking selfies. They started fighting, my wife yelled at them.

I cried out, 'Girls! Come on please!'

One pushed the other and said, 'She's such a bitch.'

I realised all was good in my world as I stared out at the ocean, and while my family bickered in the background, it suddenly occurred to me that I still had no idea which compartment does what in the washing machine drawer.

Some words
from the girls

Ruby and Lois O'Connell

What did you think when you found out you were moving to Australia?

Lois

When I first found out we were moving to the other side of the world I was slightly concerned that Dad was having a mid-life crisis, but I was mostly excited to be somewhere with new accents and good weather. Dorking sucked.

Ruby

Mid-life crisis! I even asked Mum if Dad was having one. He was having some sort of meltdown and that's when men his age do something drastic.

I overheard Mum saying she was worried about crocodiles and I'd been spying on Dad on these odd late-night phone calls to someone called 'Duncan' and Dad lying badly that it was an old friend, who he'd never ever mentioned before.

So I just asked Mum and she is not great at keeping a secret, and she couldn't wait to tell me.

What did you think about Australia before moving here?

Lois

I think my biggest concern was just that there were spiders, snakes and crocodiles in Australia and all my friends thought I would be killed by one of those in the first few months of living there. People seemed less grumpy over there.

Ruby

It looked so much sunnier! Dad and I loved watching Australian *MasterChef*, which was way more friendlier and supportive than the UK one. That was all I really knew. That and the *Border Security* show and they were cool in that too.

I thought it would make us more interesting. We'd be those people who have cool stories like 'yeah we moved to Australia when we were younger'.

What was it like starting a new school on the other side of the world?

Ruby

I thought it would be more laid-back and easier! It wasn't. New teachers and trying to understand a new timetable—awful.

Everyone else had grown up together, they had their groups all made. It was more a different world than a different school.

In the first few days we were asked all the time, 'Say this . . . Please say that . . .' because our accents were novel. That soon wore off. I missed the closeness of my old friends so much. It was really lonely at times.

Plus, Dad's poster outside the school made it really weird! Boys would come up and ask about him. I just wanted to fit in, not stand out. I still think he asked for it to be put there on purpose to annoy us.

Lois

Everybody talked the same, me and Ruby didn't. Everyone had so many questions for a while when we were a novelty.

Starting a new school is hard enough but especially when you're in a completely different country. At first, being the centre of attention because you say flip-flops instead of thongs was fun, but after a few weeks everyone still kept asking me to say things like 'yoghurt' and 'dance' and it was quite annoying.

What do you miss?

Lois

Being so far from everyone, Nanna almost dying. All our family, Christmas was really hard seeing Mum and Dad upset on Skype.

Oh, also Marks & Spencer's sausages and scotch eggs. Our local Thai takeaway.

Ruby

The countryside, my grandparents, proper Christmas, friendships that I grew up with. Our old Thai takeaway.

What's the best thing about life here?

Lois

Despite how hard it was, I don't regret moving here. Imagine just growing up in one place—boring! It gave me a chance to see how different people live, to get an idea of the whole world.

Ruby

I love being close to the beach. The people are super friendly. You chat to so many people who you don't know and I love that. The warmer weather is awesome. I've done so many things I never would've done in my old life. These insane school camps they go on here in the bush! Doing rowing! Twice a week at 6 a.m. before school—can't even imagine doing that back in England. I also learnt I can cope with more than I thought.

What have you learnt moving here?

Ruby

Grit. When I look back it's amazing seeing how I weathered all the hard times, having no friends, school changes, being homesick.

Lois

How you can make big changes in your life, like even if you're really old. Sorry, that sounds rude, but you know what I mean.

Sarah O'Connell

What did you think when Christian called you about moving to Australia?

I felt overwhelmed with excitement and then fear in case it didn't happen.

Why did you want to come?

Australia always occupied a really special place in my heart and soul. I had fallen in love with the country back in my twenties backpacking for eighteen months. I had always wanted to come back and live here one day, then the dream of emigrating was put on the back shelf. It gathered an awful lot of dust until Christian rang one afternoon and said, 'What do you think of moving to Australia?!'

How worried were you during his panic attacks?

Of course I was worried, my biggest worry wasn't our financial security, it was what it would do to him if he couldn't do what he loved most.

I told him as long as we had a roof over our heads we were going to be okay. Christian and I don't come from well-off families so just being able to have enough money to provide the basics was all I really cared about.

My biggest worry was just about his happiness, as he loves to perform.

What was it like when your mum had the heart attack?

Hell.

Did that make you question moving here?

It's really hard to explain but no matter how tough some of the times have been since we moved here, I've never questioned moving. It sounds a bit weird but it has always felt like this was where we were supposed to be.

Did you think his show would work out?

I confess I had some worrying moments and actually didn't listen for the first year as I would fret so much over anything he might have got slightly wrong in my opinion. I have some very wrong opinions at times! The honest truth is, however, I always believed the show would work out because I'm his biggest fan and I couldn't believe others wouldn't love him too!

Did you know how hard and bad things were?

Christian has a very protective side of him. It's a wonderful side of him but it can mean that he doesn't share enough when he is struggling. I think it's some sort of Irish pride! So no, I didn't know how hard things were for him and, even now, I don't ever trust that he's telling me the full story.

What do you love about life here?

How long have I got?

The spirit of Australian people—their warmth, kindness and friendliness (except when they get into cars!). Big, big skies. Swimming in the bay in the winter—a pod of dolphins swam around me, and last week I scuba-dived with octopuses. I'm so lucky.

What do you miss?

I miss my family and friends so much. I miss the small town we came from and its street of old antique shops and the old buildings. I miss Marks & Spencer's sandwiches and mini-sausages, and I truly miss our old Indian takeaway.

What have you learnt from moving here?

That you are asking a lot of teenagers to move to a new country and we were probably hopelessly naive on that front. With young children you can help them adjust to it but teenagers don't let you help and it has not been easy to watch them leave a settled school life in the UK and rebuild it here. I am so proud of them.

That I am braver than I thought.

That Australia is even more special than I remembered it.

Thank-you note

This is traditionally called the 'Acknowledgements' but that's too poncy for me.

I do need to thank some people.

To you, if you followed my story to this end point, I hope it gave you something. Thank you for you being a friend and hearing me.

If you want to drop me a line: christian@christianoconnell. com.au.

Love and thanks to my wife, Sarah, for her eternal support and giving me space to do this.

The girls, Ruby and Lois.

Proceeds from this book will be deposited into a trust that will fund your therapy in years to come, if this was all too much for you.

I love you, and thank you for being my greatest teachers x

Mum and Dad, for teaching me the joy of stories and laughter.

My sister, Louise, who I left to deal with Mum and Dad when I fucked off to the other side of the world.

I want to thank the good people of Melbourne and Australia for giving me a go. I thank the haters for testing me, keeping me honest, being the fire that forged me!

To the listeners, callers, emailers of my show, wherever you are, you're the lifeblood of my show. Thank you for giving me and my family this great chance and great life.

I'm always humbled by those still lending me their listening ears in the UK and across the world. It means so much, thank you.

To the man at Allen & Unwin, Tom Gilliatt, who told me to write this book, even when I feared it was making me uncomfortable, and for encouraging me to lean into that more. Thank you for your generous heart, here's to many more long lunches.

Tom Bailey-Smith, the editor, for his forensic eye for detail.

Mark Klemens, Stephanie and Steve Vizard at Profile Talent.

Titus O'Reily for helping me put my stories into some kind of order, without him this would be like the ramblings of a madman.

Tony Horne, my mentor and great friend, always there for me, always inspiring me.

Alan Dolan, for teaching me breath work—he has loads of great free resources at his site www.breathguru.com.

Sara Brooke at The Space In Between. My go-to for a reset, so good she's teaching me Reiki—spaceinbetween.com.au.

Andrew Smith at Blue Rose Astrology in Dublin. Purple Rain, my friend.

Duncan Campbell and Phil Dowse for having balls the size of Australia in hiring me. The big Irishman Ciaran Davies for paying me, and backing me.

At Gold FM in Melbourne, Sue Carter, I must've been terrifying to be around when I started, with my feverish allergic reaction to overplanning, wipe boards and cash giveaways.

Jack and Pats, my team on air, thank you for leaping with me every morning, my E Street Band along with Tom, Colette, Rio, Emlyn and Mel.

Brian, Bec and MDV.

My lucky rabbit's foot of a producer, Nick Daly.

Brad Hulme, for EVERYTHING x

Hamish and Andy, if I hadn't met those two bundles of joy and wondered about the country that made them and been inspired by their love of Australia, I never would've moved here.

To the man in the bar in Amsterdam, cheers! Thank you, I needed to be tested about how much I really wanted this.

Man in the shed, thank you.

Peter Logan, thank you for being a friend.

Christian x